CONTENTS

4

INTRODUCTION

Understanding the Ninja Foodi Dual Zone Air Fryer

Do you want to cut your cooking time to half? Or do you want to cook two meals at a time? Then the new Ninja Foodi Dual Zone Air fryer is the next good thing that you should buy for your kitchen. This Air fryer is designed with a dual-zone technology that will let you cook two different meals at a time either on a single cooking mode and setting or two different modes and settings. While this might sound too good to be true but Ninja Kitchen has made it possible. In a single 8 quart Ninja Air fryer, your cooking options will be multiplied up to many folds because this time, you will be having two air fryer basket and two independent cooking zones. Handling two fryer baskets at a time may sound too complicated, but Ninja kitchen has managed to create such a simple and user-friendly control system with a touch button panel that will let you choose and select any program, any cooking temperature, and time for both the cooking chambers independently or in complete sync with another. Doesn't that sound amazing? Well, it does! And if you are up for more surprises, then continue reading as we are about to discuss some major benefits of this Dual Zone Air fryer.

The Benefits of Using Ninja Foodi Dual Zone Air Fryer

The Ninja 2 basket Air Fry is known for several of its advanced features and its ultimate benefits.

1.   Smart Finish

This cooking miracle can intelligently sync the cook times of both the cooking zones so that you cook different foods at a time with the same finishing time. So, here is how it works! When you add different food to the two baskets, and each has its own cooking time. When you cook using the smart cooking function and start the operation, the basket with the longer cooking time will initiate its operation first while the other basket will stay on hold until the other chamber reaches the same cooking time. In this way, both sides finish cooking at the same time.

2.   Match Cook

The total 8 quartz capacity of this Ninja Air fryer is divided into two 4 quarts air fryer baskets, which means that you get to cook different food and the same food in the two baskets at a time. Using the match cook technology, you can use the same cooking function for both the baskets and use its XL capacity.

3.   XL 8-Qt. Capacity

The large 8 quarts capacity divide into two parts gives you a perfect space to cook food in a large and small amount. This capacity is enough to cook 2 lbs of fries and 2 lbs of wings and drumettes.

4.   Nonstick For Easy Cleaning

Both two baskets are nonstick, so they are easy to clean and wash. Crisper plates that are lined at the base of the baskets are dishwasher safe so you can wash them without damaging them.

Structural Composition of the Ninja Foodi Dual Zone Air Fryer

The Digital Ninja Foodi Air Fry has brought such a revolution into the kitchen that now the users can enjoy fresh and crispy meals in no time. It is a dual-zone air fryer technology that has merged 6 cooking functions like the Air Broil, Air Fry, Roast, Bake, Dehydrate and Reheat. This appliance is especially good for people who love to bake and cook crispy food.

The air fryer comes with 2 Fryer baskets that are marked as "1" and "2," and each should be inserted into their respective portions because of their different shapes. The baskets don't have any click button to open. You can simply remove them by pulling them out.

The control panel is present right on top of the Basket's inlets, and it covers the front top portion of the Air fryer. The top of the air fryer unit is flat, and it does not produce much heat. Do not place anything on the flat top of the air fryer unit or nearby. The control panel is designed with function and operating buttons.

The display screen is divided into two sections, each indicating the cooking status of its side of the basket. To select the settings for basket 1, press the KEY 1 on the control panel, and to select the settings for basket 2, press the KEY2 on the control. The other function and operating keys include:

Function Buttons:

- AIR BROIL: This mode gives a crispy touch to the meals and uses it to melt the toppings of the food
- AIR FRY: Cook crispy fried food without the use of the oil with the help of this mode.
- ROAST: Turn this air fryer unit into a roaster oven to cook soft and tender meat.
- BAKE: Cooked delicious baked desserts and treats.
- REHEAT: Allow you to reheat and warm your leftovers meals.
- DEHYDRATE: Use this mode to dehydrate fruits, meats, and vegetables.

Operating Buttons:

- TEMP Keys: The up and down key allows you to adjust the cooking temperature.
- TIME arrows: The up and down keys are there to adjust the cooking time.
- SMART FINISH button: This mode automatically syncs the cooking times of both the cooking zones and let them finish at the same time.
- MATCH COOK button: Allow you to automatically match the settings of zone 2 to those of the first cooking zone, which lets you cook a larger amount of the same food or different type of food in the same settings.
- START/PAUSE button: These buttons are used to initiate, stop, and resume the cooking.
- POWER BUTTON: The button is pressed to turn on or off the unit once the cooking function is completed or stopped.
- Standby Mode: In this mode, the Power button will get dimly lit, and the machine goes into standby if there is no activity for 10 minutes.
- Hold Mode: Hold sign will appear on the display screen when it is in the SMART FINISH mode. When the cooking time of one zone is greater than the other, then the hold will appear for the zone with less cooking time until its cooking time matches with the other one.

The Dual-Zone Technology

The amazing dual-zone technology of the Ninja Air fryer will let you cook using the following two modes:

- **Smart Finish Technology**

This function is used to finish cooking at the same time when foods in the two air fryer baskets have different cook temps, times, or even cooking functions:

1.   Add all the ingredients into the baskets, then insert baskets in the air fryer unit.
2.   Press the smart finish mode, and the machine will automatically sync during cooking.
3.   At first, the Zone 1 will stay illuminated. Now select the cooking function for this zone. Use the TEMP key to set the required temperature, and use the TIME keys to set the required time.
4.   Now select zone 2, and select the cooking function.
5.   Use the TEMP keys to set the temperature, then use the TIME key to set the time for zone 2.
6.   Press the start button, and the timer will start ticking for both zones according to their timings. And the cooking will be finished at one time.
7.   On smart finish mode, you can also start cooking at the same time and let it end at different times. For that, simply select their cooking time and press the start button for both zones.

- **Match Cook**

To cook a larger amount of the same food, or cook different foods using the same function, temperature, and time:

1.   Add the cooking ingredients into the baskets, then insert both the baskets into the unit.
2.   Zone 1 will stay illuminated. Press the desired function button. Use the TEMP keys to set the cooking temperature, and use the TIME keys to set the time.
3.   Press the MATCH COOK button to copy the basket one's settings to the basket 2.
4.   Then press the START/PAUSE button to initiate cooking in both the baskets.
5.   Once the cooking is completed "End" sign will appear on both the screens.

How to Use the Ninja Foodi 2 Basket Air Fryer

To use the different cooking programs of the Ninja Foodi Air Fryer, you can try the following steps:

Air Broil:

1.   Insert crisper plate in the basket, then add ingredients into the basket, and insert basket in the unit.
2.   The unit will default to zone 1, and to use zone 2 instead, select zone 2.
3.   Select the Air broil cooking mode.
4.   Use the TEMP keys to set the desired temperature.
5.   Use the TIME key to set the time from 1-minute to 1 hour and from 5-minute to 1 to 4 hours.
6.   Press the START/PAUSE button to initiate cooking.
7.   The unit will beep once the cooking is complete, and the "End" sign will appear on the display screen.
8.   Remove ingredients from the basket/s by dumping them out onto the plate or using silicone tongs/utensils.

Air Fry:

1.   Insert crisper plate in the basket, then add ingredients into the basket, and insert basket in the unit.
2.   The unit will default to zone 1, and to use basket 2 instead of just select zone 2.
3.   Select Air Fry cooking mode use the TEMP keys to set the required temperature.
4.   Use the TIME keys to set the time from 1-minute to 1 hour and from 5-minute from 1 to 4 hours.
5.   Press the START/PAUSE button to initiate cooking.
6.   The unit will beep once the cooking is completed, and the "End" sign will appear on display.

Bake:

1.   Insert crisper plate in the basket, then add ingredients into the basket, and insert basket in the unit.
2.   Select BAKE cooking mode. Use the TEMP keys to set the required temperature.
3.   Use the TIME keys to set the time in 1-minute increments up to 1 hour and in 5-minute increments from 1 to 4 hours.
4.   Press the START/PAUSE button to begin cooking.
5.   The unit will beep once the cooking is complete, and the "End" sign will appear on the display screen.
6.   Reduce the temperature by 25 degrees F while converting the traditional oven recipes.

Other Cooking Modes:

While using the other cooking modes, remember to follow the same steps, and select use the crisper plate or cooking rack as required. Then select the required mode, zone, and temperature then initiate cooking.

You can remove any of the baskets during the cooking process and shake the food inside, then reinsert the baskets to resume cooking. Press the start button to resume cooking.

The broiling function is not available for the MATCH COOK technology; you can only broil the food in one basket at a time. If your food is in a large amount and you need to broil it, then broil in batches.

Cleaning and Maintenance:

Here is how you can keep your 2 basket air fryer clean and maintained after every session of cooking:

1.   Unplug the appliance before cleaning it and allow it to cool completely.
2.   You can remove the air fryer baskets from the main unit and keep them aside to cool.
3.   Once cooled, remove their air crisper plates and wash them in the dishwasher.
4.   Clean the air fryer basket using soapy water and avoid hard scrubbing to protect their nonstick layers.
5.   Dishwash the air fryer racks in the dishwasher and use soft scrubs if the food is stuck to the rack.
6.   Wipe the main unit with a clean piece of cloth or with a lightly damp cloth.
7.   Once everything is cleaned and return the baskets to the air fryer.
8.   Now your device is ready to use.

BREAKFAST & BRUNCH RECIPES

1. Cheddar Biscuits

Servings: 4
Cooking Time: 8 Minutes
Ingredients:
- ½ cup almond flour
- ¼ cup Cheddar cheese, shredded
- ¾ teaspoon salt
- 1 egg, beaten
- 1 tablespoon mascarpone
- 1 tablespoon coconut oil, melted
- ¾ teaspoon baking powder
- ½ teaspoon apple cider vinegar
- ¼ teaspoon ground nutmeg

Directions:
1. In the big bowl mix up ground nutmeg, almond flour, salt, and baking powder. After this, add egg, apple cider vinegar, coconut oil, and mascarpone. Add cheese and knead the soft dough. Then with the help of the fingertips make the small balls (biscuits). Preheat the air fryer to 400F. Then line the air fryer basket with parchment. Place the cheese biscuits on the parchment and cook them for 8 minutes at 400F. Shake the biscuits during the cooking to avoid burning. The cooked cheese biscuits will have a golden brown color.

2. Caprese On Toast

Servings: 1
Cooking Time: 7 Minutes
Ingredients:
- 4 tomato slices
- 4 mozzarella slices
- 1 tbsp olive oil
- 1 tbsp chopped basil
- Salt and pepper, to taste

Directions:
1. Preheat air fryer to 370 F. Arrange two tomato slices on each bread slice. Season with salt and pepper. Top each slice with 2 mozzarella slices. Put in the air fryer and cook for 3 minutes. Drizzle the toasts with olive oil and top with chopped basil to serve.

3. Peanut Butter Bread

Servings: 3
Cooking Time: 15 Minutes
Ingredients:
- 1 tbsp. oil
- 2 tbsp. peanut butter
- 4 slices bread
- 1 banana, sliced

Directions:
1. Spread the peanut butter on top of each slice of bread, then arrange the banana slices on top. Sandwich two slices together, then the other two.
2. Oil the inside of the Air Fryer and cook the bread for 5 minutes at 300°F.

4. Spicy Cauliflower Rice

Servings: 2
Cooking Time: 22 Minutes
Ingredients:
- 1 cauliflower head, cut into florets
- 1/2 tsp cumin
- 1/2 tsp chili powder
- 6 onion spring, chopped
- 2 jalapenos, chopped
- 4 tbsp olive oil
- 1 zucchini, trimmed and cut into cubes
- 1/2 tsp paprika
- 1/2 tsp garlic powder
- 1/2 tsp cayenne pepper
- 1/2 tsp pepper
- 1/2 tsp salt

Directions:
1. Preheat the air fryer to 370 F.
2. Add cauliflower florets into the food processor and process until it looks like rice.
3. Transfer cauliflower rice into the air fryer baking pan and drizzle with half oil.
4. Place pan in the air fryer and cook for 12 minutes, stir halfway through.
5. Heat remaining oil in a small pan over medium heat.
6. Add zucchini and cook for 5-8 minutes.
7. Add onion and jalapenos and cook for 5 minutes.
8. Add spices and stir well. Set aside.
9. Add cauliflower rice in the zucchini mixture and stir well.
10. Serve and enjoy.

5. Mushroom Frittata

Servings: 1
Cooking Time: 13 Minutes
Ingredients:
- 1 cup egg whites
- 1 cup spinach, chopped
- 2 mushrooms, sliced
- 2 tbsp parmesan cheese, grated
- Salt

Directions:
1. Spray pan with cooking spray and heat over medium heat.
2. Add mushrooms and sauté for 2-3 minutes. Add spinach and cook for 1-2 minutes or until wilted.
3. Transfer mushroom spinach mixture into the air fryer pan.

4. Whisk egg whites in a mixing bowl until frothy. Season with a pinch of salt.
5. Pour egg white mixture into the spinach and mushroom mixture and sprinkle with parmesan cheese.
6. Place pan in air fryer basket and cook frittata at 350 F for 8 minutes.
7. Slice and serve.

6. Mozzarella Bell Peppers Mix

Servings: 4
Cooking Time: 15 Minutes
Ingredients:
- 1 red bell pepper, roughly chopped
- 1 celery stalk, chopped
- 2 green onions, sliced
- 2 tablespoons butter, melted
- ½ cup mozzarella cheese, shredded
- A pinch of salt and black pepper
- 6 eggs, whisked

Directions:
1. In a bowl, mix all the ingredients except the butter and whisk well. Preheat the air fryer at 360 degrees F, add the butter, heat it up, add the celery and bell peppers mix, and cook for 15 minutes, shaking the fryer once. Divide the mix between plates and serve for breakfast.

7. Strawberry Oatmeal

Servings: 4
Cooking Time: 10 Minutes
Ingredients:
- 1 cup strawberries, chopped
- 1 cup steel cut oats
- 1 cup almond milk
- 2 tablespoons sugar
- ½ teaspoon vanilla extract
- Cooking spray

Directions:
1. Spray your air fryer with cooking spray and then add all ingredients; toss and cover.
2. Cook at 365 degrees F for 10 minutes.
3. Divide into bowls and serve.

8. Spinach & Egg Cups

Servings: 4
Cooking Time: 23 Minutes
Ingredients:
- 1 tablespoon unsalted butter, melted
- 1 tablespoon olive oil
- 1 pound fresh baby spinach
- 4 eggs
- 7 ounces ham, sliced
- 4 teaspoons milk
- Salt and freshly ground black pepper

Directions:
1. Set the temperature of Air Fryer to 355 degrees F. Grease 4 ramekins with butter.

2. Take a skillet, heat the oil over medium heat and sauté the spinach for about 2-3 minutes or until just wilted.
3. Drain the liquid completely from the spinach.
4. Divide the spinach into the prepared ramekins, followed by the ham slices.
5. Crack 1 egg into each ramekin over ham slices.
6. Drizzle evenly with milk and sprinkle with salt and black pepper.
7. Air Fry for about 16-20 minutes or until the desired doneness of eggs.
8. Serve hot.

9. Colorful Hash Brown

Servings: 4
Cooking Time: 25 Minutes
Ingredients:
- 5 russet potatoes, peeled, cubed and soaked in water for 30 minutes
- ½ onion, chopped
- ½ jalapeño, chopped
- ½ red bell pepper, seeded and chopped
- ½ green bell pepper, seeded and chopped
- ½ tablespoon extra-virgin olive oil
- ¼ tablespoon dried oregano, crushed
- ¼ tablespoon garlic powder
- ¼ tablespoon ground cumin
- ¼ tablespoon red chili powder
- Salt and black pepper, to taste

Directions:
1. Preheat the Air fryer at 330 °F.
2. Mix together potatoes and olive oil in a bowl and toss to coat well.
3. Place the potatoes into the Air fryer basket and cook for about 5 minutes.
4. Dish out the potatoes onto a wire rack and allow them to cool.
5. Add remaining ingredients in the bowl and toss to coat well.
6. Stir in the potatoes and mash well.
7. Set the Air fryer to 390 °F and transfer the potato mixture in the Air fryer basket.
8. Cook for about 20 minutes until desired doneness and serve warm.

10. Tofu Scramble

Servings: 3
Cooking Time: 40 Minutes
Ingredients:
- 2 ½ cups red potato, chopped
- 1 tbsp. olive oil
- 1 block tofu, chopped finely
- 1tbsp. olive oil
- 2 tbsp. tamari
- 1 tsp. turmeric powder
- ½ tsp. onion powder
- ½ tsp. garlic powder

- ½ cup onion, chopped
- 4 cups broccoli florets

Directions:
1. Pre-heat the Air Fryer at 400°F.
2. Toss together the potatoes and olive oil.
3. Cook the potatoes in a baking dish for 15 minutes, shaking once during the cooking time to ensure they fry evenly.
4. Combine the tofu, olive oil, turmeric, onion powder, tamari, and garlic powder together, before stirring in the onions, followed by the broccoli.
5. Top the potatoes with the tofu mixture and allow to cook for an additional 15 minutes. Serve warm.

11. Coriander Sausages Muffins

Servings: 4
Cooking Time: 12 Minutes
Ingredients:
- 4 teaspoons coconut flour
- 1 tablespoon coconut cream
- 1 egg, beaten
- ½ teaspoon baking powder
- 6 oz sausage meat
- 1 teaspoon spring onions, chopped
- ½ teaspoon ground coriander
- 1 teaspoon sesame oil
- ½ teaspoon salt

Directions:
1. In the mixing bowl mix up coconut flour, coconut cream, egg, baking powder, minced onion, and ground coriander. Add salt and whisk the mixture until smooth. After this, add the sausage meat and stir the muffin batter. Preheat the air fryer to 385F. Brush the muffin molds with sesame oil and pour the batter inside. Place the rack in the air fryer basket. Put the muffins on a rack. Cook the meal for 12 minutes.

12. Grilled Steak With Parsley Salad

Servings: 4
Cooking Time: 45 Minutes
Ingredients:
- 1 ½ pounds flatiron steak
- 3 tablespoons olive oil
- Salt and pepper to taste
- 2 cups parsley leaves
- ½ cup parmesan cheese, grated
- 1 tablespoon fresh lemon juice

Directions:
1. Preheat the air fryer at 390 °F.
2. Place the grill pan accessory in the air fryer.
3. Mix together the steak, oil, salt and pepper.
4. Grill for 15 minutes per batch and make sure to flip the meat halfway through the cooking time.
5. Meanwhile, prepare the salad by combining in a bowl the parsley leaves, parmesan cheese and lemon juice. Season with salt and pepper.

13. Fried Flatbreads

Servings: 8
Cooking Time: 9 Minutes
Ingredients:
- 1½ tablespoons granulated sugar
- 1 tablespoon active dry yeast
- ½ teaspoon salt
- 1 2/3 cups whole milk
- 1½ tablespoons shortening*
- 1 egg, beaten
- 4-4½ cups bread flour
- 1 cup vegetable oil

Directions:
1. In a small bowl, mix well sugar, yeast, and salt.
2. In a small pan, add the milk and shortening over medium heat and cook for about 2-3 minutes or until shortening just melts, stirring continuously.
3. Once done, move away the pan from the heat and set aside until just warm.
4. Take the bowl of a stand mixer, attached with the dough hook, add in the yeast mixture, and milk mixture. Mix them well and set aside for about 10 minutes.
5. Add the egg and 1½ cups of flour and mix on low speed until combined.
6. Gradually, add the remaining flour and blend until non-sticky dough ball forms.
7. Place the dough into a lightly greased bowl and turn to coat.
8. With a clean kitchen towel, cover the bowl and set aside for about 1-2 hours or until doubled in size.
9. Set the temperature of Air Fryer to 300 degrees F.
10. Make 2 golf ball sized balls from the dough and place on a lightly floured surface.
11. Now, roll each ball into a circle using a rolling pin and coat both sides with a little oil.
12. Arrange both rolled knead in an Air fryer basket.
13. Air Fry for about 9 minutes or until puffy and browned.
14. Repeat with the remaining dough.
15. Serve warm.

14. Herbed Omelet

Servings: 4
Cooking Time: 20 Minutes
Ingredients:
- 10 eggs, whisked
- ½ cup cheddar, shredded

- 2 tablespoons parsley, chopped
- 2 tablespoons chives, chopped
- 2 tablespoons basil, chopped
- Cooking spray
- Salt and black pepper to the taste

Directions:
1. In a bowl, mix the eggs with all the ingredients except the cheese and the cooking spray and whisk well. Preheat the air fryer at 350 degrees F, grease it with the cooking spray, and pour the eggs mixture inside. Sprinkle the cheese on top and cook for 20 minutes. Divide everything between plates and serve.

15. Tomato Egg Breakfast

Servings: 2
Cooking Time: 30 Minutes
Ingredients:
- 2 eggs
- ½ cup tomatoes, chopped
- ¼ cup coconut milk
- 2 tbsp onion, chopped
- ½ cup cheddar cheese, shredded
- Pepper
- Salt

Directions:
1. In a large bowl, add all ingredients except cheese and stir to combine.
2. Pour bowl mixture into the air fryer baking dish and sprinkle cheese on top.
3. Place in the air fryer and cook at 350 F for 30 minutes.
4. Serve and enjoy.

16. Sweet Rosemary Cornbread

Servings:4
Cooking Time: 25 Minutes
Ingredients:
- ¾ cup fine yellow cornmeal
- ½ cup sorghum flour
- ¼ cup tapioca starch
- ½ teaspoon xanthan gum*
- ¼ cup granulated sugar
- 2 teaspoons baking powder
- ¼ teaspoon salt
- 1 cup plain almond milk
- 3 tablespoons olive oil
- 2 teaspoons fresh rosemary, minced

Directions:
1. In a large bowl, mix together the cornmeal, sorghum flour, tapioca starch, xanthan gum, sugar, baking powder, and salt.
2. Add the almond milk, oil, and rosemary. Mix until well combined.
3. Set the temperature of Air Fryer to 400 degrees F. Grease 4 ramekins.
4. Put the mixture evenly into the prepared ramekins.

5. Place the ramekins into an Air Fryer basket.
6. Air Fry for about 20-25 minutes or until a toothpick inserted in the center comes out clean.
7. Remove from Air Fryer and place the ramekins onto a wire rack for about 10-15 minutes.
8. Carefully, invert the breads into serving plates.
9. Enjoy!

17. Ham And Egg Toast Cups

Servings:2
Cooking Time:5 Minutes
Ingredients:
- 2 eggs
- 2 slices of ham
- 2 tablespoons butter
- Cheddar cheese, for topping
- Salt, to taste
- Black pepper, to taste

Directions:
1. Preheat the Air fryer to 400 °F and grease both ramekins with melted butter.
2. Place each ham slice in the greased ramekins and crack each egg over ham slices.
3. Sprinkle with salt, black pepper and cheddar cheese and transfer into the Air fryer basket.
4. Cook for about 5 minutes and remove the ramekins from the basket.
5. Serve warm.

18. Mini Tomato Quiche

Servings:2
Cooking Time:30 Minutes
Ingredients:
- 4 eggs
- ¼ cup onion, chopped
- ½ cup tomatoes, chopped
- ½ cup milk
- 1 cup Gouda cheese, shredded
- Salt, to taste

Directions:
1. Preheat the Air fryer to 340 °F and grease a large ramekin with cooking spray.
2. Mix together all the ingredients in a ramekin and transfer into the air fryer basket.
3. Cook for about 30 minutes and dish out to serve hot.

19. Medium Rare Simple Salt And Pepper Steak

Servings:3
Cooking Time: 30 Minutes
Ingredients:
- 1 ½ pounds skirt steak

- Salt and pepper to taste

Directions:
1. Preheat the air fryer at 390 °F.
2. Place the grill pan accessory in the air fryer.
3. Season the skirt steak with salt and pepper.
4. Place on the grill pan and cook for 15 minutes per batch.
5. Flip the meat halfway through the cooking time.

20. Easy & Tasty Salsa Chicken

Servings: 4
Cooking Time: 30 Minutes
Ingredients:
- 1 lb chicken thighs, boneless and skinless
- 1 cup salsa
- Pepper
- Salt

Directions:
1. Preheat the air fryer to 350 F.
2. Place chicken thighs into the air fryer baking dish and season with pepper and salt. Top with salsa.
3. Place in the air fryer and cook for 30 minutes.
4. Serve and enjoy.

21. Turkey And Mushroom Sandwich

Servings:1
Cooking Time: 15 Minutes
Ingredients:
- ⅓ cup sliced mushrooms
- 1 tbsp butter, divided
- 2 tomato slices
- ½ tsp red pepper flakes
- ¼ tsp salt
- ¼ tsp black pepper
- 1 hamburger bun

Directions:
1. Melt half of the butter and add the mushrooms. Cook for 4 minutes. Cut the bun in half and spread the remaining butter on the outside of the bun. Place the turkey on one half of the bun.
2. Arrange mushroom slices on top of the turkey. Place the tomato slices over the mushrooms. Sprinkle with salt pepper and red pepper flakes. Top with the other bun half. Cook for 5 minutes at 350 F.

22. Herbed Cheese Balls

Servings: 3
Cooking Time: 9 Minutes
Ingredients:
- 1 teaspoon garlic powder
- 1 oz Parmesan, grated
- ½ cup Cheddar cheese, shredded
- 1 egg, beaten
- 1 tablespoon cream cheese

- 1 teaspoon dried dill
- 1 teaspoon dried cilantro
- 1 teaspoon dried parsley
- Cooking spray

Directions:
1. Mix up Parmesan and Cheddar cheese. Add garlic powder, egg, cream cheese, dried dill, cilantro, and parsley. Stir the mixture until homogenous. With the help of the scoop make the cheese balls and put them in the freezer for 15 minutes. Preheat the air fryer to 400F. Then spray the air fryer basket with cooking spray. Put the frozen cheese balls in the air fryer basket. Cook them for 9 minutes or until they are golden brown.

23. Butter Donuts

Servings: 4
Cooking Time: 10 Minutes
Ingredients:
- 1 cup almond flour
- 1 tablespoon flax meal
- 2 tablespoons Erythritol
- 2 eggs, beaten
- 1 teaspoon baking powder
- 1 teaspoon vanilla extract
- 1 teaspoon heavy cream
- 1 teaspoon butter, melted
- 1 tablespoon Psyllium husk powder

Directions:
1. Make the dough: mix up almond flour, flax meal, eggs, baking powder, vanilla extract, heavy cream, and butter. Add Psyllium husk and knead the soft but non-sticky dough. Then make the donuts balls and leave them for 10 minutes in a warm place. Preheat the air fryer to 355F. Line the air fryer basket with baking paper. Put the donuts inside and cook them for 10 minutes or until they are light brown. Then coat every donut in Erythritol.

24. Kale Omelet

Servings: 1
Cooking Time: 10 Minutes
Ingredients:
- 3 eggs, lightly beaten
- 1 tbsp parsley, chopped
- 1 tbsp basil, chopped
- 3 tbsp kale, chopped
- 3 tbsp cottage cheese, crumbled
- Pepper
- Salt

Directions:
1. Spray air fryer baking dish with cooking spray.
2. In a bowl, whisk eggs with pepper and salt.
3. Add remaining ingredients into the egg and stir to combine.

4. Pour egg mixture into the prepared dish and place into the air fryer.
5. Cook at 330 F for 10 minutes.
6. Serve and enjoy.

25. Chicken And Cream Lasagna

Servings: 2
Cooking Time: 25 Minutes
Ingredients:
- 1 egg, beaten
- 1 tablespoon heavy cream
- 1 teaspoon cream cheese
- 2 tablespoons almond flour
- ¼ teaspoon salt
- ¼ cup coconut cream
- 1 teaspoon dried basil
- 1 teaspoon keto tomato sauce
- ¼ cup Mozzarella, shredded
- 1 teaspoon butter, melted
- ½ cup ground chicken

Directions:
1. Make the lasagna batter: in the bowl mix up egg, heavy cream, cream cheese, and almond flour. Add coconut cream. Stir the liquid until smooth. Then preheat the air fryer to 355F. Brush the air fryer basket with butter. Pour ½ part of lasagna batter in the air fryer basket and flatten it in one layer. Then in the separated bowl mix up tomato sauce, basil, salt, and ground chicken. Put the chicken mixture over the batter in the air fryer. Add beaten egg. Then top it with remaining lasagna batter and sprinkle with shredded Mozzarella. Cook the lasagna for 25 minutes.

26. Egg Cups

Servings: 12
Cooking Time: 18 Minutes
Ingredients:
- 12 eggs
- 4 oz cream cheese
- 12 bacon strips, uncooked
- 1/4 cup buffalo sauce
- 2/3 cup cheddar cheese, shredded
- Pepper
- Salt

Directions:
1. In a bowl, whisk together eggs, pepper, and salt.
2. Line each silicone muffin mold with one bacon strip.
3. Pour egg mixture into each muffin mold and place in the air fryer basket. (In batches)
4. Cook at 350 F for 8 minutes.
5. In another bowl, mix together cheddar cheese and cream cheese and microwave for 30 seconds. Add buffalo sauce and stir well.

6. Remove muffin molds from air fryer and add 2 tsp cheese mixture in the center of each egg cup.
7. Return muffin molds to the air fryer and cook for 10 minutes more.
8. Serve and enjoy.

27. Homemade Crispy Croutons

Servings: 4
Cooking Time: 20 Minutes
Ingredients:
- 2 tbsp butter, melted
- Garlic salt and black pepper to taste

Directions:
1. Mix bread with butter, garlic salt, and pepper until well-coated. Place in the air fryer, cook for 12 minutes at 380 F until golden brown and crispy.

28. Orange-flavored Cupcakes

Servings: 5
Cooking Time: 25 Minutes
Ingredients:
- 1 cup natural yogurt
- Sugar to taste
- 1 orange, juiced
- 1 tbsp orange zest
- 7 oz cream cheese
- Cake:
- 2 lemons, quartered
- ½ cup flour + extra for basing
- ¼ tsp salt
- 2 tbsp sugar
- 1 tsp baking powder
- 1 tsp vanilla extract
- 2 eggs
- ½ cup softened butter
- 2 tbsp milk

Directions:
1. In a bowl, add the yogurt and cream cheese. Mix until smooth. Add the orange juice and zest; mix well. Gradually add the sweetener to your taste while stirring until smooth. Make sure the frost is not runny. Set aside.
2. For cupcakes: Place the lemon quarters in a food processor and process it until pureed. Add the baking powder, softened butter, milk, eggs, vanilla extract, sugar, and salt. Process again until smooth.
3. Preheat the air fryer to 400 F. Flour the bottom of 10 cupcake cases and spoon the batter into the cases ¾ way up. Place them in the air fryer and bake for 7 minutes. Once ready, remove and let cool. Design the cupcakes with the frosting.

29. Crustless Mediterranean Quiche

Servings: 2
Cooking Time: 40 Minutes

Ingredients:
- ½ cup chopped tomatoes
- 1 cup crumbled feta cheese
- 1 tbsp chopped basil
- 1 tbsp chopped oregano
- ¼ cup chopped kalamata olives
- ¼ cup chopped onion
- 2 tbsp olive oil
- ½ cup milk
- Salt and pepper to taste

Directions:
1. Preheat air fryer to 340 F. Brush a pie pan with olive oil. Beat eggs along with milk and some salt and pepper. Stir in all of the remaining ingredients. Pour the egg mixture into the pan. Cook for 30 minutes.

30. Yogurt Banana Bread

Servings:5
Cooking Time: 35 Minutes
Ingredients:
- ½ cup all-purpose flour
- ¼ cup whole-wheat flour
- ¼ teaspoon baking soda
- ½ teaspoon salt
- 1 large egg
- ½ cup granulated sugar
- ¼ cup plain yogurt
- ¼ cup vegetable oil
- ½ teaspoon pure vanilla extract
- 2 ripe bananas, peeled and mashed
- 2 tablespoons turbinado sugar

Directions:
1. In a bowl, sift together the flours, baking soda, and salt.
2. In another large bowl, mix well the egg, granulated sugar, yogurt, oil, and vanilla extract.
3. Add in the bananas and beat until well combined.
4. Now, add the flour mixture and mix until just combined.
5. Set the temperature of Air Fryer to 310 degrees F.
6. Place the mixture evenly into a cake pan and sprinkle with the turbinado sugar.
7. Arrange the cake pan into an Air Fryer basket.
8. Air Fry for about 30-35 minutes or until a toothpick inserted in the center comes out clean, turning the pan once halfway through.
9. Carefully, take out the bread from pan and put onto a wire rack until it is completely cool before slicing.
10. Cut the bread into desired size slices and serve.

31. Bistro Wedges

Servings: 4

Cooking Time: 20 Minutes
Ingredients:
- 1 lb. fingerling potatoes, cut into wedges
- 1 tsp. extra virgin olive oil
- ½ tsp. garlic powder
- Salt and pepper to taste
- ½ cup raw cashews, soaked in water overnight
- ½ tsp. ground turmeric
- ½ tsp. paprika
- 1 tbsp. nutritional yeast
- 1 tsp. fresh lemon juice
- 2 tbsp. to ¼ cup water

Directions:
1. Pre-heat your Air Fryer at 400°F.
2. In a bowl, toss together the potato wedges, olive oil, garlic powder, and salt and pepper, making sure to coat the potatoes well.
3. Transfer the potatoes to the basket of your fryer and fry for 10 minutes.
4. In the meantime, prepare the cheese sauce. Pulse the cashews, turmeric, paprika, nutritional yeast, lemon juice, and water together in a food processor. Add more water to achieve your desired consistency.
5. When the potatoes are finished cooking, move them to a bowl that is small enough to fit inside the fryer and add the cheese sauce on top. Cook for an additional 3 minutes.

32. Mushroom Bake

Servings: 4
Cooking Time: 20 Minutes
Ingredients:
- 2 garlic cloves, minced
- 1 teaspoon olive oil
- 2 celery stalks, chopped
- ½ cup white mushrooms, chopped
- ½ cup red bell pepper, chopped
- Salt and black pepper to the taste
- 1 teaspoon oregano, dried
- 7 ounces mozzarella, shredded
- 1 tablespoon lemon juice

Directions:
1. Preheat the Air Fryer at 350 degrees F, add the oil and heat it up. Add garlic, celery, mushrooms, bell pepper, salt, pepper, oregano, mozzarella and the lemon juice, toss and cook for 20 minutes. Divide between plates and serve for breakfast.

33. Breakfast Spinach Pie

Servings: 4
Cooking Time: 19 Minutes
Ingredients:
- 7 ounces white flour
- 7 ounces spinach, torn
- 2 tablespoons olive oil
- 2 eggs, whisked

- 2 tablespoons milk
- 3 ounces mozzarella cheese, crumbled
- Salt and black pepper to taste
- 1 red onion, chopped

Directions:
1. In your food processor, mix the flour with 1 tablespoon of the oil, eggs, milk, salt, and pepper; pulse, then transfer to a bowl.
2. Knead the mixture a bit, cover, and keep in the fridge for 10 minutes.
3. Heat up a pan with the remaining 1 tablespoon of oil over medium heat, and then add all remaining ingredients.
4. Stir, cook for 4 minutes, and remove from heat.
5. Divide the dough into 4 pieces, roll each piece, and place in the bottom of a ramekin.
6. Divide the spinach mixture between the ramekins, place them in your air fryer's basket, and cook at 360 degrees F for 15 minutes.
7. Serve and enjoy!

34. Air Fried Calzone

Servings:4
Cooking Time: 20 Minutes
Ingredients:
- 4 oz cheddar cheese, grated
- 1 oz mozzarella cheese
- 1 oz bacon, diced
- 2 cups cooked and shredded turkey
- 1 egg, beaten
- 4 tbsp tomato paste
- 1 tsp basil
- 1 tsp oregano
- Salt and pepper, to taste

Directions:
1. Preheat the air fryer to 350 F. Divide the pizza dough into 4 equal pieces so you have the dough for 4 small pizza crusts. Combine the tomato paste, basil, and oregano in a small bowl.
2. Brush the mixture onto the crusts, just make sure not to go all the way and avoid brushing near the edges on one half of each crust, place ½ turkey, and season the meat with some salt and pepper. Top the meat with bacon. Divide mozzarella and cheddar cheeses between pizzas. Brush the edges with beaten egg. Fold the crust and seal with a fork. Cook for 10 minutes.

35. Breakfast Omelet

Servings: 2
Cooking Time: 30 Minutes
Ingredients:
- 1 large onion, chopped
- 2 tbsp. cheddar cheese, grated
- 3 eggs

- ½ tsp. soy sauce
- Salt
- Pepper powder
- Cooking spray

Directions:
1. In a bowl, mix the salt, pepper powder, soy sauce and eggs with a whisk.
2. Take a small pan small enough to fit inside the Air Fryer and spritz with cooking spray. Spread the chopped onion across the bottom of the pan, then transfer the pan to the Fryer. Cook at 355°F for 6-7 minutes, ensuring the onions turn translucent.
3. Add the egg mixture on top of the onions, coating everything well. Add the cheese on top, then resume cooking for another 5 or 6 minutes.
4. Take care when taking the pan out of the fryer. Enjoy with some toasted bread.

36. Spiced Pudding

Servings: 2
Cooking Time: 12 Minutes
Ingredients:
- ½ teaspoon cinnamon powder
- ¼ teaspoon allspice, ground
- 4 tablespoons erythritol
- 4 eggs, whisked
- 2 tablespoons heavy cream
- Cooking spray

Directions:
1. In a bowl, mix all the ingredients except the cooking spray, whisk well and pour into a ramekin greased with cooking spray. Add the basket to your Air Fryer, put the ramekin inside and cook at 400 degrees F for 12 minutes. Divide into bowls and serve for breakfast.

37. Turmeric Mozzarella Sticks

Servings: 2
Cooking Time: 7 Minutes
Ingredients:
- 4 oz Mozzarella
- 2 tablespoons coconut flakes
- 1 egg, beaten
- 1 teaspoon turmeric powder
- 1 tablespoon heavy cream
- ½ teaspoon ground black pepper
- Cooking spray

Directions:
1. Cut Mozzarella into 2 sticks. Then in the mixing bowl mix up heavy cream, egg, and ground black pepper. Dip the cheese sticks in the liquid. After this, coat every cheese stick with coconut flakes. Preheat the air fryer to 400F. Then spray the air fryer basket with cooking spray. Put Mozzarella

sticks in the air fryer and cook them for 7 minutes or until they are light brown.

38. Choco Bars

Servings: 8
Cooking Time: 30 Minutes
Ingredients:
- 2 cups old-fashioned oats
- ½ cup quinoa, cooked
- ½ cup chia seeds
- ½ cup s, sliced
- ½ cup dried cherries, chopped
- ½ cup dark chocolate, chopped
- ¾ cup butter
- ⅓ cup honey
- 2 tbsp. coconut oil
- ¼ tsp. salt
- ½ cup prunes, pureed

Directions:
1. Pre-heat your Air Fryer at 375°F.
2. Put the oats, quinoa, s, cherries, chia seeds, and chocolate in a bowl and mix well.
3. Heat the butter, honey, and coconut oil in a saucepan, gently stirring together. Pour this over the oats mixture.
4. Mix in the salt and pureed prunes and combine well.
5. Transfer this to a baking dish small enough to fit inside the fryer and cook for 15 minutes. Remove from the fryer and allow to cool completely. Cut into bars and enjoy.

39. Chicken Meatballs

Servings: 4
Cooking Time: 12 Minutes
Ingredients:
- 1 lb ground chicken
- 1/3 cup frozen spinach, drained and thawed
- 1/3 cup feta cheese, crumbled
- 1 tsp greek seasoning
- ½ oz pork rinds, crushed
- Pepper
- Salt

Directions:
1. Spray air fryer basket with cooking spray.
2. Add all ingredients into the large bowl and mix until well combined.
3. Make small balls from meat mixture and place into the air fryer basket and cook for 12 minutes.
4. Serve and enjoy.

40. Yummy Savory French Toasts

Servings: 2
Cooking Time: 4 Minutes
Ingredients:
- ¼ cup chickpea flour
- 3 tablespoons onion, chopped finely
- 2 teaspoons green chili, seeded and chopped finely
- Water, as required
- 4 bread slices
- ½ teaspoon red chili powder
- ¼ teaspoon ground turmeric
- ¼ teaspoon ground cumin
- Salt, to taste

Directions:
1. Preheat the Air fryer to 375 °F and line an Air fryer pan with a foil paper.
2. Mix together all the ingredients in a large bowl except the bread slices.
3. Spread the mixture over both sides of the bread slices and transfer into the Air fryer pan.
4. Cook for about 4 minutes and remove from the Air fryer to serve.

41. Baked Kale Omelet

Servings: 1
Cooking Time: 15 Minutes
Ingredients:
- 3 tbsp cottage cheese
- 3 tbsp chopped kale
- ½ tbsp chopped basil
- ½ tbsp chopped parsley
- Salt and pepper to taste

Directions:
1. Beat the eggs, salt and pepper in a bowl. Stir in the rest of the ingredients. Pour the mixture into the greased air fryer basket and cook for 10 minutes at 330 F, until slightly golden and set. Serve.

42. Cheesy Omelet

Servings: 1
Cooking Time: 15 Minutes
Ingredients:
- Black pepper to taste
- 1 cup cheddar cheese, shredded
- 1 whole onion, chopped
- 2 tbsp soy sauce

Directions:
1. Preheat your air fryer to 340 F. Drizzle soy sauce over the chopped onions. Place the onions in your air fryer's cooking basket and cook for 8 minutes. In a bowl, mix the beaten eggs with salt and pepper.
2. Pour the egg mixture over onions (in the cooking basket) and cook for 3 minutes. Add cheddar cheese over eggs and bake for 2 more minutes. Serve with fresh basil and enjoy!

43. French Toast With Vanilla Filling

Servings: 3
Cooking Time: 15 Minutes
Ingredients:

- 2 eggs
- ¼ cup heavy cream
- ⅓ cup sugar mixed with 1 tsp ground cinnamon
- 6 tbsp caramel
- 1 tsp vanilla extract
- Cooking spray

Directions:
1. In a bowl, whisk eggs and cream. Dip each piece of bread into the egg and cream. Dip the bread into the sugar and cinnamon mixture until well-coated. On a clean board, lay the coated slices and spread three of the slices with about 2 tbsp of caramel each, around the center.
2. Place the remaining three slices on top to form three sandwiches. Spray the air fryer basket with oil. Arrange the sandwiches into the fryer and cook for 10 minutes at 340 F, turning once.

44. Air Fryer Sausage

Servings:5
Cooking Time:20 Minutes
Ingredients:
- 5 raw and uncooked sausage links
- 1 tablespoon olive oil

Directions:
1. Preheat the Air fryer to 360 °F and grease an Air fryer basket with olive oil.
2. Cook for about 15 minutes and flip the sausages.
3. Cook for 5 more minutes and serve warm.

45. Greek-style Frittata

Servings:2
Cooking Time: 10 Minutes
Ingredients:
- 2 tbsp heavy cream
- 2 cups spinach, chopped
- 1 cup chopped mushrooms
- 3 oz feta cheese, crumbled
- A handful of fresh parsley, chopped
- Salt and black pepper

Directions:
1. Spray your air fryer basket with cooking spray. In a bowl, whisk eggs and until combined. Stir in spinach, mushrooms, feta, parsley, salt, and black pepper.
2. Pour into the basket and cook for 6 minutes at 350 F. Serve immediately with a touch of tomato relish.

46. Spinach Spread

Servings: 4
Cooking Time: 10 Minutes
Ingredients:
- 2 tablespoons coconut cream
- 3 cups spinach leaves

- 2 tablespoons cilantro
- 2 tablespoons bacon, cooked and crumbled
- Salt and black pepper to the taste

Directions:
1. In a pan that fits the air fryer, combine all the ingredients except the bacon, put the pan in the machine and cook at 360 degrees F for 10 minutes. Transfer to a blender, pulse well, divide into bowls and serve with bacon sprinkled on top.

47. Zucchini Omelet

Servings:2
Cooking Time: 14 Minutes
Ingredients:
- 1 teaspoon butter
- 1 zucchini, julienned
- 4 eggs
- ¼ teaspoon fresh basil, chopped
- ¼ teaspoon red pepper flakes, crushed
- Salt and ground black pepper, as required

Directions:
1. Set the temperature of Air Fryer to 355 degrees F. Grease an Air Fryer pan.
2. Take a skillet, melt the butter over medium heat and cook the zucchini for about 3-4 minutes.
3. Meanwhile, in a bowl, mix together the eggs, basil, red pepper flakes, salt, and black pepper.
4. Add the cooked zucchini and gently, stir to combine.
5. Transfer the mixture into the prepared pan.
6. Air Fry for 10 minutes or until done completely.
7. Serve hot.

48. Clean Breakfast Sandwich

Servings:1
Cooking Time: 10 Minutes
Ingredients:
- 1 slice English bacon
- Salt and pepper to taste
- 1 slice bread
- ½ cup butter

Directions:
1. Preheat your air fryer to 400 F. Spread butter on one side of the bread slice. Add the cracked egg on top and season with salt and pepper. Place bacon on top. Arrange the bread slice in your air fryer's cooking basket and cook for 3-5 minutes. Serve and enjoy!

49. Carrot Oatmeal

Servings: 4
Cooking Time: 15 Minutes
Ingredients:
- 2 cups almond milk

- ½ cup steel cut oats
- 1 cup carrots, shredded
- 1 teaspoon cardamom, ground
- 2 teaspoons sugar
- Cooking spray

Directions:
1. Spray your air fryer with cooking spray, add all ingredients, toss, and cover.
2. Cook at 365 degrees F for 15 minutes.
3. Divide into bowls and serve.

50. Rice Paper Bacon

Servings: 4
Cooking Time: 30 Minutes
Ingredients:
- 3 tbsp. soy sauce or tamari
- 2 tbsp. cashew butter
- 2 tbsp. liquid smoke
- 2 tbsp. water
- 4 pc white rice paper, cut into 1-inch thick strips

Directions:
1. Pre-heat your Air Fryer at 350°F.
2. Mix together the soy sauce/tamari, liquid smoke, water, and cashew butter in a large bowl.

3. Take the strips of rice paper and soak them for 5 minutes. Arrange in one layer in the bottom of your fryer.
4. Cook for 15 minutes, ensuring they become crispy, before serving with some vegetables.

51. Peppers And Lettuce Salad

Servings: 4
Cooking Time: 10 Minutes
Ingredients:
- 1 tablespoon lime juice
- 4 red bell peppers
- 1 lettuce head, torn
- Salt and black pepper to taste
- 3 tablespoons heavy cream
- 2 tablespoons olive oil
- 2 ounces rocket leaves

Directions:
1. Place the bell peppers in your air fryer's basket and cook at 400 degrees F for 10 minutes.
2. Remove the peppers, peel, cut them into strips, and put them in a bowl.
3. Add all remaining ingredients, toss, and serve.

LUNCH & DINNER RECIPES

52. Rosemary Chicken Stew

Servings: 4
Cooking Time: 20 Minutes
Ingredients:
- 2 cups okra
- 2 garlic cloves, minced
- 1 pound chicken breasts, skinless, boneless and cubed
- 4 tomatoes, cubed
- 1 tablespoon olive oil
- 1 teaspoon rosemary, dried
- Salt and black pepper to the taste
- 1 tablespoon parsley, chopped

Directions:
1. Heat up a pan that fits your air fryer with the oil over medium-high heat, add the chicken, garlic, rosemary, salt and pepper, toss and brown for 5 minutes. Add the remaining ingredients, toss again, place the pan in the air fryer and cook at 380 degrees F for 15 minutes more. Divide the stew into bowls and serve for lunch.

53. Vegan Ravioli

Servings: 4
Cooking Time: 15 Minutes
Ingredients:
- ½ cup bread crumbs
- 2 tsp. nutritional yeast
- 1 tsp. dried basil
- 1 tsp. dried oregano
- 1 tsp. garlic powder
- Salt and pepper to taste
- ¼ cup aquafaba
- 8 oz. vegan ravioli
- Cooking spray

Directions:
1. Cover the Air Fryer basket with aluminum foil and coat with a light brushing of oil.
2. Pre-heat the Air Fryer to 400°F. Combine together the panko breadcrumbs, nutritional yeast, basil, oregano, and garlic powder. Sprinkle on salt and pepper to taste.
3. Put the aquafaba in a separate bowl. Dip the ravioli in the aquafaba before coating it in the panko mixture. Spritz with cooking spray and transfer to the Air Fryer.
4. Cook for 6 minutes ensuring to shake the Air Fryer basket halfway.

54. Paprika Tofu

Servings: 4
Cooking Time: 25 Minutes
Ingredients:
- 2 block extra firm tofu, pressed to remove excess water and cubed
- ¼ cup cornstarch
- 1 tbsp. smoked paprika
- Salt and pepper to taste

Directions:
1. Cover the Air Fryer basket with aluminum foil and coat with a light brushing of oil.
2. Pre-heat the Air Fryer to 370°F.
3. Combine all ingredients in a bowl, coating the tofu well.
4. Put in the Air Fryer basket and allow to cook for 12 minutes.

55. Olives Mix

Servings: 4
Cooking Time: 20 Minutes
Ingredients:
- 2 cups black olives, pitted and halved
- 1 red bell pepper, chopped
- 3 celery stalks, chopped
- Salt and black pepper to the taste
- 4 cups spinach, torn
- 2 tomatoes, chopped
- ½ cup keto tomato sauce

Directions:
1. In a pan that fits your air fryer, mix all the ingredients except the spinach, toss, introduce the pan in the air fryer and cook at 370 degrees F for 15 minutes. Add the spinach, toss, cook for 5-6 minutes more, divide into bowls and serve.

56. Sweet & Sour Tofu

Servings: 2
Cooking Time: 55 Minutes
Ingredients:
- 2 tsp. apple cider vinegar
- 1 tbsp. sugar
- 1 tbsp. soy sauce
- 3 tsp. lime juice
- 1 tsp. ground ginger
- 1 tsp. garlic powder
- ½ block firm tofu, pressed to remove excess liquid and cut into cubes
- 1 tsp. cornstarch
- 2 green onions, chopped
- Toasted sesame seeds for garnish

Directions:
1. In a bowl, thoroughly combine the apple cider vinegar, sugar, soy sauce, lime juice, ground ginger, and garlic powder.
2. Cover the tofu with this mixture and leave to marinate for at least 30 minutes.
3. Transfer the tofu to the Air Fryer, keeping any excess marinade for the sauce. Cook at 400°F for 20 minutes or until crispy.
4. In the meantime, thicken the sauce with the cornstarch over a medium-low heat.

5. Serve the cooked tofu with the sauce, green onions, sesame seeds, and some rice.

57. Chicken And Coconut Casserole

Servings: 4
Cooking Time:35 Minutes
Ingredients:
- 1 lb. chicken breast; skinless, boneless and cut into thin strips
- 4 lime leaves; torn
- 1 cup veggie stock
- 1 lemongrass stalk; chopped
- 1-inch piece; grated
- 8 oz. mushrooms; chopped.
- 4 Thai chilies; chopped.
- 4 tbsp. fish sauce
- 6 oz. coconut milk
- 1/4 cup lime juice
- 1/4 cup cilantro; chopped
- Salt and black pepper to the taste

Directions:
1. Put stock into a pan that fits your air fryer; bring to a simmer over medium heat, add lemongrass, ginger and lime leaves; stir and cook for 10 minutes.
2. Strain soup, return to pan, add chicken, mushrooms, milk, chilies, fish sauce, lime juice, cilantro, salt and pepper; stir, introduce in your air fryer and cook at 360 °F, for 15 minutes. Divide into bowls and serve.

58. Jarlsberg Lunch Omelet

Servings: 2
Cooking Time: 10 Minutes
Ingredients:
- 4 medium mushrooms, sliced, 2 oz
- 1 green onion, sliced
- 2 eggs, beaten
- 1 oz Jarlsberg or Swiss cheese, shredded
- 1 oz ham, diced

Directions:
1. In a skillet, cook the mushrooms and green onion until tender.
2. Add the eggs and mix well.
3. Sprinkle with salt and top with the mushroom mixture, cheese and the ham.
4. When the egg is set, fold the plain side of the omelet on the filled side.
5. Turn off the heat and let it stand until the cheese has melted.
6. Serve!

59. Thyme Green Beans

Servings: 6
Cooking Time: 20 Minutes
Ingredients:
- 1 pound green beans, trimmed and halved
- 2 eggplants, cubed

- 1 cup veggie stock
- 1 tablespoon olive oil
- 1 red chili pepper
- 1 red bell pepper, chopped
- ½ teaspoon thyme, dried
- Salt and black pepper to the taste

Directions:
1. In a pan that fits your air fryer, mix all the ingredients, toss, introduce the pan in the machine and cook at 350 degrees F for 20 minutes. Divide into bowls and serve for lunch.

60. Cheese Pizza

Servings: 4
Cooking Time: 15 Minutes
Ingredients:
- 1 pc. bread
- ½ lb. mozzarella cheese
- 1 tbsp. olive oil
- 2 tbsp. ketchup
- ⅓ cup sausage
- 1 tsp. garlic powder

Directions:
1. Using a tablespoon, spread the ketchup over the pita bread.
2. Top with the sausage and cheese. Season with the garlic powder and 1 tablespoon of olive oil.
3. Pre-heat the Air Fryer to 340°F.
4. Put the pizza in the fryer basket and cook for 6 minutes. Enjoy!

61. Eggplant Sandwich

Servings: 2
Cooking Time: 7 Minutes
Ingredients:
- 1 large eggplant
- ½ cup mozzarella, shredded
- 1 tablespoon fresh basil, chopped
- 1 teaspoon minced garlic
- 1 teaspoon salt
- 1 tablespoon nut oil
- 1 tomato

Directions:
1. Slice the tomato on 4 slices. Then slice along the eggplant on 4 slices. Then rub every eggplant slice with salt, minced garlic, and brush with nut oil. Preheat the air fryer to 400F. Put the eggplant slices in one layer and cook for 2 minutes at 400F. Then flip the vegetables on another side and cook for 2 minutes more. Transfer the cooked eggplant slices on the plate. Sprinkle 2 eggplant slices with basil and mozzarella. Then add 2 tomato slices on 2 eggplant slices. Cover the tomato slices with the remaining 2 eggplant slices and put in the

air fryer basket. Cook the sandwich for 3 minutes at 400F.

62. Summer Rolls

Servings: 4
Cooking Time: 25 Minutes
Ingredients:
- 1 cup shiitake mushroom, sliced thinly
- 1 celery stalk, chopped
- 1 medium carrot, shredded
- ½ tsp. ginger, finely chopped
- 1 tsp. sugar
- 1 tbsp. soy sauce
- 1 tsp. nutritional yeast
- 8 spring roll sheets
- 1 tsp. corn starch
- 2 tbsp. water

Directions:
1. In a bowl, combine the ginger, soy sauce, nutritional yeast, carrots, celery, and sugar.
2. Mix together the cornstarch and water to create an adhesive for your spring rolls.
3. Scoop a tablespoonful of the vegetable mixture into the middle of the spring roll sheets. Brush the edges of the sheets with the cornstarch adhesive and enclose around the filling to make spring rolls.
4. Pre-heat your Air Fryer at 400°F. When warm, place the rolls inside and cook for 15 minutes or until crisp.

63. Quinoa And Spinach Salad

Servings: 4
Cooking Time: 15 Minutes
Ingredients:
- 1½ cups quinoa, cooked
- 1 red bell pepper, chopped
- 3 celery stalks, chopped
- Salt and black pepper to taste
- 4 cups spinach, torn
- 2 tomatoes, chopped
- ½ cup chicken stock
- ½ cup black olives, pitted and chopped
- ½ cup feta cheese, crumbled
- ⅓ cup basil pesto
- ¼ cup almonds, sliced

Directions:
1. In a pan that fits your air fryer, combine the quinoa, bell peppers, celery, salt, pepper, spinach, tomatoes, chicken stock, olives, and basil pesto.
2. Sprinkle the almonds and the cheese on top, and then place the pan in the air fryer and cook at 380 degrees F for 15 minutes.
3. Divide between plates and serve.

64. Risotto

Servings: 2
Cooking Time: 40 Minutes

Ingredients:
- 1 onion, diced
- 2 cups chicken stock, boiling
- ½ cup parmesan cheese or cheddar cheese, grated
- 1 clove garlic, minced
- ¾ cup arborio rice
- 1 tbsp. olive oil
- 1 tbsp. butter, unsalted

Directions:
1. Turn the Air Fryer to 390°F and set for 5 minutes to warm.
2. Grease a round baking tin with oil and stir in the butter, garlic, and onion.
3. Put the tin in the fryer and allow to cook for 4 minutes.
4. Pour in the rice and cook for a further 4 minutes, stirring three times throughout the cooking time.
5. Turn the temperature down to 320°F.
6. Add the chicken stock and give the dish a gentle stir. Cook for 22 minutes, leaving the fryer uncovered.
7. Pour in the cheese, stir once more and serve.

65. Seasoned Chicken Thighs

Servings: 4
Cooking Time: 22 Minutes
Ingredients:
- 4 chicken thighs, skinless, boneless
- 1 teaspoon jerk seasonings
- 1 teaspoon Jerk sauce
- Cooking spray

Directions:
1. Sprinkle the chicken thighs with Jerk seasonings and Jerk sauce and leave them for 10 minutes to marinate. Meanwhile, preheat the air fryer to 385F. Place the marinated chicken thighs in the air fryer and spray them with the cooking spray. Cook the chicken thighs for 12 minutes. Then flip them on another side and cook for 10 minutes more.

66. Chicken-mushroom Casserole

Servings: 4
Cooking Time: 30 Minutes
Ingredients:
- 4 chicken breasts
- ½ cup shredded cheese
- Salt to taste
- 1 cup coconut milk
- 1 cup mushrooms
- 1 broccoli, cut into florets
- 1 tbsp. curry powder

Directions:
1. Pre-heat your Air Fryer to 350°F. Spritz a casserole dish with some cooking spray.

2. Cube the chicken breasts and combine with curry powder and coconut milk in a bowl. Season with salt.
3. Add in the broccoli and mushroom and mix well.
4. Pour the mixture into the casserole dish. Top with the cheese.
5. Transfer to your Air Fryer and cook for about 20 minutes.
6. Serve warm.

67. Paprika Chicken

Servings: 6
Cooking Time: 35 Minutes
Ingredients:
- 3 pounds chicken thighs, bone-in
- ½ cup butter, melted
- 1 tablespoon smoked paprika
- 1 teaspoon lemon juice

Directions:
1. In a bowl, mix the chicken thighs with the paprika, toss, put all the pieces in your air fryer's basket and cook them at 360 degrees F for 25 minutes shaking the fryer from time to time and basting the meat with the butter. Divide between plates and serve.

68. Roasted Garlic, Broccoli & Lemon

Servings: 6
Cooking Time: 25 Minutes
Ingredients:
- 2 heads broccoli, cut into florets
- 2 tsp. extra virgin olive oil
- 1 tsp. salt
- ½ tsp. black pepper
- 1 clove garlic, minced
- ½ tsp. lemon juice

Directions:
1. Cover the Air Fryer basket with aluminum foil and coat with a light brushing of oil.
2. Pre-heat the fryer to 375°F.
3. In a bowl, combine all ingredients save for the lemon juice and transfer to the fryer basket. Allow to cook for 15 minutes.
4. Serve with the lemon juice.

69. Fat Bombs

Servings: 2
Cooking Time: 100 Minutes
Ingredients:
- 1 cup coconut butter
- 1 cup coconut milk (full fat, canned)
- 1 tsp vanilla extract (gluten free)
- ½ tsp nutmeg
- ½ cup coconut shreds

Directions:
1. Pour some water into pot and put a glass bowl on top.

2. Add all the ingredients except the shredded coconut into the glass bowl and cook on a medium heat.
3. Stir and melt until they start melting.
4. Then, take them off of the heat.
5. Put the glass bowl into your refrigerator until the mix can be rolled into doughy balls. Usually this happens after around 30 minutes.
6. Roll the dough into 1-inch balls through the coconut shreds.
7. Place the balls on a plate and refrigerate for one hour.
8. Serve!

70. Falafel

Servings: 8
Cooking Time: 30 Minutes
Ingredients:
- 1 tsp. cumin seeds
- ½ tsp. coriander seeds
- 2 cups chickpeas from can, drained and rinsed
- ½ tsp. red pepper flakes
- 3 cloves garlic
- ¼ cup parsley, chopped
- ¼ cup coriander, chopped
- ½ onion, diced
- 1 tbsp. juice from freshly squeezed lemon
- 3 tbsp. flour
- ½ tsp. salt cooking spray

Directions:
1. Fry the cumin and coriander seeds over medium heat until fragrant.
2. Grind using a mortar and pestle.
3. Put all of ingredients, except for the cooking spray, in a food processor and blend until a fine consistency is achieved.
4. Use your hands to mold the mixture into falafels and spritz with the cooking spray.
5. Preheat your Air Fryer at 400°F.
6. Transfer the falafels to the fryer in one single layer.
7. Cook for 15 minutes, serving when they turn golden brown.

71. Cheese & Bacon Rolls

Servings: 4
Cooking Time: 25 Minutes
Ingredients:
- 8 oz. refrigerated crescent roll dough [usually 1 can]
- 6 oz. very sharp cheddar cheese, grated
- 1 lb. bacon, cooked and chopped

Directions:
1. Roll out the crescent dough flat and slice it into 1" x 1 ½" pieces.
2. In a bowl, mix together the cheese and bacon. Take about ¼ cup of this mixture

and spread it across one slice of dough. Repeat with the rest of the mixture and dough.

3. Set your Air Fryer to 330°F and allow to warm.
4. Place the rolls on the Air Fry tray and transfer to the fryer. Alternatively, you can put them in the food basket.
5. Bake for roughly 6 – 8 minutes until a golden brown color is achieved. Watch them carefully to prevent burning, as they may cook very quickly.

72. Chili Potato Wedges

Servings: 4
Cooking Time: 50 Minutes
Ingredients:
- 1 lb. fingerling potatoes, washed and cut into wedges
- 1 tsp. olive oil
- 1 tsp. salt
- 1 tsp. black pepper
- 1 tsp. cayenne pepper
- 1 tsp. nutritional yeast
- ½ tsp. garlic powder

Directions:
1. Pre-heat the Air Fryer at 400°F.
2. Coat the potatoes with the rest of the ingredients.
3. Transfer to the basket of your fryer and allow to cook for 16 minutes, shaking the basket at the halfway point.

73. Air Fryer Bacon Pudding

Servings: 6
Cooking Time:40 Minutes
Ingredients:
- 4 bacon strips; cooked and chopped.
- 1 tbsp. butter; soft
- 2 cups corn
- 3 eggs; whisked
- 3 cups bread; cubed
- 4 tbsp. parmesan; grated
- 1 yellow onion; chopped.
- 1/4 cup celery; chopped.
- 1/2 cup red bell pepper; chopped.
- 1 tsp. thyme; chopped.
- 2 tsp. garlic; minced
- 1/2 cup heavy cream
- 1 ½ cups milk
- Cooking spray
- Salt and black pepper to the taste

Directions:
1. Grease your air fryer's pan with cooking spray.
2. In a bowl; mix bacon with butter, corn, onion, bell pepper, celery, thyme, garlic, salt, pepper, milk, heavy cream, eggs and bread

cubes; toss, pour into greased pan and sprinkle cheese all over

3. Add this to your preheated air fryer at 320 degrees and cook for 30 minutes. Divide among plates and serve warm for a quick lunch.

74. Bacon-wrapped Hot Dog

Servings: 4
Cooking Time: 25 Minutes
Ingredients:
- 4 slices sugar-free bacon
- 4 beef hot dogs

Directions:
1. Take a slice of bacon and wrap it around the hot dog, securing it with a toothpick. Repeat with the other pieces of bacon and hot dogs, placing each wrapped dog in the basket of your fryer.
2. Cook at 370°F for ten minutes, turning halfway through to fry the other side.
3. Once hot and crispy, the hot dogs are ready to serve. Enjoy!

75. Tofu & Sweet Potatoes

Servings: 8
Cooking Time: 50 Minutes
Ingredients:
- 8 sweet potatoes, scrubbed
- 2 tbsp. olive oil
- 1 large onion, chopped
- 2 green chilies, deseeded and chopped
- ½ lb. tofu, crumbled
- 2 tbsp. Cajun seasoning
- cup tomatoes
- 1 can kidney beans, drained and rinsed
- Salt and pepper to taste

Directions:
1. Pre-heat the Air Fryer at 400°F.
2. With a knife, pierce the skin of the sweet potatoes in numerous places and cook in the fryer for half an hour, making sure they become soft. Remove from the fryer, halve each potato, and set to one side.
3. Over a medium heat, fry the onions and chilis in a little oil for 2 minutes until fragrant.
4. Add in the tofu and Cajun seasoning and allow to cook for a further 3 minutes before incorporating the kidney beans and tomatoes. Sprinkle some salt and pepper as desire.
5. Top each sweet potato halve with a spoonful of the tofu mixture and serve.

76. Beef And Green Onions Casserole

Servings: 4
Cooking Time: 21 Minutes
Ingredients:

- 10 oz lean ground beef
- 1 oz green onions, chopped
- 2 low carb tortillas
- 1 cup Mexican cheese blend, shredded
- 1 teaspoon fresh cilantro, chopped
- 1 teaspoon butter
- 1 tablespoon mascarpone
- 1 tablespoon heavy cream
- ¼ teaspoon garlic powder
- 1 teaspoon Mexican seasonings
- 1 teaspoon olive oil

Directions:
1. Pour olive oil in the skillet and heat it up over the medium heat. Then add ground beef and sprinkle it with garlic powder and Mexican seasonings. Cook the ground beef for 7 minutes over the medium heat. Stir it from time to time Then chop the low carb tortillas. Grease the air fryer pan with butter and put the tortillas in one layer inside. Put the ground beef mixture over the tortillas and spread it gently with the help of the spoon. Then sprinkle it with cilantro, green onions, mascarpone, and heavy cream. Top the casserole with Mexican cheese blend and cover with baking paper. Secure the edges of the pan well. Preheat the air fryer to 360F. Cook the casserole for 10 minutes at 360F and then remove the baking paper and cook the meal for 5 minutes more to reach the crunchy crust.

77. Zucchini Casserole

Servings: 4
Cooking Time: 30 Minutes
Ingredients:
- 1 cup ground chicken
- ½ cup ground pork
- 2 oz celery stalk, chopped
- 1 zucchini, grated
- 1 tablespoon coconut oil, melted
- ½ teaspoon salt
- 1 teaspoon ground black pepper
- ½ teaspoon chili flakes
- 1 teaspoon dried dill
- ½ teaspoon dried parsley
- ½ cup beef broth

Directions:
1. In the mixing bowl mix up ground chicken, ground pork, celery stalk, and salt. Add ground black pepper, chili flakes, dried dill, and dried parsley. Stir the meat mixture until homogenous. Then brush the air fryer pan with coconut oil and put ½ part of all grated zucchini. Then spread it with all ground pork mixture. Sprinkle the meat with remaining grated zucchini and cover with foil. Preheat the air fryer to 375F. Place the pan with casserole in the air fryer and

cook it for 25 minutes. When the time is finished, remove the foil and cook the casserole for 5 minutes more.

78. Rosemary Zucchini Mix

Servings: 4
Cooking Time: 12 Minutes
Ingredients:
- ¼ cup keto tomato sauce
- 1 tablespoon olive oil
- 8 zucchinis, roughly cubed
- Salt and black pepper to the taste
- ¼ teaspoon rosemary, dried
- ½ teaspoon basil, chopped

Directions:
1. Grease a pan that fits your air fryer with the oil, add all the ingredients, toss, introduce the pan in the fryer and cook at 350 degrees F for 12 minutes. Divide into bowls and serve for lunch.

79. Butternut Squash Stew

Servings: 5
Cooking Time: 15 Minutes
Ingredients:
- 1½ pounds butternut squash, cubed
- ½ cup green onions, chopped
- 3 tablespoons butter, melted
- ½ cup carrots, chopped
- ½ cup celery, chopped
- 1 garlic clove, minced
- ½ teaspoon Italian seasoning
- 15 ounces canned tomatoes, chopped
- Salt and black pepper to taste
- ⅛ teaspoon red pepper flakes, dried
- 1 cup quinoa, cooked
- 1½ cups heavy cream
- 1 cup chicken meat, already cooked and shredded

Directions:
1. Place all the ingredients in a pan that fits your air fryer and toss.
2. Put the pan into the fryer and cook at 400 degrees F for 15 minutes.
3. Divide the stew between bowls, serve, and enjoy.

80. Sweet Potatoes

Servings: 4
Cooking Time: 55 Minutes
Ingredients:
- 2 potatoes, peeled and cubed
- 4 carrots, cut into chunks
- 1 head broccoli, cut into florets
- 4 zucchinis, sliced thickly
- Salt and pepper to taste
- ¼ cup olive oil
- 1 tbsp. dry onion powder

Directions:

1. Pre-heat the Air Fryer to 400°F.
2. In a baking dish small enough to fit inside the fryer, add all the ingredients and combine well.
3. Cook for 45 minutes in the fryer, ensuring the vegetables are soft and the sides have browned before serving.

81. Monkey Salad

Servings: 1
Cooking Time: 10 Minutes
Ingredients:
- 2 tbsp butter
- 1 cup unsweetened coconut flakes
- 1 cup raw, unsalted cashews
- 1 cup raw, unsalted s
- 1 cup 90% dark chocolate shavings

Directions:
1. In a skillet, melt the butter on a medium heat.
2. Add the coconut flakes and sauté until lightly browned for 4 minutes.
3. Add the cashews and s and sauté for 3 minutes. Remove from the heat and sprinkle with dark chocolate shavings.
4. Serve!

82. Eggplant Lasagna

Servings: 6
Cooking Time: 30 Minutes
Ingredients:
- 2 medium eggplants
- ½ cup keto tomato sauce
- 1 cup Cheddar cheese, shredded
- ½ cup Mozzarella cheese, shredded
- 1 cup ground pork
- 1 teaspoon Italian seasonings
- 1 teaspoon sesame oil

Directions:
1. Slice the eggplants into the long slices. Then brush the air fryer pan with sesame oil. In the mixing bowl mix up ground pork and Italian seasonings. Then make the layer from the sliced eggplants in the air fryer pan. Top it with a small amount of ground pork and mozzarella cheese. Then sprinkle mozzarella with the tomato sauce Place the second eggplant layer over the sauce and repeat all the steps again. Cover the last layer with remaining eggplant and top with Cheddar cheese. Cover the lasagna with foil and place it in the air fryer. Cook the meal for 20 minutes at 365F. Then remove the foil from the lasagna and cook it for 10 minutes more. Let the cooked lasagna cool for 10 minutes before serving.

83. Faux Rice

Servings: 8

Cooking Time: 60 Minutes
Ingredients:
- 1 medium-to-large head of cauliflower
- ½ lemon, juiced
- garlic cloves, minced
- 2 cans mushrooms, 8 oz. each
- 1 can water chestnuts, 8 oz.
- ¾ cup peas
- ½ cup egg substitute or 1 egg, beaten
- 4 tbsp. soy sauce
- 1 tbsp. peanut oil
- 1 tbsp. sesame oil
- 1 tbsp. ginger, fresh and minced
- High quality cooking spray

Directions:
1. Mix together the peanut oil, soy sauce, sesame oil, minced ginger, lemon juice, and minced garlic to combine well.
2. Peel and wash the cauliflower head before cutting it into small florets.
3. In a food processor, pulse the florets in small batches to break them down to resemble rice grains.
4. Pour into your Air Fryer basket.
5. Drain the can of water chestnuts and roughly chop them. Pour into the basket.
6. Cook at 350°F for 20 minutes.
7. In the meantime, drain the mushrooms. When the 20 minutes are up, add the mushrooms and the peas to the fryer and continue to cook for another 15 minutes.
8. Lightly spritz a frying pan with cooking spray. Prepare an omelet with the egg substitute or the beaten egg, ensuring it is firm. Lay on a cutting board and slice it up.
9. When the cauliflower is ready, throw in the omelet and cook for an additional 5 minutes. Serve hot.

84. Broccoli Salad

Servings: 2
Cooking Time: 18 Minutes
Ingredients:
- 1 cup broccoli florets
- 1 teaspoon olive oil
- 1 tablespoon hazelnuts, chopped
- 4 bacon slices
- ½ teaspoon salt
- ½ teaspoon lemon zest, grated
- ½ teaspoon sesame oil

Directions:
1. Mix up broccoli florets with olive oil, salt, and lemon zest. Shake the vegetables well. Preheat the air fryer to 385F. Put the broccoli in the air fryer basket and cook for 8 minutes. Shake the broccoli after 4 minutes of cooking. Then transfer the broccoli in the salad bowl. Place the bacon in the air fryer and cook it at 400F for 10

minutes or until it is crunchy. Chop the cooked bacon and add in the broccoli. After this, add hazelnuts and sesame oil. Stir the salad gently.

85. Tomato And Peppers Stew

Servings: 4
Cooking Time: 15 Minutes
Ingredients:
- 4 spring onions, chopped
- 2 pound tormatoes, cubed
- 1 teaspoon sweet paprika
- Salt and black pepper to the taste
- 2 red bell peppers, cubed
- 1 tablespoon cilantro, chopped

Directions:
1. In a pan that fits your air fryer, mix all the ingredients, toss, introduce the pan in the fryer and cook at 360 degrees F for 15 minutes. Divide into bowls and serve for lunch.

86. Chickpeas

Servings: 4
Cooking Time: 20 Minutes
Ingredients:
- 1 15-oz. can chickpeas, drained but not rinsed
- 2 tbsp. olive oil
- 1 tsp. salt
- 2 tbsp. lemon juice

Directions:
1. Pre-heat the Air Fryer at 400°F.
2. Add all the ingredients together in a bowl and mix. Transfer this mixture to the basket of the fryer.
3. Cook for 15 minutes, ensuring the chickpeas become nice and crispy.

87. Rocket Salad

Servings: 4
Cooking Time: 35 Minutes
Ingredients:
- 8 fresh figs, halved
- 1 ½ cups chickpeas, cooked
- 1 tsp. cumin seeds, roasted then crushed
- 4 tbsp. balsamic vinegar
- 2 tbsp. extra-virgin olive oil
- Salt and pepper to taste
- 3 cups arugula rocket, washed and dried

Directions:
1. Pre-heat the Air Fryer to 375°F.
2. Cover the Air Fryer basket with aluminum foil and grease lightly with oil. Put the figs in the fryer and allow to cook for 10 minutes.
3. In a bowl, combine the chickpeas and cumin seeds.

4. Remove the cooked figs from the fryer and replace with chickpeas. Cook for 10 minutes. Leave to cool.
5. In the meantime, prepare the dressing. Mix together the balsamic vinegar, olive oil, salt and pepper.
6. In a salad bowl combine the arugula rocket with the cooled figs and chickpeas.
7. Toss with the sauce and serve right away.

88. Chicken In A Blanket

Servings: 3
Cooking Time: 60 Minutes
Ingredients:
- 3 boneless chicken breasts
- 1 package bacon
- 1 8-oz package cream cheese
- 3 jalapeno peppers
- Salt, pepper, garlic powder or other seasonings

Directions:
1. Cut the chicken breast in half lengthwise to create two pieces.
2. Cut the jalapenos in half lengthwise and remove the seeds.
3. Dress each breast with a half-inch slice of cream cheese and half a slice of jalapeno. Sprinkle with garlic powder, salt and pepper.
4. Roll the chicken and wrap 2 to 3 pieces of bacon around it—secure with toothpicks.
5. Bake in a preheated 375°F/190°C fryer for 50 minutes.
6. Serve!

89. Chicken & Veggies

Servings: 4
Cooking Time: 30 Minutes
Ingredients:
- 8 chicken thighs
- 5 oz. mushrooms, sliced
- 1 red onion, diced
- Fresh black pepper, to taste
- 10 medium asparagus
- ½ cup carrots, diced
- ¼ cup balsamic vinegar
- 2 red bell peppers, diced
- ½ tsp. sugar
- 2 tbsp. extra-virgin olive oil
- 1 ½ tbsp. fresh rosemary
- 2 cloves garlic, chopped
- ½ tbsp. dried oregano
- 1 tsp. kosher salt
- 2 fresh sage, chopped

Directions:
1. Pre-heat the Air Fryer to 400°F.
2. Grease the inside of a baking tray with the oil.
3. Season the chicken with salt and pepper.

4. Put all of the vegetables in a large bowl and throw in the oregano, garlic, sugar, mushrooms, vinegar, and sage. Combine everything well before transferring to the baking tray.
5. Put the chicken thighs in the baking tray. Cook in the Air Fryer for about 20 minutes.
6. Serve hot.

90. 'i Love Bacon'

Servings: 4
Cooking Time: 90 Minutes
Ingredients:
- 30 slices thick-cut bacon
- 12 oz steak
- 10 oz pork sausage
- 4 oz cheddar cheese, shredded

Directions:
1. Lay out 5 x 6 slices of bacon in a woven pattern and bake at 400°F/200°C for 20 minutes until crisp.
2. Combine the steak, bacon and sausage to form a meaty mixture.
3. Lay out the meat in a rectangle of similar size to the bacon strips. Season with salt/peppe.
4. Place the bacon weave on top of the meat mixture.
5. Place the cheese in the center of the bacon.
6. Roll the meat into a tight roll and refrigerate.
7. Make a 7 x 7 bacon weave and roll the bacon weave over the meat, diagonally.
8. Bake at 400°F/200°C for 60 minutes or 165°F/75°C internally.
9. Let rest for 5 minutes before serving.

91. Potato Salad

Servings: 4
Cooking Time:35 Minutes
Ingredients:
- 2 lb. red potatoes; halved
- 2 tbsp. olive oil
- 1/3 cup lemon juice
- 3 tbsp. mustard
- Salt and black pepper to the taste
- 2 green onions; chopped
- 1 red bell pepper; chopped

Directions:
1. On your air fryer's basket; mix potatoes with half of the olive oil, salt and pepper and cook at 350 °F, for 25 minutes shaking the fryer once.
2. In a bowl; mix onions with bell pepper and roasted potatoes and toss.
3. In a small bowl; mix lemon juice with the rest of the oil and mustard and whisk really well. Add this to potato salad; toss well and serve for lunch.

92. Cauliflower Steak

Servings: 2
Cooking Time: 30 Minutes
Ingredients:
- 1 cauliflower, sliced into two
- 1 tbsp. olive oil
- 2 tbsp. onion, chopped
- ¼ tsp. vegetable stock powder
- ¼ cup milk
- Salt and pepper to taste

Directions:
1. Place the cauliflower in a bowl of salted water and allow to absorb for at least 2 hours.
2. Pre-heat the Air Fryer to 400°F.
3. Rinse off the cauliflower, put inside the fryer and cook for 15 minutes.
4. In the meantime, fry the onions over medium heat, stirring constantly, until they turn translucent. Pour in the vegetable stock powder and milk. Bring to a boil and then lower the heat.
5. Let the sauce reduce and add in salt and pepper.
6. Plate up the cauliflower steak and top with the sauce.

93. Pasta Salad

Servings: 8
Cooking Time: 2 Hours 25 Minutes
Ingredients:
- 4 tomatoes, medium and cut in eighths
- 3 eggplants, small
- 3 zucchinis, medium sized
- 2 bell peppers, any color
- 4 cups large pasta, uncooked in any shape
- 1 cup cherry tomatoes, sliced
- ½ cup Italian dressing, fat-free
- 8 tbsp. parmesan, grated
- 2 tbsp. extra virgin olive oil
- 2 tsp. pink Himalayan salt
- 1 tsp. basil, dried
- High quality cooking spray

Directions:
1. Wash and dry the eggplant. Cut off the stem and throw it away. Do not peel the eggplant. Cut it into half-inch-thick round slices.
2. Coat the eggplant slices with 1 tbsp. of extra virgin olive oil, and transfer to the Air Fryer basket.
3. Cook the eggplant for 40 minutes at 350°F. Once it is tender and cooked through, remove from the fryer and set to one side.
4. Wash and dry the zucchini. Cut off the stem and throw it away. Do not peel the zucchini. Cut the zucchini into half-inch-thick round slices.
5. Combine with the olive oil to coat, and put it in the Air Fryer basket.
6. Cook the zucchini for about 25 minutes at 350°F. Once it is tender and cooked through, remove from the fryer and set to one side.
7. Wash the tomatoes and cut them into eight equal slices. Transfer them to the fryer basket and spritz lightly with high quality cooking spray. Cook the tomatoes for 30 minutes at 350°F. Once they have shrunk

and are beginning to turn brown, set them to one side.

8. Cook the pasta and drain it. Rinse with cold water and set it aside to cool.
9. Wash, dry and halve the bell peppers. Remove the stems and seeds.
10. Wash and halve the cherry tomatoes.
11. In a large bowl, mix together the bell peppers and cherry tomatoes. Stir in the roasted vegetables, cooked pasta, pink Himalayan salt, dressing, chopped basil leaves, and grated parmesan, ensuring to incorporate everything well.
12. Let the salad cool and marinate in the refrigerator.
13. Serve the salad cold or at room temperature.

94. Garlic Pork And Sprouts Stew

Servings: 4
Cooking Time: 25 Minutes
Ingredients:
- 2 tablespoons olive oil
- 2 tomatoes, cubed
- 2 garlic cloves, minced
- ½ pound Brussels sprouts, halved
- 1 pound pork stew meat, cubed
- ¼ cup veggie stock
- ¼ cup keto tomato sauce
- Salt and black pepper to the taste
- 1 tablespoon chives, chopped

Directions:
1. Heat up a pan that fits the air fryer with the oil over medium-high heat, add the meat, garlic, salt and pepper, stir and brown for 5 minutes. Add all the other ingredients except the chives, toss, introduce in the fryer and cook at 380 degrees F for 20 minutes. Divide the stew into bowls and serve with chives sprinkled on top.

95. Sausage-chicken Casserole

Servings: 8
Cooking Time: 30 Minutes
Ingredients:
- 2 cloves minced garlic
- 10 eggs
- 1 cup broccoli, chopped
- ½ tbsp. salt
- 1 cup cheddar, shredded and divided
- ¼ tbsp. pepper
- ¾ cup whipping cream
- 1 x 12-oz. package cooked chicken sausage

Directions:
1. Pre-heat the Air Fryer to 400°F.
2. In a large bowl, beat the eggs with a whisk. Pour in the whipping cream and cheese. Combine well.
3. In a separate bowl, mix together the garlic, broccoli, salt, pepper and cooked sausage.
4. Place the chicken sausage mix in a casserole dish. Top with the cheese mixture.
5. Transfer to the Air Fryer and cook for about 20 minutes.

96. Cabbage & Beef Casserole

Servings: 6
Cooking Time: 40 Minutes
Ingredients:
- ½ lb ground beef
- ½ cup chopped onion
- ½ bag coleslaw mix
- 1-1/2 cups tomato sauce
- 1 tbsp lemon juice

Directions:
1. In a skillet, cook the ground beef until browned and to the side.
2. Mix in the onion and cabbage to the skillet and sauté until soft.
3. Add the ground beef back in along with the tomato sauce and lemon juice.
4. Bring the mixture to a boil, then cover and simmer for 30 minutes.
5. Enjoy!

97. Eggplant Bowls

Servings: 4
Cooking Time: 15 Minutes
Ingredients:
- 2 cups eggplants, cubed
- 1 cup keto tomato sauce
- 1 teaspoon olive oil
- 1 cup mozzarella, shredded

Directions:
1. In a pan that fits the air fryer, combine all the ingredients except the mozzarella and toss. Sprinkle the cheese on top, introduce the pan in the machine and cook at 390 degrees F for 15 minutes. Divide between plates and serve for lunch.

98. Lamb Ribs

Servings: 4
Cooking Time: 25 Minutes
Ingredients:
- 1 lb. lamb ribs
- 2 tbsp. mustard
- 1 tsp. rosemary, chopped
- Salt and pepper
- ¼ cup mint leaves, chopped
- 1 cup Green yogurt

Directions:
1. Pre-heat the fryer at 350°F.
2. Use a brush to apply the mustard to the lamb ribs, and season with rosemary, as well as salt and pepper as desired.
3. Cook the ribs in the fryer for eighteen minutes.
4. Meanwhile, combine together the mint leaves and yogurt in a bowl.
5. Remove the lamb ribs from the fryer when cooked and serve with the mint yogurt. Enjoy!

99. Coconut Chicken

Servings: 4
Cooking Time: 20 Minutes

Ingredients:
- 4 chicken breasts, skinless, boneless and cubed
- Salt and black pepper to the taste
- ¼ cup coconut cream
- 1 teaspoon olive oil
- 1 and ½ teaspoon sweet paprika

Directions:
1. Grease a pan that fits your air fryer with the oil, mix all the ingredients inside, introduce the pan in the fryer and cook at 370 degrees F for 17 minutes. Divide between plates and serve for lunch.

100.Tofu Bites

Servings: 3
Cooking Time: 65 Minutes
Ingredients:
- 2 tbsp. sesame oil
- ¼ cup maple syrup
- 3 tbsp. peanut butter
- ¼ cup liquid aminos
- 3tbsp. chili garlic sauce
- 2 tbsp. rice wine vinegar
- 2 cloves of garlic, minced
- 1 inch fresh ginger, peeled and grated
- 1 tsp. red pepper flakes
- 1 block extra firm tofu, pressed to remove excess water and cubed
- Toasted peanuts, chopped
- 1 tsp. sesame seeds
- 1 sprig cilantro, chopped

Directions:
1. Whisk together the first 9 ingredients in a large bowl to well combine.
2. Transfer to an airtight bag along with the cubed tofu. Allow to marinate for a minimum of a half hour.
3. Pre-heat the Air Fryer to 425°F.
4. Put the tofu cubes in the fryer, keep any excess marinade for the sauce. Cook for 15 minutes.
5. In the meantime, heat the marinade over a medium heat to reduce by half.
6. Plate up the cooked tofu with some cooked rice and serve with the sauce. Complete the dish with the sesame seeds, cilantro and peanuts.

101.Cheesy Calzone

Servings: 2

Cooking Time: 8 Minutes
Ingredients:
- 2 tablespoons almond flour
- 2 tablespoons flax meal
- 1 tablespoon coconut oil, softened
- ¼ teaspoon salt
- ¼ teaspoon baking powder
- 2 ham slices, chopped
- 1 oz Parmesan, grated
- 1 egg yolk, whisked
- 1 tablespoon spinach, chopped
- Cooking spray

Directions:
1. Make calzone dough: mix up almond flour, flax meal, coconut oil, salt, and baking powder. Knead the dough until soft and smooth. Then roll it up with the help of the rolling pin and cut into halves. Fill every dough half with chopped ham, grated Parmesan, and spinach. Fold the dough in the shape of calzones and secure the edges. Then brush calzones with the whisked egg yolk. Preheat the air fryer basket to 350F. Place the calzones in the air fryer basket and spray them with cooking spray. Cook them for 8 minutes or until they are light brown. Flip the calzones on another side after 4 minutes of cooking.

102.Salmon Skewers

Servings: 4
Cooking Time: 10 Minutes
Ingredients:
- 1-pound salmon fillet
- 4 oz bacon, sliced
- 2 mozzarella balls, sliced
- ½ teaspoon avocado oil
- ½ teaspoon chili flakes

Directions:
1. Cut the salmon into the medium size cubes (4 cubes per serving) Then sprinkle salmon cubes with chili flakes and wrap in the sliced bacon. String the wrapped salmon cubes on the skewers and sprinkle with avocado oil. After this, preheat the air fryer to 400F. Put the salmon skewers in the preheat air fryer basket and cook them at 400F for 4 minutes. Then flip the skewers on another side and cook them for 6 minutes at 385F.

VEGETABLE & SIDE DISHES

103.Brussels Sprout Salad With Pancetta

Servings: 4
Cooking Time: 35 Minutes + Chilling Time
Ingredients:
- 2/3 pound Brussels sprouts
- 1 tablespoon olive oil
- Coarse sea salt and ground black pepper, to taste
- 2 ounces baby arugula
- 1 shallot, thinly sliced
- 4 ounces pancetta, chopped
- Lemon Vinaigrette:
- 2 tablespoons extra virgin olive oil
- 2 tablespoons fresh lemon juice
- 1 tablespoon honey
- 1 teaspoon Dijon mustard

Directions:
1. Start by preheating your Air Fryer to 380 degrees F.
2. Add the Brussels sprouts to the cooking basket. Brush with olive oil and cook for 15 minutes. Let it cool to room temperature about 15 minutes.
3. Toss the Brussels sprouts with the salt, black pepper, baby arugula, and shallot.
4. Mix all ingredients for the dressing. Then, dress your salad, garnish with pancetta, and serve well chilled. Bon appétit!

104.Three-cheese Stuffed Mushrooms

Servings: 3
Cooking Time: 15 Minutes
Ingredients:
- 9 large button mushrooms, stems removed
- 1 tablespoon olive oil
- Salt and ground black pepper, to taste
- 1/2 teaspoon dried rosemary
- 6 tablespoons Swiss cheese shredded
- 6 tablespoons Romano cheese, shredded
- 6 tablespoons cream cheese
- 1 teaspoon soy sauce
- 1 teaspoon garlic, minced
- 3 tablespoons green onion, minced

Directions:
1. Brush the mushroom caps with olive oil; sprinkle with salt, pepper, and rosemary.
2. In a mixing bowl, thoroughly combine the remaining ingredients; mix to combine well and divide the filling mixture among the mushroom caps.
3. Cook in the preheated Air Fryer at 390 degrees F for 7 minutes.
4. Let the mushrooms cool slightly before serving. Bon appétit!

105.Herby Meatballs

Servings:4
Cooking Time: 30 Minutes
Ingredients:
- 1 onion, finely chopped
- 3 garlic cloves, finely chopped
- 2 eggs
- 1 cup breadcrumbs
- ½ cup fresh mixed herbs
- Salt and pepper to taste
- Olive oil

Directions:
1. In a bowl, add beef, onion, garlic, eggs, crumbs, herbs, salt and pepper and mix with hands to combine. Shape into balls and arrange them in the air fryer's basket. Drizzle with oil and cook for 16 minutes at 380 F, turning once halfway through.

106.Fava Bean Falafel Bites

Servings:4
Cooking Time: 20 Minutes
Ingredients:
- 1 can (15.5-oz) fava beans, drained
- 1 red onion, chopped
- 2 tsp chopped fresh cilantro
- 1 tsp ground cumin
- Salt to taste
- 1 garlic clove, minced
- 3 tbsp flour
- 4 lemon wedges, to serve

Directions:
1. Preheat the Air fryer to 380 F. Grease the air fryer basket with cooking spray.
2. In a food processor, blitz all the ingredients until a thick paste is formed. Shape the mixture into ping pong-sized balls. Brush with olive oil and insert in the air fryer basket. Cook for 12 minutes, flipping once. Remove to a platter and serve with lemon wedges.

107.Crunchy Chicken Egg Rolls

Servings:6
Cooking Time: 30 Minutes
Ingredients:
- 2 garlic cloves, minced
- ¼ cup soy sauce
- 2 tsp grated fresh ginger
- 1 pound ground chicken
- 2 cups white cabbage, shredded
- 1 onion, chopped
- 1 egg, beaten
- 12 egg roll wrappers

Directions:

1. Heat olive oil in a pan over medium heat and add garlic, onion, and ginger, and ground chicken. Cook for 5 minutes until the chicken is no longer pink. Pour in soy sauce and cabbage and continue cooking for 5-6 minutes until the cabbage is tender, stirring occasionally. Fill each wrapper with chicken mixture, arranging the mixture just below the center of the wrappers.
2. Fold in both sides and tightly roll-up. Use the beaten egg to seal the edges. Place the rolls into a greased air fryer basket, spray them with cooking spray and cook for 12 minutes at 370 F, turning once halfway through. Let cool and serve.

108.Creamy Broccoli And Cauliflower

Servings: 4
Cooking Time: 20 Minutes
Ingredients:
- 15 ounces broccoli florets
- 10 ounces cauliflower florets
- 1 leek, chopped
- 2 spring onions, chopped
- Salt and black pepper to the taste
- 2 ounces butter, melted
- 2 tablespoons mustard
- 1 cup sour cream
- 5 ounces mozzarella cheese, shredded

Directions:
1. In a baking pan that fits the air fryer, add the butter and spread it well. Add the broccoli, cauliflower and the rest of the ingredients except the mozzarella and toss. Sprinkle the cheese on top, introduce the pan in the air fryer and cook at 380 degrees F for 20 minutes. Divide between plates and serve as a side dish.

109.Chili Cauliflower

Servings: 4
Cooking Time: 20 Minutes
Ingredients:
- 2 cups cauliflower florets, roughly chopped
- 1 tablespoon olive oil
- Salt and black pepper to the taste
- 4 garlic cloves, minced
- 1 red chili pepper, chopped
- 2 tomatoes, cubed
- 1 teaspoon cumin powder
- ½ teaspoon chili powder
- 1 tablespoon coriander, chopped
- 1 avocado, peeled, pitted and sliced
- 1 tablespoon lime juice

Directions:
1. In a pan that fits the air fryer, combine the cauliflower with the other ingredients except the coriander, avocado and lime juice, toss, introduce the pan in the machine

and cook at 380 degrees F for 20 minutes. Divide between plates, top each serving with coriander, avocado and lime juice and serve as a side dish.

110.Homemade Croquettes

Servings:4
Cooking Time: 45 Minutes
Ingredients:
- 1 brown onion, chopped
- 2 garlic cloves, chopped
- 2 eggs, lightly beaten
- ½ cup grated Parmesan cheese
- Salt and pepper to taste
- ½ cup breadcrumbs
- 1 tsp dried mixed herbs

Directions:
1. Combine rice, onion, garlic, eggs, Parmesan, salt and pepper. Shape into 10 croquettes. Spread the crumbs onto a plate and coat each croquette in the crumbs. Spray each croquette with oil.
2. Arrange the croquettes in the air fryer and cook for 16 minutes at 380 F, turning once halfway through cooking. They should be golden and crispy. Serve with plum sauce.

111.Shrimp And Cauliflower Casserole

Servings: 4
Cooking Time: 25 Minutes
Ingredients:
- 1 pound shrimp cleaned and deveined
- 2 cups cauliflower, cut into florets
- 2 bell pepper, sliced
- 1 shallot, sliced
- 2 tablespoons sesame oil
- 1 cup tomato paste

Directions:
1. Start by preheating your Air Fryer to 360 degrees F. Spritz the baking pan with cooking spray.
2. Now, arrange the shrimp and vegetables in the baking pan. Then, drizzle the sesame oil over the vegetables. Pour the tomato paste over the vegetables.
3. Cook for 10 minutes in the preheated Air Fryer. Stir with a large spoon and cook for a further 12 minutes. Serve warm.

112.Creamy Spinach

Servings: 6
Cooking Time: 16 Minutes
Ingredients:
- 1 lb fresh spinach
- 6 oz gouda cheese, shredded
- 8 oz cream cheese
- 1 tsp garlic powder
- 1 tbsp onion, minced
- Pepper

- Salt

Directions:
1. Preheat the air fryer to 370 F.
2. Spray air fryer baking dish with cooking spray and set aside.
3. Spray a large pan with cooking spray and heat over medium heat.
4. Add spinach to the pan and cook until wilted.
5. Add cream cheese, garlic powder, and onion and stir until cheese is melted.
6. Remove pan from heat and add Gouda cheese and season with pepper and salt.
7. Transfer spinach mixture to the prepared baking dish and place into the air fryer.
8. Cook for 16 minutes.
9. Serve and enjoy.

113.Zucchini Bites

Servings: 4
Cooking Time: 15 Minutes
Ingredients:
- 4 zucchinis
- 1 egg
- ½ cup parmesan cheese, grated
- 1 tbsp. Italian herbs
- 1 cup coconut, grated

Directions:
1. 1 Thinly grate the zucchini and dry with a cheesecloth, ensuring to remove all of the moisture.
2. 2 In a bowl, combine the zucchini with the egg, parmesan, Italian herbs, and grated coconut, mixing well to incorporate everything. Using your hands, mold the mixture into balls.
3. 3 Pre-heat the fryer at 400°F and place a rack inside. Lay the zucchini balls on the rack and cook for ten minutes. Serve hot.

114.South Asian Pork Momos

Servings:4
Cooking Time: 45 Minutes
Ingredients:
- 1 tbsp olive oil
- 1 shredded carrot
- 1 onion, chopped
- 1 tsp soy sauce
- 16 wonton wrappers
- Salt and black pepper to taste

Directions:
1. Preheat the Air fryer to 320 F.
2. Warm oil in a pan over medium heat and cook ground pork, onion, carrot, salt, and pepper for 10 minutes until the meat is browned, stirring occasionally. Divide the filling between the wrappers. Fold them around the pork mixture to form momo shapes. Seal the edges. Spray momos with

cooking spray and arrange them on the air fryer basket. Cook for 10 minutes, flipping once halfway through. Serve.

115.Tomato Bites With Creamy Parmesan Sauce

Servings: 4
Cooking Time: 20 Minutes
Ingredients:
- For the Sauce:
- 1/2 cup Parmigiano-Reggiano cheese, grated
- 4 tablespoons pecans, chopped
- 1 teaspoon garlic puree
- 1/2 teaspoon fine sea salt
- 1/3 cup extra-virgin olive oil
- For the Tomato Bites:
- 2 large-sized Roma tomatoes, cut into thin slices and pat them dry
- 8 ounces Halloumi cheese, cut into thin slices
- 1/3 cup onions, sliced
- 1 teaspoon dried basil
- 1/4 teaspoon red pepper flakes, crushed
- 1/8 teaspoon sea salt

Directions:
1. Start by preheating your Air Fryer to 385 degrees F.
2. Make the sauce by mixing all ingredients, except the extra-virgin olive oil, in your food processor.
3. While the machine is running, slowly and gradually pour in the olive oil; puree until everything is well - blended.
4. Now, spread 1 teaspoon of the sauce over the top of each tomato slice. Place a slice of Halloumi cheese on each tomato slice. Top with onion slices. Sprinkle with basil, red pepper, and sea salt.
5. Transfer the assembled bites to the Air Fryer cooking basket. Drizzle with a nonstick cooking spray and cook for approximately 13 minutes.
6. Arrange these bites on a nice serving platter, garnish with the remaining sauce and serve at room temperature. Bon appétit!

116.Smoked Paprika Chicken Wings

Servings:4
Cooking Time: 35 Minutes
Ingredients:
- Salt and black pepper to taste
- 1 tsp smoked paprika
- 1 pinch dry mustard
- 1 pinch cayenne pepper
- 1 tsp ground cumin
- 1 cup mayonnaise mixed with 1 tbsp lemon juice

Directions:

1. Preheat the Air fryer to 380 F. Grease the air fryer basket with cooking spray.
2. In a bowl, mix together smoked paprika, dry mustard, cayenne pepper, cumin, salt, and pepper. Add the chicken wings and toss to coat. Place in the air fryer basket and cook for 20 minutes, flipping once halfway through. Let cool for a few minutes before serving with mayo for dipping.

117.Swiss Chard And Cheese Omelet

Servings:2
Cooking Time:25 Minutes
Ingredients:
- 1 teaspoon garlic paste
- 1 ½ tablespoons olive oil
- 1/2 cup crème fraîche
- 1/3 teaspoon ground black pepper, to your liking
- 1/3 cup Swiss cheese, crumbled
- 1 teaspoon cayenne pepper
- 1/3 cup Swiss chard, torn into pieces
- 5 eggs
- 1/4 cup yellow onions, chopped
- 1 teaspoon fine sea salt

Directions:
1. Crack your eggs into a mixing dish; then, add the crème fraîche, salt, ground black pepper, and cayenne pepper.
2. Next, coat the inside of a baking dish with olive oil and tilt it to spread evenly. Scrape the egg/cream mixture into the baking dish. Add the other ingredients; mix to combine well.
3. Bake for 18 minutes at 292 degrees F. Serve immediately.

118.Rutabaga And Cherry Tomatoes Mix Recipe

Servings: 4
Cooking Time:25 Minutes
Ingredients:
- 1 tbsp. shallot; chopped
- 1 garlic clove; minced
- 3/4 cup cashews; soaked for a couple of hours and drained
- 2 tbsp. nutritional yeast
- 1/2 cup veggie stock
- 2 tsp. lemon juice
- Salt and black pepper to the taste
- For the pasta:
- 1 cup cherry tomatoes; halved
- 2 rutabagas; peeled and cut into thick noodles
- 5 tsp. olive oil
- 1/4 tsp. garlic powder

Directions:
1. Place tomatoes and rutabaga noodles into a pan that fits your air fryer, drizzle the oil over them, season with salt, black pepper and garlic powder, toss to coat and cook in your air fryer at 350 °F, for 15 minutes
2. Meanwhile; in a food processor, mix garlic with shallots, cashews, veggie stock, nutritional yeast, lemon juice, a pinch of sea salt and black pepper to the taste and blend well
3. Divide rutabaga pasta on plates, top with tomatoes, drizzle the sauce over them and serve.

119.Kabocha Fries

Servings: 2
Cooking Time: 11 Minutes
Ingredients:
- 6 oz Kabocha squash, peeled
- ½ teaspoon olive oil
- ½ teaspoon salt

Directions:
1. Cut the Kabocha squash into the shape of the French fries and sprinkle with olive oil. Preheat the air fryer to 390F. Put the Kabocha squash fries in the air fryer basket and cook them for 5 minutes. Then shake them well and cook for 6 minutes more. Sprinkle the cooked Kabocha fries with salt and mix up well.

120.Crumbed Beans

Servings: 4
Cooking Time: 10 Minutes
Ingredients:
- ½ cup flour
- 1 tsp. smoky chipotle powder
- ½ tsp. ground black pepper
- 1 tsp. sea salt flakes
- 2 eggs, beaten
- ½ cup crushed saltines
- 10 oz. wax beans

Directions:
1. Combine the flour, chipotle powder, black pepper, and salt in a bowl. Put the eggs in a second bowl. Place the crushed saltines in a third bowl.
2. Wash the beans with cold water and discard any tough strings.
3. Coat the beans with the flour mixture, before dipping them into the beaten egg. Lastly cover them with the crushed saltines.
4. Spritz the beans with a cooking spray.
5. Air-fry at 360°F for 4 minutes. Give the cooking basket a good shake and continue to cook for 3 minutes. Serve hot.

121.Cheddar Asparagus

Servings: 4
Cooking Time: 10 Minutes
Ingredients:

- 2 pounds asparagus, trimmed
- 2 tablespoons olive oil
- 1 cup cheddar cheese, shredded
- 4 garlic cloves, minced
- 4 bacon slices, cooked and crumbled

Directions:
1. In a bowl, mix the asparagus with the other ingredients except the bacon, toss and put in your air fryer's basket. Cook at 400 degrees F for 10 minutes, divide between plates, sprinkle the bacon on top and serve.

122.Pantano Romanesco With Goat Cheese Appetizer

Servings:4
Cooking Time:20 Minutes
Ingredients:
- 6 ounces goat cheese, sliced
- 2 shallots, thinly sliced
- 2 Pantano Romanesco tomatoes, cut into 1/2-inch slices
- 1 ½ tablespoons extra-virgin olive oil
- 3/4 teaspoon sea salt
- Fresh parsley, for garnish
- Fresh basil, chopped

Directions:
1. Preheat your air fryer to 380 degrees F.
2. Now, pat each tomato slice dry using a paper towel. Sprinkle each slice with salt and chopped basil. Top with a slice of goat cheese.
3. Top with the shallot slices; drizzle with olive oil. Add the prepared tomato and feta "bites" to the air fryer food basket.
4. Cook in the air fryer for about 14 minutes. Lastly, adjust seasonings to taste and serve garnished with fresh parsley leaves. Enjoy!

123.Lime Green Beans And Sauce

Servings: 4
Cooking Time: 8 Minutes
Ingredients:
- 1 pound green beans, trimmed
- 1 tablespoon lime juice
- A pinch of salt and black pepper
- 2 tablespoons ghee, melted
- 1 teaspoon chili powder

Directions:
1. In a bowl, mix the ghee with the rest of the ingredients except the green beans and whisk really well. Mix the green beans with the lime sauce, toss, put them in your air fryer's basket and cook at 400 degrees F for 8 minutes. Serve right away.

124.Baked Potato For One

Servings:1
Cooking Time: 35 Minutes
Ingredients:

- 1 medium russet potato
- 1 teaspoon canola oil
- ¼ teaspoon onion powder
- Salt and pepper, to taste
- 1 tablespoon cream cheese
- 1 tablespoon chopped chives

Directions:
1. Scrub the potato under running water to remove debris.
2. Place the baking dish in the air fryer and add the potato.
3. Brush with oil over entire surface and season with onion powder, salt, and pepper.
4. Close the air fryer and cook for 35 minutes at 350 °F.
5. Once cooked, slice through the potato and serve with cream cheese and chives.

125.Garlic Balsamic Tomatoes

Servings: 4
Cooking Time: 15 Minutes
Ingredients:
- 1 tablespoon olive oil
- 1 pound cherry tomatoes, halved
- 1 tablespoon dill, chopped
- 6 garlic cloves, minced
- 1 tablespoon balsamic vinegar
- Salt and black pepper to the taste

Directions:
1. In a pan that fits the air fryer, combine all the ingredients, toss gently, put the pan in the air fryer and cook at 380 degrees F for 15 minutes. Divide between plates and serve.

126.Basil Zucchini Noodles

Servings: 4
Cooking Time: 15 Minutes
Ingredients:
- 4 zucchinis, cut with a spiralizer
- 1 tablespoon olive oil
- 4 garlic cloves, minced
- 1 and ½ cups tomatoes, crushed
- Salt and black pepper to the taste
- 1 tablespoon basil, chopped
- ¼ cup green onions, chopped

Directions:
1. In a pan that fits your air fryer, mix zucchini noodles with the other ingredients, toss, introduce in the fryer and cook at 380 degrees F for 15 minutes. Divide between plates and serve as a side dish.

127.Herbed Potatoes Mix

Servings: 4
Cooking Time: 30 Minutes
Ingredients:
- 3 large potatoes, peeled and cut into chunks
- 1 teaspoon parsley, chopped

- 1 teaspoon chives, chopped
- 1 teaspoon oregano, chopped
- 1 tablespoon garlic, minced
- Salt and black pepper to taste
- 2 tablespoons olive oil

Directions:
1. Mix all of the ingredients in your air fryer, and stir well.
2. Cook at 370 degrees F for 30 minutes.
3. Divide between plates and serve as a side dish.

128. Fried Pimiento-stuffed Green Olives

Servings:4
Cooking Time: 15 Minutes
Ingredients:
- ¼ cup flour
- ¼ cup Parmesan cheese
- Salt and black pepper to taste
- ½ cup panko breadcrumbs
- 1 egg, beaten
- 1 tsp cayenne pepper

Directions:
1. Preheat the Air fryer to 390 F. Grease the air fryer basket with cooking spray.
2. In a bowl, combine flour, cayenne pepper, salt, and black pepper. In another bowl, add the beaten egg. Place panko breadcrumbs with Parmesan cheese in a third bowl.
3. Drain and pat dry the olives using a paper towel. Dredge olives in flour, then in egg, and finally in the breadcrumbs. Place in the air fryer cooking basket, spray them with cooking spray, and cook for 5 minutes, shake and continue cooking for another 3 minutes. Allow to cool before serving.

129. Simple Stuffed Bell Peppers

Servings: 2
Cooking Time: 20 Minutes
Ingredients:
- 2 bell peppers, tops and seeds removed
- Salt and pepper, to taste
- 2/3 cup cream cheese
- 2 tablespoons mayonnaise
- 1 tablespoon fresh celery stalks, chopped

Directions:
1. Arrange the peppers in the lightly greased cooking basket. Cook in the preheated Air Fryer at 400 degrees F for 15 minutes, turning them over halfway through the cooking time.
2. Season with salt and pepper.
3. Then, in a mixing bowl, combine the cream cheese with the mayonnaise and chopped celery. Stuff the pepper with the cream cheese mixture and serve.

130. Tater Tots For Two

Servings:2
Cooking Time: 20 Minutes
Ingredients:
- 2 cups frozen tater tots
- ½ teaspoon cooking oil

Directions:
1. Place all ingredients into the air fryer baking dish. Toss to coat the tater tots in the oil.
2. Close the air fryer and cook for 20 minutes at 350 °F.
3. Halfway through the cooking time, give the baking dish a good shake.

131. Portobello Mushrooms Recipe

Servings: 4
Cooking Time:22 Minutes
Ingredients:
- 4 Portobello mushrooms; stems removed and chopped.
- 10 basil leaves
- 1 cup baby spinach
- 3 garlic cloves; chopped
- 1 cup almonds; roughly chopped.
- 1 tbsp. parsley
- 1/4 cup olive oil
- 8 cherry tomatoes; halved
- Salt and black pepper to the taste

Directions:
1. In your food processor, mix basil with spinach, garlic, almonds, parsley, oil, salt, black pepper to the taste and mushroom stems and blend well
2. Stuff each mushroom with this mix, place them in your air fryer and cook at 350 °F, for 12 minutes. Divide mushrooms on plates and serve.

132. Sweet Potato Chips With Greek Yogurt Dip

Servings: 2
Cooking Time: 20 Minutes
Ingredients:
- 4 sweet potatoes, sliced
- 2 tablespoons olive oil
- Coarse sea salt and freshly ground black pepper, to taste
- 1 teaspoon paprika
- Dipping Sauce:
- 1/2 cup Greek-style yogurt
- 1 clove garlic, minced
- 1 tablespoon fresh chives, chopped

Directions:
1. Soak the sweet potato slices in icy cold water for 20 to 30 minutes. Drain the sweet potatoes and pat them dry with kitchen towels.

2. Toss the sweet potato slices with olive oil, salt, black pepper, and paprika.
3. Place in the lightly greased cooking basket. Cook in the preheated Air Fryer at 360 degrees F for 14 minutes.
4. Meanwhile, make the sauce by whisking the remaining ingredients. Serve the sweet potato chips with the sauce for dipping and enjoy!

133.Homemade Peanut Corn Nuts

Servings:4
Cooking Time: 30 Minutes
Ingredients:
- 3 tbsp peanut oil
- 2 tbsp old bay seasoning
- Salt to taste

Directions:
1. Preheat the Air Fryer to 390 F.
2. Pat dry hominy and season with salt and old bay seasoning. Drizzle with oil and toss to coat. Spread in the air fryer basket. Cook for 14 minutes. Slide out the basket and shake; cook for another 10 minutes until crispy. Remove to a towel-lined plate to soak up the excess fat. Leave to cool before serving.

134.Mint-butter Stuffed Mushrooms

Servings:3
Cooking Time:19 Minutes
Ingredients:
- 3 garlic cloves, minced
- 1 teaspoon ground black pepper, or more to taste
- 1/3 cup seasoned breadcrumbs
- 1½ tablespoons fresh mint, chopped
- 1 teaspoon salt, or more to taste
- 1½ tablespoons melted butter
- 14 medium-sized mushrooms, cleaned, stalks removed

Directions:
1. Mix all of the above ingredients, minus the mushrooms, in a mixing bowl to prepare the filling.
2. Then, stuff the mushrooms with the prepared filling.
3. Air-fry stuffed mushrooms at 375 degrees F for about 12 minutes. Taste for doneness and serve at room temperature as a vegetarian appetizer.

135.Broccoli Hash Recipe

Servings: 2
Cooking Time:38 Minutes
Ingredients:
- 10 oz. mushrooms; halved
- 1 broccoli head; florets separated
- 1 garlic clove; minced
- 1 tbsp. balsamic vinegar

- 1 avocado; peeled and pitted
- A pinch of red pepper flakes
- 1 yellow onion; chopped.
- 1 tbsp. olive oil
- Salt and black pepper
- 1 tsp. basil; dried

Directions:
1. In a bowl; mix mushrooms with broccoli, onion, garlic and avocado.
2. In another bowl, mix vinegar, oil, salt, pepper and basil and whisk well
3. Pour this over veggies, toss to coat, leave aside for 30 minutes; transfer to your air fryer's basket and cook at 350 °F, for 8 minutes; Divide among plates and serve with pepper flakes on top

136.Sweet Potato And Chickpea Tacos

Servings: 4
Cooking Time: 15 Minutes
Ingredients:
- 2 cups sweet potato puree
- 2 tablespoons butter, melted
- 14 ounces canned chickpeas, rinsed
- 1 cup Colby cheese, shredded
- 1 teaspoon garlic powder
- 1 teaspoon onion powder
- Salt and freshly cracked black pepper, to taste
- 8 corn tortillas
- 1/4 cup Pico de gallo
- 2 tablespoons fresh coriander, chopped

Directions:
1. Mix the sweet potatoes with the butter, chickpeas, cheese, garlic powder, onion powder, salt, black pepper.
2. Divide the sweet potato mixture between the tortillas. Bake in the preheated Air Fryer at 390 degrees F for 7 minutes.
3. Garnish with Pico de gallo and coriander. Bon appétit!

137.Easy Mushroom Cakes

Servings: 8
Cooking Time:18 Minutes
Ingredients:
- 4 oz. mushrooms; chopped
- 1 yellow onion; chopped.
- 1/2 tsp. nutmeg; ground
- 2 tbsp. olive oil
- 1 tbsp. butter
- 1 ½ tbsp. flour
- 1 tbsp. bread crumbs
- 14 oz. milk
- Salt and black pepper to the taste

Directions:
1. Heat up a pan with the butter over medium high heat; add onion and mushrooms; stir,

cook for 3 minutes, add flour, stir well again and take off heat.
2. Add milk gradually, salt, pepper and nutmeg; stir and leave aside to cool down completely.
3. In a bowl; mix oil with bread crumbs and whisk.
4. Take spoonfuls of the mushroom filling, add to breadcrumbs mix, coat well, shape patties out of this mix; place them in your air fryer's basket and cook at 400 °F, for 8 minutes. Divide among plates and serve as a side for a steak

138.Cabbage Slaw

Servings: 4
Cooking Time: 20 Minutes
Ingredients:
- 1 green cabbage head, shredded
- Juice of ½ lemon
- A pinch of salt and black pepper
- ½ cup coconut cream
- ½ teaspoon fennel seeds
- 1 tablespoon mustard

Directions:
1. In a pan that fits the air fryer, combine the cabbage with the rest of the ingredients, toss, introduce the pan in the machine and cook at 350 degrees F for 20 minutes. Divide between plates and serve right away as a side dish.

139.Air-fried Chicken Breasts

Servings:4
Cooking Time: 30 Minutes
Ingredients:
- Cooking spray
- Salt and black pepper to taste
- 1 tsp garlic powder

Directions:
1. Spray the breasts and the air fryer tray, with cooking spray. Rub chicken with salt, garlic powder, and black pepper. Arrange the breasts in the basket, without overcrowding. Cook in batches if needed. Cook for 20 minutes at 360°F, until nice and crispy.

140.Sage Artichoke

Servings: 4
Cooking Time: 12 Minutes
Ingredients:
- 4 artichokes
- 1 tablespoon sage
- 4 teaspoons avocado oil
- 1 teaspoon chives, chopped
- ½ teaspoon salt

Directions:
1. Cut the artichoke into halves and rub them with sage avocado oil, minced garlic, and

salt. Preheat the air fryer to 375F. Place the artichoke halves in the air fryer basket and cook them for 12 minutes.

141.Cumin Artichokes

Servings: 4
Cooking Time: 15 Minutes
Ingredients:
- 12 ounces artichoke hearts
- ½ teaspoon olive oil
- 1 teaspoon coriander, ground
- ½ teaspoon cumin seeds
- Salt and black pepper to the taste
- 1 tablespoon lemon juice

Directions:
1. In a pan that fits your air fryer, mix all the ingredients, toss, introduce the pan in the fryer and cook at 370 degrees F for 15 minutes. Divide the mix between plates and serve as a side dish.

142.Asian Fennel And Noodle Salad

Servings: 3
Cooking Time: 20 Minutes + Chilling Time
Ingredients:
- 1 fennel bulb, quartered
- Salt and white pepper, to taste
- 1 clove garlic, finely chopped
- 1 green onion, thinly sliced
- 2 cups Chinese cabbage, shredded
- 2 tablespoons rice wine vinegar
- 1 tablespoon honey
- 2 tablespoons sesame oil
- 1 teaspoon ginger, freshly grated
- 1 tablespoon soy sauce
- 1 cup chow mein noodles, for serving

Directions:
1. Start by preheating your Air Fryer to 370 degrees F.
2. Now, cook the fennel bulb in the lightly greased cooking basket for 15 minutes, shaking the basket once or twice.
3. Let it cool completely and toss with the remaining ingredients. Serve well chilled.

143.Turmeric Cauliflower

Servings: 4
Cooking Time: 8 Minutes
Ingredients:
- 1-pound cauliflower head
- 1 tablespoon ground turmeric
- 1 tablespoon coconut oil
- ½ teaspoon dried cilantro
- ¼ teaspoon salt

Directions:
1. Slice the cauliflower head on 4 steaks. Then rub every cauliflower steak with dried cilantro, salt, and ground turmeric. Sprinkle the steaks with coconut oil. Preheat the air

fryer to 400F. Place the cauliflower steaks in the air fryer basket and cook for 4 minutes from each side.

144.Quick Cheese Sticks

Servings:12
Cooking Time: 5 Minutes
Ingredients:
- 2 tbsp butter, melted
- 2 cups panko crumbs

Directions:
1. With a knife, cut the cheese into equal sized sticks. Brush each stick with melted butter and dip into panko crumbs. Arrange the cheese sticks in a single layer on the fryer basket. Cook at 390 F for 10 minutes. Flip them halfway through, to brown evenly; serve warm.

145.Bacon Cabbage

Servings: 2
Cooking Time: 12 Minutes
Ingredients:
- 8 oz Chinese cabbage, roughly chopped
- 2 oz bacon, chopped
- 1 tablespoon sunflower oil
- ½ teaspoon onion powder
- ½ teaspoon salt

Directions:
1. Cook the bacon at 400F for 10 minutes. Stir it from time to time. Then sprinkle it with onion powder and salt. Add Chinese cabbage and shake the mixture well. Cook it for 2 minutes. Then add sunflower oil, stir the meal and place in the serving plates.

146.Delicious Ratatouille

Servings: 6
Cooking Time: 15 Minutes
Ingredients:
- 1 eggplant, diced
- 3 garlic cloves, chopped
- 1 onion, diced
- 3 tomatoes, diced
- 2 bell peppers, diced
- 1 tbsp vinegar
- 1 1/2 tbsp olive oil
- 2 tbsp herb de Provence
- Pepper
- Salt

Directions:
1. Preheat the air fryer to 400 F.
2. Add all ingredients into the bowl and toss well and transfer into the air fryer baking dish.
3. Place dish into the air fryer and cook for 15 minutes. Stir halfway through.
4. Serve and enjoy.

147.Mediterranean Tomatoes With Feta Cheese

Servings: 2
Cooking Time: 20 Minutes
Ingredients:
- 3 medium-sized tomatoes, cut into four slices, pat dry
- 1 teaspoon dried basil
- 1 teaspoon dried oregano
- 1/4 teaspoon red pepper flakes, crushed
- 1/2 teaspoon sea salt
- 3 slices Feta cheese

Directions:
1. Spritz the tomatoes with cooking oil and transfer them to the Air Fryer basket. Sprinkle with seasonings.
2. Cook at 350 degrees F approximately 8 minutes turning them over halfway through the cooking time.
3. Top with the cheese and cook an additional 4 minutes. Bon appétit!

148.Horseradish Mayo & Gorgonzola Mushrooms

Servings: 5
Cooking Time: 15 Minutes
Ingredients:
- ½ cup of bread crumbs
- 2 cloves garlic, pressed
- 2 tbsp. fresh coriander, chopped
- ⅓ tsp. kosher salt
- ½ tsp. crushed red pepper flakes
- 1 ½ tbsp. olive oil
- 20 medium-sized mushrooms, stems removed
- ½ cup Gorgonzola cheese, grated
- ¼ cup low-fat mayonnaise
- 1 tsp. prepared horseradish, well-drained
- tbsp. fresh parsley, finely chopped

Directions:
1. Combine the bread crumbs together with the garlic, coriander, salt, red pepper, and the olive oil.
2. Take equal-sized amounts of the bread crumb mixture and use them to stuff the mushroom caps. Add the grated Gorgonzola on top of each.
3. Put the mushrooms in the Air Fryer grill pan and transfer to the fryer.
4. Grill them at 380°F for 8-12 minutes, ensuring the stuffing is warm throughout.
5. In the meantime, prepare the horseradish mayo. Mix together the mayonnaise, horseradish and parsley.
6. When the mushrooms are ready, serve with the mayo.

149.Yellow Squash Chips

Servings:4
Cooking Time: 15 Minutes
Ingredients:
- ½ cup flour
- Salt and black pepper to taste
- 2 eggs
- 1 tbsp soy sauce
- ¾ cup panko breadcrumbs
- 1 tbsp dried dill
- ¼ cup Parmesan cheese, grated
- Greek yogurt dressing, for serving

Directions:
1. Preheat your Air Fryer to 380 F. Spray the air fryer basket with cooking spray.
2. In a bowl, mix the flour, dill, salt, and black pepper. In another bowl, beat the eggs with soy sauce. In a third, pour the panko breadcrumbs and Parmesan cheese.
3. Dip the squash rounds in the flour, then in the eggs, and then coat with the breadcrumbs. Place in the air fryer basket. Cook for 10 minutes, flipping once halfway through. Serve with Greek yogurt dressing.

150.Nutmeg Kale

Servings: 4
Cooking Time: 15 Minutes
Ingredients:
- 1 tablespoon butter, melted
- ½ cup almond milk
- Salt and black pepper to the taste
- 3 garlic cloves
- 10 cups kale, roughly chopped
- ¼ teaspoon nutmeg, ground
- 1/3 cup parmesan, grated
- ¼ cup walnuts, chopped

Directions:
1. In a pan that fits the air fryer, combine all the ingredients, toss, introduce the pan in the machine and cook at 360 degrees F for 15 minutes. Divide between plates and serve.

151.Artichokes And Tarragon Sauce Dish

Servings: 4
Cooking Time:28 Minutes
Ingredients:
- 4 artichokes; trimmed
- 2 tbsp. tarragon; chopped
- 2 tbsp. lemon juice
- 1 celery stalk; chopped.
- 1/2 cup olive oil
- 2 tbsp. chicken stock
- Lemon zest from 2 lemons; grated

- Salt to the taste

Directions:
1. In your food processor; mix tarragon, chicken stock, lemon zest, lemon juice, celery, salt and olive oil and pulse very well.
2. In a bowl; mix artichokes with tarragon and lemon sauce; toss well, transfer them to your air fryer's basket and cook at 380 °F, for 18 minutes.
3. Divide artichokes on plates; drizzle the rest of the sauce all over and serve as a side dish.

152.Artichoke Sauté

Servings: 4
Cooking Time: 10 Minutes
Ingredients:
- 4 artichoke hearts, chopped
- 4 teaspoons lemon juice
- 2 teaspoons avocado oil
- ¼ teaspoon lemon zest, grated

Directions:
1. Preheat the air fryer to 360F. Meanwhile, sprinkle the chopped artichoke hearts with lemon juice, avocado oil, and lemon zest. Shake them well and leave for 10 minutes to marinate. After this, put the artichoke hearts in the preheated air fryer and cook them for 8 minutes. Shake them well and cook for an additional 2 minutes.

153.Air Fried Vegetable Tempura

Servings:3
Cooking Time: 20 Minutes
Ingredients:
- 1 cup broccoli florets
- 1 red bell pepper, cut into strips
- 1 small sweet potato, peeled and cut into thick slices
- 1 small zucchini, cut into thick slices
- ⅔ cup cornstarch
- ⅓ cup all-purpose flour
- 1 egg, beaten
- ¾ cup club soda
- 1½ cups panko breadcrumbs
- Non-stick cooking spray

Directions:
1. Mix the cornstarch and all-purpose flour. Dredge the vegetables in this mixture.
2. Mix egg and club soda. Dip each flour-coated vegetable into this mixture soda before dredging in bread crumbs.
3. Place the vegetables on the double layer rack accessory and spray with cooking oil.
4. Place inside the air fryer.
5. Close and cook for 20 minutes at 350 °F.

VEGAN & VEGETARIAN RECIPES

154.Parmesan Broccoli

Servings:2
Cooking Time:20 Minutes
Ingredients:
- 10 ounces frozen broccoli
- 2 tablespoons Parmesan cheese, grated
- 3 tablespoons balsamic vinegar
- 1 tablespoon olive oil
- 1/8 teaspoon cayenne pepper
- Salt and black pepper, as required

Directions:
1. Preheat the Air fryer to 400 °F and grease an Air fryer basket.
2. Mix broccoli, vinegar, oil, cayenne, salt, and black pepper in a bowl and toss to coat well.
3. Arrange broccoli into the Air fryer basket and cook for about 20 minutes.
4. Dish out in a bowl and top with Parmesan cheese to serve.

155.Mixed Veggie Salad

Servings:8
Cooking Time:1 Hour 20 Minutes
Ingredients:
- 3 medium carrots, cut into ½-inch thick rounds
- 3 small radishes, sliced into ½-inch thick rounds
- 8 cherry tomatoes, cut in eighths
- 2 red bell peppers, seeded and chopped
- ½ cup Parmesan cheese, grated
- 2 tablespoons olive oil, divided
- ½ cup Italian dressing
- Salt, as required

Directions:
1. Preheat the Air fryer to 365 °F and grease an Air fryer basket.
2. Mix carrots and 1 tablespoon of olive oil in a bowl and toss to coat well.
3. Arrange the carrots in the Air fryer basket and cook for about 25 minutes.
4. Mix radishes and 1 tablespoon of olive oil in another bowl and toss to coat well.
5. Arrange the radishes in the Air fryer basket and cook for about 40 minutes.
6. Set the Air fryer to 330 °F and place the cherry tomatoes into the Air fryer basket.
7. Cook for about 15 minutes and combine all the Air fried vegetables.
8. Stir in the remaining ingredients except Parmesan cheese and refrigerate covered for at least 2 hours to serve.
9. Garnish with Parmesan cheese and serve.

156.Crispy Wings With Lemony Old Bay Spice

Servings:4
Cooking Time: 25 Minutes
Ingredients:
- ½ cup butter
- ¾ cup almond flour
- 1 tablespoon old bay spices
- 1 teaspoon lemon juice, freshly squeezed
- 3 pounds chicken wings
- Salt and pepper to taste

Directions:
1. Preheat the air fryer for 5 minutes.
2. In a mixing bowl, combine all ingredients except for the butter.
3. Place in the air fryer basket.
4. Cook for 25 minutes at 350 °F.
5. Halfway through the cooking time, shake the fryer basket for even cooking.
6. Once cooked, drizzle with melted butter.

157.Vegetable Skewers With Asian-style Peanut Sauce

Servings: 4
Cooking Time: 30 Minutes
Ingredients:
- 2 bell peppers, diced into 1-inch pieces
- 4 pearl onions, halved
- 8 small button mushrooms, cleaned
- 2 tablespoons extra-virgin olive oil
- Sea salt and ground black pepper, to taste
- 1 teaspoon red pepper flakes, crushed
- 1 teaspoon dried rosemary, crushed
- 1/3 teaspoon granulated garlic
- Peanut Sauce:
- 2 tablespoons peanut butter
- 1 tablespoon balsamic vinegar
- 1 tablespoon soy sauce
- 1/2 teaspoon garlic salt

Directions:
1. Soak the wooden skewers in water for 15 minutes.
2. Thread the vegetables on skewers; drizzle the olive oil all over the vegetable skewers; sprinkle with spices.
3. Cook in the preheated Air Fryer at 400 degrees F for 13 minutes.
4. Meanwhile, in a small dish, whisk the peanut butter with the balsamic vinegar, soy sauce, and garlic salt. Serve your skewers with the peanut sauce on the side. Enjoy!

158.Broccoli With Cauliflower

Servings:4
Cooking Time:20 Minutes

Ingredients:
- 1½ cups broccoli, cut into 1-inch pieces
- 1½ cups cauliflower, cut into 1-inch pieces
- 1 tablespoon olive oil
- Salt, as required

Directions:
1. Preheat the Air fryer to 375 °F and grease an Air fryer basket.
2. Mix the vegetables, olive oil, and salt in a bowl and toss to coat well.
3. Arrange the veggie mixture in the Air fryer basket and cook for about 20 minutes, tossing once in between.
4. Dish out in a bowl and serve hot.

159.Rich Asparagus And Mushroom Patties

Servings: 4
Cooking Time: 15 Minutes
Ingredients:
- 3/4 pound asparagus spears
- 1 tablespoon canola oil
- 1 teaspoon paprika
- Sea salt and freshly ground black pepper, to taste
- 1 teaspoon garlic powder
- 3 tablespoons scallions, chopped
- 1 cup button mushrooms, chopped
- 1/2 cup parmesan cheese, grated
- 2 tablespoons flax seeds
- 2 eggs, beaten
- 4 tablespoons sour cream, for garnish

Directions:
1. Place the asparagus spears in the lightly greased cooking basket. Toss the asparagus with the canola oil, paprika, salt, and black pepper.
2. Cook in the preheated Air Fryer at 400 degrees F for 5 minutes. Chop the asparagus spears and add the garlic powder, scallions, mushrooms, parmesan, flax seeds, and eggs.
3. Mix until everything is well incorporated and form the asparagus mixture into patties.
4. Cook in the preheated Air Fryer at 400 degrees F for 5 minutes, flipping halfway through the cooking time. Serve with well-chilled sour cream. Bon appétit!

160.Elegant Garlic Mushroom

Servings:3
Cooking Time: 20 Minutes
Ingredients:
- 2 tbsp vermouth
- ½ tsp garlic powder
- 1 tbsp olive oil
- 2 tsp herbs
- 1 tbsp duck fat

Directions:

1. Preheat your air fryer to 350 F, add duck fat, garlic powder and herbs in a blender, and process. Pour the mixture over the mushrooms and cover with vermouth. Place the mushrooms in the cooking basket and cook for 10 minutes. Top with more vermouth and cook for 5 more minutes.

161.Beans & Veggie Burgers

Servings:4
Cooking Time: 22 Minutes
Ingredients:
- 1 cup cooked black beans
- 2 cups boiled potatoes, peeled and mashed
- 1 cup fresh spinach, chopped
- 1 cup fresh mushrooms, chopped
- 2 teaspoons Chile lime seasoning
- Olive oil cooking spray
- 6 cups fresh baby greens

Directions:
1. In a large bowl, add the beans, potatoes, spinach, mushrooms, and seasoning and with your hands, mix until well combined.
2. Make 4 equal-sized patties from the mixture.
3. Set the temperature of air fryer to 370 degrees F. Grease an air fryer basket.
4. Arrange patties into the prepared air fryer basket in a single layer and spray with the cooking spray.
5. Air fry for about 12 minutes, shaking once halfway through.
6. Flip the patties and air fry for another 6-7 minutes.
7. Now, set the temperature of air fryer to 90 degrees F and air fry for 3 more minutes.
8. Remove from air fryer and transfer the burgers onto serving plates.
9. Serve warm alongside the baby greens.

162.Pesto Tomatoes

Servings:4
Cooking Time: 16 Minutes
Ingredients:
- For Pesto:
- ½ cup plus 1 tablespoon olive oil, divided
- 3 tablespoons pine nuts
- Salt, to taste
- ½ cup fresh basil, chopped
- ½ cup fresh parsley, chopped
- 1 garlic clove, chopped
- ½ cup Parmesan cheese, grated
- For Tomatoes:
- 2 heirloom tomatoes, cut into ½ inch thick slices
- 8 ounces feta cheese, cut into ½ inch thick slices.
- ½ cup red onions, thinly sliced
- 1 tablespoon olive oil
- Salt, to taste

Directions:
1. Set the temperature of air fryer to 390 degrees F. Grease an air fryer basket.
2. In a bowl, mix together one tablespoon of oil, pine nuts and pinch of salt.
3. Arrange pine nuts into the prepared air fryer basket.
4. Air fry for about 1-2 minutes.
5. Remove from air fryer and transfer the pine nuts onto a paper towel-lined plate.
6. In a food processor, add the toasted pine nuts, fresh herbs, garlic, Parmesan, and salt and pulse until just combined.
7. While motor is running, slowly add the remaining oil and pulse until smooth.
8. Transfer into a bowl, covered and refrigerate until serving.
9. Spread about one tablespoon of pesto onto each tomato slice.
10. Top each tomato slice with one feta and onion slice and drizzle with oil.
11. Arrange tomato slices into the prepared air fryer basket in a single layer.
12. Air fry for about 12-14 minutes.
13. Remove from air fryer and transfer the tomato slices onto serving plates.
14. Sprinkle with a little salt and serve with the remaining pesto.

163.Couscous Stuffed Tomatoes

Servings:4
Cooking Time:25 Minutes
Ingredients:
- 4 tomatoes, tops and seeds removed
- 1 parsnip, peeled and finely chopped
- 1 cup mushrooms, chopped
- 1½ cups couscous
- 1 teaspoon olive oil
- 1 garlic clove, minced
- 1 tablespoon mirin sauce

Directions:
1. Preheat the Air fryer to 355 °F and grease an Air fryer basket.
2. Heat olive oil in a skillet on low heat and add parsnips, mushrooms and garlic.
3. Cook for about 5 minutes and stir in the mirin sauce and couscous.
4. Stuff the couscous mixture into the tomatoes and arrange into the Air fryer basket.
5. Cook for about 20 minutes and dish out to serve warm.

164.Rice Flour Crusted Tofu

Servings:3
Cooking Time: 28 Minutes
Ingredients:
- 1 (14-ounces) block firm tofu, pressed and cubed into ½-inch size
- 2 tablespoons cornstarch

- ¼ cup rice flour
- Salt and ground black pepper, as required
- 2 tablespoons olive oil

Directions:
1. In a bowl, mix together cornstarch, rice flour, salt, and black pepper.
2. Coat the tofu evenly with flour mixture.
3. Drizzle the tofu with oil.
4. Set the temperature of air fryer to 360 degrees F. Grease an air fryer basket.
5. Arrange tofu cubes into the prepared air fryer basket in a single layer.
6. Air fry for about 14 minutes per side.
7. Remove from air fryer and transfer the tofu onto serving plates.
8. Serve warm.

165.Sweet 'n Nutty Marinated Cauliflower-tofu

Servings:2
Cooking Time: 20 Minutes
Ingredients:
- ¼ cup brown sugar
- ¼ cup low sodium soy sauce
- ½ teaspoon chili garlic sauce
- 1 package extra firm tofu, pressed to release extra water and cut into cubes
- 1 small head cauliflower, cut into florets
- 1 tablespoon sesame oil
- 2 ½ tablespoons almond butter
- 2 cloves of garlic, minced

Directions:
1. Place the garlic, sesame oil, soy sauce, sugar, chili garlic sauce, and almond butter in a mixing bowl. Whisk until well combined.
2. Place the tofu cubes and cauliflower in the marinade and allow to soak up the sauce for at least 30 minutes.
3. Preheat the air fryer to 400 °F. Add tofu and cauliflower. Coo for 20 minutes. Shake basket halfway through cooking time.
4. Meanwhile, place the remaining marinade in a saucepan and bring to a boil over medium heat. Adjust the heat to low once boiling and stir until the sauce thickens.
5. Pour the sauce over the tofu and cauliflower.
6. Serve with rice or noodles.

166.Roasted Peppers With Greek Mayo Sauce

Servings: 4
Cooking Time: 35 Minutes
Ingredients:
- 2 bell peppers, cut into strips
- 1 teaspoon avocado oil
- 1/2 teaspoon celery salt
- 1/4 teaspoon red pepper flakes, crushed
- 1/2 cup mayonnaise
- 1 clove garlic, minced

- 1 teaspoon lemon juice

Directions:
1. Toss the peppers with avocado oil, celery salt, and red pepper flakes.
2. Air-fry them at 380 degrees F for 10 minutes. Shake the cooking basket and cook for 20 minutes more.
3. In the meantime, thoroughly combine the mayonnaise, garlic, and lemon juice.
4. When the peppers come out of the Air Fryer, check them for doneness. Serve with chilled mayonnaise sauce and enjoy!

167. Famous Buffalo Cauliflower

Servings: 4
Cooking Time: 30 Minutes
Ingredients:
- 1 pound cauliflower florets
- 1/2 cup all-purpose flour
- 1/2 cup rice flour
- Sea salt and cracked black pepper, to taste
- 1/2 teaspoon cayenne pepper
- 1/2 teaspoon chili powder
- 1/2 cup soy milk
- 2 tablespoons soy sauce
- 2 tablespoons tahini
- 1 teaspoon vegetable oil
- 2 cloves garlic, minced
- 6 scotch bonnet peppers, seeded and sliced
- 1 small-sized onion, minced
- 1/2 teaspoon salt
- 1 cup water
- 2 tablespoons white vinegar
- 1 tablespoon granulated sugar

Directions:
1. Rinse the cauliflower florets and pat them dry. Spritz the Air Fryer basket with cooking spray.
2. In a mixing bowl, combine the all purpose flour and rice flour; add the salt, black pepper, cayenne pepper, and chili powder.
3. Add the soy milk, soy sauce, and tahini. Stir until a thick batter is formed. Dip the cauliflower florets in the batter.
4. Cook the cauliflower at 400 degrees F for 16 minutes, turning them over halfway through the cooking time.
5. Meanwhile, heat the vegetable oil in a saucepan over medium-high heat; then, sauté the garlic, peppers, and onion for a minute or so or until they are fragrant.
6. Add the remaining ingredients and bring the mixture to a rapid boil. Now, reduce the heat to simmer, and continue cooking for 10 minutes more or until the sauce has reduced by half.
7. Pour the sauce over the prepared cauliflower and serve. Bon appétit!

168. Classic Onion Rings

Servings: 8
Cooking Time: 30 Minutes
Ingredients:
- 2 medium-sized yellow onions, cut into rings
- 1 cup almond flour
- 1/2 teaspoon baking soda
- 1 teaspoon baking powder
- 1 ½ teaspoons sea salt flakes
- 2 medium-sized eggs
- 1 ½ cups plain milk
- 1 ¼ cups grated parmesan cheese
- 1/2 teaspoon green peppercorns, freshly cracked
- 1/2 teaspoon dried dill weed
- 1/4 teaspoon paprika

Directions:
1. Begin by preheating your Air Fryer to 356 degrees F.
2. Place the onion rings into the bowl with icy cold water; let them stay 15 to 20 minutes; drain the onion rings and dry them using a kitchen towel.
3. In a shallow bowl, mix the flour together with baking soda, baking powder and sea salt flakes. Then, coat each onion ring with the flour mixture;
4. In another shallow bowl, beat the eggs with milk; add the mixture to the remaining flour mixture and whisk well. Dredge the coated onion rings into this batter.
5. In a third bowl, mix the parmesan cheese, green peppercorns, dill, and paprika. Roll the onion rings over the parmesan cheese mixture, covering well.
6. Air-fry them in the cooking basket for 8 to 11 minutes or until thoroughly cooked to golden.

169. Easy Crispy Shawarma Chickpeas

Servings: 4
Cooking Time: 25 Minutes
Ingredients:
- 1 (12-ounce) can chickpeas, drained and rinsed
- 2 tablespoons canola oil
- 1 teaspoon cayenne pepper
- 1 teaspoon sea salt
- 1 tablespoon Shawarma spice blend

Directions:
1. Toss all ingredients in a mixing bowl.
2. Roast in the preheated Air Fryer at 380 degrees F for 10 minutes, shaking the basket halfway through the cooking time.
3. Work in batches. Bon appétit!

170.Cottage And Mayonnaise Stuffed Peppers

Servings: 2
Cooking Time: 20 Minutes
Ingredients:
- 1 red bell pepper, top and seeds removed
- 1 yellow bell pepper, top and seeds removed
- Salt and pepper, to taste
- 1 cup Cottage cheese
- 4 tablespoons mayonnaise
- 2 pickles, chopped

Directions:
1. Arrange the peppers in the lightly greased cooking basket. Cook in the preheated Air Fryer at 400 degrees F for 15 minutes, turning them over halfway through the cooking time.
2. Season with salt and pepper.
3. Then, in a mixing bowl, combine the cream cheese with the mayonnaise and chopped pickles. Stuff the pepper with the cream cheese mixture and serve. Enjoy!

171.Barbecue Roasted Almonds

Servings: 6
Cooking Time: 20 Minutes
Ingredients:
- 1 ½ cups raw almonds
- Sea salt and ground black pepper, to taste
- 1/4 teaspoon garlic powder
- 1/4 teaspoon mustard powder
- 1/2 teaspoon cumin powder
- 1/4 teaspoon smoked paprika
- 1 tablespoon olive oil

Directions:
1. Toss all ingredients in a mixing bowl.
2. Line the Air Fryer basket with baking parchment. Spread out the coated almonds in a single layer in the basket.
3. Roast at 350 degrees F for 6 to 8 minutes, shaking the basket once or twice. Work in batches. Enjoy!

172.Ultimate Vegan Calzone

Servings: 1
Cooking Time: 25 Minutes
Ingredients:
- 1 teaspoon olive oil
- 1/2 small onion, chopped
- 2 sweet peppers, seeded and sliced
- Sea salt, to taste
- 1/4 teaspoon ground black pepper
- 1/4 teaspoon dried oregano
- 4 ounces prepared Italian pizza dough
- 1/4 cup marinara sauce
- 2 ounces plant-based cheese Mozzarella-style, shredded

Directions:
1. Heat the olive oil in a nonstick skillet. Once hot, cook the onion and peppers until tender and fragrant, about 5 minutes. Add salt, black pepper, and oregano.
2. Sprinkle some flour on a kitchen counter and roll out the pizza dough.
3. Spoon the marinara sauce over half of the dough; add the sautéed mixture and sprinkle with the vegan cheese. Now, gently fold over the dough to create a pocket; make sure to seal the edges.
4. Use a fork to poke the dough in a few spots. Add a few drizzles of olive oil and place in the lightly greased cooking basket.
5. Bake in the preheated Air Fryer at 330 degrees F for 12 minutes, turning the calzones over halfway through the cooking time. Bon appétit!

173.Italian-style Risi E Bisi

Servings: 4
Cooking Time: 20 Minutes
Ingredients:
- 2 cups brown rice
- 4 cups water
- 1/2 cup frozen green peas
- 3 tablespoons soy sauce
- 1 tablespoon olive oil
- 1 cup brown mushrooms, sliced
- 2 garlic cloves, minced
- 1 small-sized onion, chopped
- 1 tablespoon fresh parsley, chopped

Directions:
1. Heat the brown rice and water in a pot over high heat. Bring it to a boil; turn the stove down to simmer and cook for 35 minutes. Allow your rice to cool completely.
2. Transfer the cold cooked rice to the lightly greased Air Fryer pan. Add the remaining ingredients and stir to combine.
3. Cook in the preheated Air Fryer at 360 degrees F for 18 to 22 minutes. Serve warm.

174.Zucchini Topped With Coconut Cream 'n Bacon

Servings:3
Cooking Time: 20 Minutes
Ingredients:
- 1 tablespoon lemon juice
- 3 slices bacon, fried and crumbled
- 3 tablespoons olive oil
- 3 zucchini squashes
- 4 tablespoons coconut cream
- Salt and pepper to taste

Directions:
1. Preheat the air fryer for 5 minutes.
2. Line up chopsticks on both sides of the zucchini and slice thinly until you hit the

stick. Brush the zucchinis with olive oil. Set aside.
3. Place the zucchini in the air fryer. Bake for 20 minutes at 350 °F.
4. Meanwhile, combine the coconut cream and lemon juice in a mixing bowl. Season with salt and pepper to taste.
5. Once the zucchini is cooked, scoop the coconut cream mixture and drizzle on top.
6. Sprinkle with bacon bits.

175.Almond Flour Battered Wings

Servings:4
Cooking Time: 25 Minutes
Ingredients:
- ¼ cup butter, melted
- ¾ cup almond flour
- 16 pieces chicken wings
- 2 tablespoons stevia powder
- 4 tablespoons minced garlic
- Salt and pepper to taste

Directions:
1. Preheat the air fryer for 5 minutes.
2. In a mixing bowl, combine the chicken wings, almond flour, stevia powder, and garlic Season with salt and pepper to taste.
3. Place in the air fryer basket and cook for 25 minutes at 400 °F.
4. Halfway through the cooking time, make sure that you give the fryer basket a shake.
5. Once cooked, place in a bowl and drizzle with melted butter. Toss to coat.

176.Vegetable Tortilla Pizza

Servings:1
Cooking Time: 15 Minutes
Ingredients:
- ¼ cup grated cheddar cheese
- ¼ cup grated mozzarella cheese
- 1 tbsp cooked sweet corn
- 4 zucchini slices
- 4 eggplant slices
- 4 red onion rings
- ½ green bell pepper, chopped
- 3 cherry tomatoes, quartered
- 1 tortilla
- ¼ tsp basil
- ¼ tsp oregano

Directions:
1. Preheat the air fryer to 350 F. Spread the tomato paste on the tortilla. Arrange the zucchini and eggplant slices first, then green peppers, and onion rings.
2. Arrange the cherry tomatoes and sprinkle the sweet corn over. Sprinkle with oregano and basil and top with cheddar and mozzarella. Place in the fryer and cook for 10 minutes.

177.Stuffed Tomatoes

Servings:4
Cooking Time: 22 Minutes
Ingredients:
- 4 tomatoes
- 1 teaspoon olive oil
- 1 carrot, peeled and finely chopped
- 1 onion, chopped
- 1 cup frozen peas, thawed
- 1 garlic clove, minced
- 2 cups cold cooked rice
- 1 tablespoon soy sauce

Directions:
1. Cut the top of each tomato and scoop out pulp and seeds.
2. In a skillet, heat oil over low heat and sauté the carrot, onion, garlic, and peas for about 2 minutes.
3. Stir in the soy sauce and rice and remove from heat.
4. Set the temperature of air fryer to 355 degrees F. Grease an air fryer basket.
5. Stuff each tomato with the rice mixture.
6. Arrange tomatoes into the prepared air fryer basket.
7. Air fry for about 20 minutes.
8. Remove from air fryer and transfer the tomatoes onto a serving platter.
9. Set aside to cool slightly.
10. Serve warm.

178.Minty Green Beans With Shallots

Servings:6
Cooking Time: 25 Minutes
Ingredients:
- 1 tablespoon fresh mint, chopped
- 1 tablespoon sesame seeds, toasted
- 1 tablespoon vegetable oil
- 1 teaspoon soy sauce
- 1-pound fresh green beans, trimmed
- 2 large shallots, sliced
- 2 tablespoons fresh basil, chopped
- 2 tablespoons pine nuts

Directions:
1. Preheat the air fryer to 330 °F.
2. Place the grill pan accessory in the air fryer.
3. In a mixing bowl, combine the green beans, shallots, vegetable oil, and soy sauce.
4. Dump in the air fryer and cook for 25 minutes.
5. Once cooked, garnish with basil, mints, sesame seeds, and pine nuts.

179.Crispy & Tasty Tofu

Servings:4
Cooking Time: 25 Minutes
Ingredients:
- 1 tbsp potato starch
- Salt and pepper to taste

- 2 tsp rice vinegar
- 2 tsp soy sauce
- 2 tsp sesame oil
- 1 green onion, chopped
- A bunch of basil, chopped

Directions:
1. Preheat air fryer to 370 F.
2. Open your tofu pack and transfer to a plate. In a bowl, make a marinade of sesame oil, soy sauce and rice vinegar. Add spices to the marinade and pour the marinade over the tofu block. Set aside for 10 minutes to get tasty. Toss the marinated tofu with the potato starch; place into the fryer's basket and cook for 20 minutes, shaking after 10 minutes. Serve with a topping of chopped onion and basil.

180. Spicy Pepper, Sweet Potato Skewers

Servings:1
Cooking Time: 20 Minutes
Ingredients:
- 1 beetroot
- 1 green bell pepper
- 1 tsp chili flakes
- ¼ tsp black pepper
- ½ tsp turmeric
- ¼ tsp garlic powder
- ¼ tsp paprika
- 1 tbsp olive oil

Directions:
1. Preheat air fryer to 350 F. Peel the veggies and cut them into bite-sized chunks. Place the chunks in a bowl, along with the remaining ingredients; mix until fully coated. Thread the veggies onto skewers in this order: potato, pepper, beetroot. Place in the air fryer and cook for 15 minutes, shaking once.

181. Chili Bean Burritos

Servings:6
Cooking Time: 30 Minutes
Ingredients:
- 1 cup grated cheddar cheese
- 1 can (8 oz) beans
- 1 tsp seasoning, any kind

Directions:
1. Preheat the air fryer to 350 F, and mix the beans with the seasoning. Divide the bean mixture between the tortillas and top with cheddar cheese. Roll the burritos and arrange them on a lined baking dish.Place in the air fryer and cook for 5 minutes, or to your liking.

182. Jacket Potatoes

Servings:2
Cooking Time: 15 Minutes

Ingredients:
- 2 potatoes
- 1 tablespoon mozzarella cheese, shredded
- 3 tablespoons sour cream
- 1 tablespoon butter, softened
- 1 teaspoon chives, minced
- Salt and ground black pepper, as required

Directions:
1. Set the temperature of air fryer to 355 degrees F. Grease an air fryer basket.
2. With a fork, prick the potatoes.
3. Arrange potatoes into the prepared air fryer basket.
4. Air fry for about 15 minutes.
5. In a bowl, add the remaining ingredients and mix until well combined.
6. Remove from air fryer and transfer the potatoes onto a platter.
7. Open potatoes from the center and stuff them with cheese mixture.
8. Serve immediately

183. Crispy Butternut Squash Fries

Servings: 4
Cooking Time: 25 Minutes
Ingredients:
- 1 cup all-purpose flour
- Salt and ground black pepper, to taste
- 3 tablespoons nutritional yeast flakes
- 1/2 cup almond milk
- 1/2 cup almond meal
- 1/2 cup bread crumbs
- 1 tablespoon herbs (oregano, basil, rosemary, chopped)
- 1 pound butternut squash, peeled and cut into French fry shapes

Directions:
1. In a shallow bowl, combine the flour, salt, and black pepper. In another shallow dish, mix the nutritional yeast flakes with the almond milk until well combined.
2. Mix the almond meal, breadcrumbs, and herbs in a third shallow dish. Dredge the butternut squash in the flour mixture, shaking off the excess. Then, dip in the milk mixture; lastly, dredge in the breadcrumb mixture.
3. Spritz the butternut squash fries with cooking oil on all sides.
4. Cook in the preheated Air Fryer at 400 degrees F approximately 12 minutes, turning them over halfway through the cooking time.
5. Serve with your favorite sauce for dipping. Bon appétit!

184. Garlic 'n Basil Crackers

Servings:6
Cooking Time: 15 Minutes

Ingredients:
- ¼ teaspoon dried basil powder
- ½ teaspoon baking powder
- 1 ¼ cups almond flour
- 1 clove of garlic, minced
- 3 tablespoons coconut oil
- A pinch of cayenne pepper powder
- Salt and pepper to taste

Directions:
1. Preheat the air fryer for 5 minutes.
2. Mix everything in a mixing bowl to create a dough.
3. Transfer the dough on a clean and flat working surface and spread out until 2mm thick. Cut into squares.
4. Place gently in the air fryer basket. Do this in batches if possible.
5. Cook for 15 minutes at 325 °F.

185. Spiced Soy Curls

Servings:2
Cooking Time: 10 Minutes
Ingredients:
- 3 cups boiling water
- 4 ounces soy curls
- ¼ cup nutritional yeast
- ¼ cup fine ground cornmeal
- 2 teaspoons Cajun seasoning
- 1 teaspoon poultry seasoning
- Salt and ground white pepper, as required

Directions:
1. In a heatproof bowl, add the boiling water and soak the soy curls for about 10 minutes.
2. Through a strainer, drain the soy curls and then with a large spoon, press to release the extra water.
3. In a bowl, mix well nutritional yeast, cornmeal, seasonings, salt, and white pepper.
4. Add the soy curls and generously coat with the mixture.
5. Set the temperature of air fryer to 380 degrees F. Grease an air fryer basket.
6. Arrange soy curls into the prepared air fryer basket in a single layer.
7. Air fry for about 10 minutes, shaking once halfway through.
8. Remove from air fryer and transfer the soy curls onto serving plates.
9. Serve warm.

186. Cheesy Spinach

Servings:3
Cooking Time: 15 Minutes
Ingredients:
- 1 (10-ounces) package frozen spinach, thawed
- ½ cup onion, chopped
- 2 teaspoons garlic, minced

- 4 ounces cream cheese, chopped
- ½ teaspoon ground nutmeg
- Salt and ground black pepper, as required
- ¼ cup Parmesan cheese, shredded

Directions:
1. In a bowl, mix well spinach, onion, garlic, cream cheese, nutmeg, salt, and black pepper.
2. Set the temperature of air fryer to 350 degrees F. Grease an air fryer pan.
3. Place spinach mixture into the prepared air fryer pan.
4. Air fry for about 10 minutes.
5. Remove from air fryer and stir the mixture well.
6. Sprinkle the spinach mixture evenly with Parmesan cheese.
7. Now, set the temperature of air fryer to 400 degrees F and air fry for 5 more minutes.
8. Remove from air fryer and transfer the spinach mixture onto serving plates.
9. Serve hot.

187. Air Fried Vegetables With Garlic

Servings:6
Cooking Time: 25 Minutes
Ingredients:
- ¾ lb tomatoes
- 1 medium onion
- 1 tbsp lemon juice
- 1 tbsp olive oil
- ½ tbsp salt
- 1 tbsp coriander powder

Directions:
1. Preheat air fryer to 360 F. Place peppers, tomatoes, and onion in the basket. Cook for 5 minutes, then flip and cook for 5 more minutes. Remove and peel the skin. Place the vegetables in a blender and sprinkle with the salt and coriander powder. Blend to smooth and season with salt and olive oil.

188. Family Favorite Potatoes

Servings:4
Cooking Time:20 Minutes
Ingredients:
- 1¾ pound waxy potatoes, cubed and boiled
- ½ cup Greek plain yoghurt
- 2 tablespoons olive oil, divided
- 1 tablespoon paprika, divided
- Salt and black pepper, to taste

Directions:
1. Preheat the Air fryer to 355 °F and grease an Air fryer basket.
2. Mix 1 tablespoon olive oil, 1/3 tablespoon of paprika and black pepper in a bowl and toss to coat well.
3. Transfer into the Air fryer basket and cook for about 20 minutes.

pepper in a bowl and serve with potatoes.

189.The Best Crispy Tofu

Servings: 4
Cooking Time: 55 Minutes
Ingredients:
- 16 ounces firm tofu, pressed and cubed
- 1 tablespoon vegan oyster sauce
- 1 tablespoon tamari sauce
- 1 teaspoon cider vinegar
- 1 teaspoon pure maple syrup
- 1 teaspoon sriracha
- 1/2 teaspoon shallot powder
- 1/2 teaspoon porcini powder
- 1 teaspoon garlic powder
- 1 tablespoon sesame oil
- 5 tablespoons cornstarch

Directions:
1. Toss the tofu with the oyster sauce, tamari sauce, vinegar, maple syrup, sriracha, shallot powder, porcini powder, garlic powder, and sesame oil. Let it marinate for 30 minutes.
2. Toss the marinated tofu with the cornstarch.
3. Cook at 360 degrees F for 10 minutes; turn them over and cook for 12 minutes more. Bon appétit!

190.Buttered Carrot-zucchini With Mayo

Servings:4
Cooking Time: 25 Minutes
Ingredients:
- 1 tablespoon grated onion
- 2 tablespoons butter, melted
- 1/2-pound carrots, sliced
- 1-1/2 zucchinis, sliced
- 1/4 cup water
- 1/4 cup mayonnaise
- 1/4 teaspoon prepared horseradish
- 1/4 teaspoon salt
- 1/4 teaspoon ground black pepper
- 1/4 cup Italian bread crumbs

Directions:
1. Lightly grease baking pan of air fryer with cooking spray. Add carrots. For 8 minutes, cook on 360°F. Add zucchini and continue cooking for another 5 minutes.
2. Meanwhile, in a bowl whisk well pepper, salt, horseradish, onion, mayonnaise, and water. Pour into pan of veggies. Toss well to coat.
3. In a small bowl mix melted butter and bread crumbs. Sprinkle over veggies.
4. Cook for 10 minutes at 390°F until tops are lightly browned.
5. Serve and enjoy.

Servings:4
Cooking Time:31 Minutes
Ingredients:
- 4 potatoes, peeled
- 1 tablespoon butter
- ½ of brown onion, chopped
- 2 tablespoons chives, chopped
- ½ cup Parmesan cheese, grated
- 3 tablespoons canola oil

Directions:
1. Preheat the Air fryer to 390 °F and grease an Air fryer basket.
2. Coat the potatoes with canola oil and arrange into the Air fryer basket.
3. Cook for about 20 minutes and transfer into a platter.
4. Cut each potato in half and scoop out the flesh from each half.
5. Heat butter in a frying pan over medium heat and add onions.
6. Sauté for about 5 minutes and dish out in a bowl.
7. Mix the onions with the potato flesh, chives, and half of cheese.
8. Stir well and stuff the potato halves evenly with the onion potato mixture.
9. Top with the remaining cheese and arrange the potato halves into the Air fryer basket.
10. Cook for about 6 minutes and dish out to serve warm.

192.Vegetable Bake With Cheese And Olives

Servings: 3
Cooking Time: 25 Minutes
Ingredients:
- 1/2 pound cauliflower, cut into 1-inch florets
- 1/4 pound zucchini, cut into 1-inch chunks
- 1 red onion, sliced
- 2 bell peppers, cut into 1-inch chunks
- 2 tablespoons extra-virgin olive oil
- 1 cup dry white wine
- 1 teaspoon dried rosemary
- Sea salt and freshly cracked black pepper, to taste
- 1/2 teaspoon dried basil
- 1/2 cup tomato, pureed
- 1/2 cup cheddar cheese, grated
- 1 ounce Kalamata olives, pitted and halved

Directions:
1. Toss the vegetables with the olive oil, wine, rosemary, salt, black pepper, and basil until well coated.
2. Add the pureed tomatoes to a lightly greased baking dish; spread to cover the bottom of the baking dish.

3. Add the vegeta...
cheese. Scatter the Kalamata o...
top.
4. Bake in the preheated Air Fryer at 390 degrees F for 20 minutes, rotating the dish halfway through the cooking time. Serve warm and enjoy!

193.Spicy Tofu

Servings:3
Cooking Time:13 Minutes
Ingredients:
- 1 (14-ounces) block extra-firm tofu, pressed and cut into ¾-inch cubes
- 3 teaspoons cornstarch
- 1½ tablespoons avocado oil
- 1½ teaspoons paprika
- 1 teaspoon onion powder
- 1 teaspoon garlic powder
- Salt and black pepper, to taste

Directions:
1. Preheat the Air fryer to 390 °F and grease an Air fryer basket.
2. Mix the tofu, oil, cornstarch, and spices in a bowl and toss to coat well.
3. Arrange the tofu pieces in the Air fryer basket and cook for about 13 minutes, tossing twice in between.
4. Dish out the tofu onto serving plates and serve hot.

194.Authentic Churros With Hot Chocolate

Servings: 3
Cooking Time: 25 Minutes
Ingredients:
- 1/2 cup water
- 2 tablespoons granulated sugar
- 1/4 teaspoon sea salt
- 1 teaspoon lemon zest
- 1 tablespoon canola oil
- 1 cup all-purpose flour
- 2 ounces dark chocolate
- 1 cup milk
- 1 tablespoon cornstarch
- 1/3 cup sugar
- 1 teaspoon ground cinnamon

Directions:
1. To make the churro dough, boil the water in a pan over medium-high heat; now, add the sugar, salt and lemon zest; cook until dissolved.
2. Add the canola oil and remove the pan from the heat. Gradually stir in the flour, whisking continuously until the mixture forms a ball.
3. Pour the mixture into a piping bag with a large star tip. Squeeze 4-inch strips of dough into the greased Air Fryer pan.
4. Cook at 410 degrees F for 6 minutes.

...elt the chocolate and 1/2 cup of milk in a pan over low heat.
6. Dissolve the cornstarch in the remaining 1/2 cup of milk; stir into the hot chocolate mixture. Cook on low heat approximately 5 minutes.
7. Mix the sugar and cinnamon; roll the churros in this mixture. Serve with the hot chocolate on the side. Enjoy!

195.Paneer Cutlet

Servings:1
Cooking Time: 15 Minutes
Ingredients:
- 1 cup grated cheese
- ½ tsp chai masala
- 1 tsp butter
- ½ tsp garlic powder
- 1 small onion, finely chopped
- ½ tsp oregano
- ½ tsp salt

Directions:
1. Preheat the air fryer to 350 F, and grease a baking dish. Mix all ingredients in a bowl, until well incorporated. Make cutlets out of the mixture and place them on the greased baking dish. Place the baking dish in the air fryer and cook the cutlets for 10 minutes, until crispy.

196.Roasted Bell Peppers 'n Onions In A Salad

Servings:4
Cooking Time: 10 Minutes
Ingredients:
- ½ lemon, juiced
- 1 tablespoon baby capers
- 1 tablespoon extra-virgin olive oil
- 1 teaspoon paprika
- 2 large red onions sliced
- 2 yellow pepper, sliced
- 4 long red pepper, sliced
- 6 cloves of garlic, crushed
- 6 plum tomatoes, halved
- salt and pepper to taste

Directions:
1. Preheat the air fryer to 420 °F.
2. Place the tomatoes, onions, peppers, and garlic in a mixing bowl.
3. Add in the extra virgin olive oil, paprika, and lemon juice. Season with salt and pepper to taste.
4. Transfer into the air fryer lined with aluminum foil and cook for 10 minutes or until the edges of the vegetables have browned.
5. Place in a salad bowl and add the baby capers. Toss to combine all ingredients.

197. Hungarian Mushroom Pilaf

Servings: 4
Cooking Time: 50 Minutes
Ingredients:
- 1 ½ cups white rice
- 3 cups vegetable broth
- 2 tablespoons olive oil
- 1 pound fresh porcini mushrooms, sliced
- 2 tablespoons olive oil
- 2 garlic cloves
- 1 onion, chopped
- 1/4 cup dry vermouth
- 1 teaspoon dried thyme
- 1/2 teaspoon dried tarragon
- 1 teaspoon sweet Hungarian paprika

Directions:
1. Place the rice and broth in a large saucepan, add water; and bring to a boil. Cover, turn the heat down to low, and continue cooking for 16 to 18 minutes more. Set aside for 5 to 10 minutes.
2. Now, stir the hot cooked rice with the remaining ingredients in a lightly greased baking dish.
3. Cook in the preheated Air Fryer at 370 degrees for 20 minutes, checking periodically to ensure even cooking.
4. Serve in individual bowls. Bon appétit!

198. Hummus Mushroom Pizza

Servings: 4
Cooking Time: 6 Minutes
Ingredients:
- 4 Portobello mushroom caps, stemmed and gills removed
- 1 tablespoon balsamic vinegar
- Salt and ground black pepper, as required
- 4 tablespoons pasta sauce
- 1 garlic clove, minced
- 3 ounces zucchini, shredded
- 2 tablespoons sweet red pepper, seeded and chopped
- 4 Kalamata olives, sliced
- 1 teaspoon dried basil
- ½ cup hummus

Directions:
1. Coat both sides of each mushroom cap with vinegar.
2. Now, sprinkle the inside of each mushroom cap with salt and black pepper.
3. Place one tablespoon of pasta sauce inside each mushroom and sprinkle with garlic.
4. Set the temperature of air fryer to 330 degrees F. Grease an air fryer basket.
5. Arrange mushroom caps into the prepared air fryer basket.
6. Air fry for about 3 minutes.

7. Remove from the air fryer and top each mushroom cap with zucchini, peppers and olives.
8. Then, sprinkle with basil, salt, and black pepper.
9. Place back mushroom caps into the air fryer basket.
10. Air fry for about 3 more minutes.
11. Remove from air fryer and transfer the mushrooms onto a serving platter.
12. Top each mushroom pizza with hummus and serve.

199. Easy Vegan "chicken"

Servings: 4
Cooking Time: 20 Minutes
Ingredients:
- 8 ounces soy chunks
- 1/2 cup cornmeal
- 1/4 cup all-purpose flour
- 1 teaspoon cayenne pepper
- 1/2 teaspoon mustard powder
- 1 teaspoon celery seeds
- Sea salt and ground black pepper, to taste

Directions:
1. Boil the soya chunks in lots of water in a saucepan over medium-high heat. Remove from the heat and let them soak for 10 minutes.
2. Drain, rinse, and squeeze off the excess water.
3. Mix the remaining ingredients in a bowl. Roll the soy chunks over the breading mixture, pressing to adhere.
4. Arrange the soy chunks in the lightly greased Air Fryer basket.
5. Cook in the preheated Air Fryer at 390 degrees for 10 minutes, turning them over halfway through the cooking time; work in batches. Bon appétit!

200. Grilled Drunken Mushrooms

Servings: 4
Cooking Time: 20 Minutes
Ingredients:
- 2 garlic cloves, finely chopped
- 3 tablespoons chopped fresh thyme and/or rosemary leaves
- Large pinch of crushed red pepper flakes
- 1 teaspoon kosher salt, plus more to taste
- 6 scallions, cut crosswise into 2-inch pieces
- 1-pint cherry tomatoes
- 1-pint cremini, button, or other small mushrooms
- 1/2 cup extra-virgin olive oil
- 1/2 teaspoon freshly ground black pepper, plus more to taste
- 1/4 cup red wine or Sherry vinegar

Directions:

1. In Ziploc bag, mix well black pepper, salt, red pepper flakes, thyme, vinegar, oil, and garlic. Add mushrooms, tomatoes, and scallions. Mix well and let it marinate for half an hour.
2. Thread mushrooms, tomatoes, and scallions. Reserve sauce for basting. Place on skewer rack in air fryer. If needed, cook in batches.
3. For 10 minutes, cook on 360°F. Halfway through cooking time, turnover skewers and baste with reserved sauce.
4. Serve and enjoy.

201.Sweet And Sour Brussel Sprouts

Servings:2
Cooking Time:10 Minutes
Ingredients:
- 2 cups Brussels sprouts, trimmed and halved lengthwise
- 1 tablespoon balsamic vinegar
- 1 tablespoon maple syrup
- Salt, as required

Directions:
1. Preheat the Air fryer to 400 °F and grease an Air fryer basket.
2. Mix all the ingredients in a bowl and toss to coat well.
3. Arrange the Brussel sprouts in the Air fryer basket and cook for about 10 minutes, shaking once halfway through.
4. Dish out in a bowl and serve hot.

202.Thai Zucchini Balls

Servings: 4
Cooking Time: 30 Minutes
Ingredients:
- 1 pound zucchini, grated
- 1 tablespoon orange juice
- 1/2 teaspoon ground cinnamon
- 1/4 teaspoon ground cloves
- 1/2 cup almond meal
- 1 teaspoon baking powder
- 1 cup coconut flakes

Directions:
1. In a mixing bowl, thoroughly combine all ingredients, except for coconut flakes.
2. Roll the balls in the coconut flakes.

3. Bake in the preheated Air Fryer at 360 degrees F for 15 minutes or until thoroughly cooked and crispy.
4. Repeat the process until you run out of ingredients. Bon appétit!

203.Shepherd's Pie Vegetarian Approved

Servings:3
Cooking Time: 35 Minutes
Directions:
1. Boil potatoes until tender. Drain and transfer to a bowl. Mash potatoes with salt, vegan cream cheese, olive oil, soy milk, and vegan mayonnaise. Mix well until smooth. Set aside.
2. Lightly grease baking pan of air fryer with cooking spray. Add carrot, celery, onions, tomato, and peas. For 10 minutes, cook on 360°F. Stirring halfway through cooking time.
3. Stir in pepper, garlic, and Italian seasoning.
4. Stir in vegetarian ground beef substitute. Cook for 5 minutes while halfway through cooking time crumbling and mixing the beef substitute.
5. Evenly spread the beef and veggie mixture in pan. Top evenly with mashed potato mixture.
6. Cook for another 20 minutes or until mashed potatoes are lightly browned.
7. Serve and enjoy.

204.Easy Roast Winter Vegetable Delight

Servings:2
Cooking Time: 30 Minutes
Ingredients:
- 1 cup chopped butternut squash
- 2 small red onions, cut in wedges
- 1 cup chopped celery
- 1 tbsp chopped fresh thyme
- Salt and pepper to taste
- 2 tsp olive oil

Directions:
1. Preheat the air fryer to 200 F, and in a bowl, add turnip, squash, red onions, celery, thyme, pepper, salt, and olive oil; mix well. Pour the vegetables into the fryer's basket and cook for 16 minutes, tossing once halfway through.

POULTRY RECIPES

205.Crumbed Sage Chicken Scallopini4

Servings:4
Cooking Time: 12 Minutes
Ingredients:
- 3 oz breadcrumbs
- 2 tbsp grated Parmesan cheese
- 2 oz flour
- 2 eggs, beaten
- 1 tbsp fresh, chopped sage

Directions:
1. Preheat the air fryer to 370 F. Place some plastic wrap underneath and on top of the chicken breasts. Using a rolling pin, beat the meat until it becomes really thin. In a bowl, combine the Parmesan cheese, sage and breadcrumbs.
2. Dip the chicken in the egg first, and then in the sage mixture. Spray with cooking oil and arrange the meat in the air fryer. Cook for 7 minutes.

206.Potato Cakes & Cajun Chicken Wings

Servings: 4
Cooking Time: 40 Minutes
Ingredients:
- 4 large-sized chicken wings
- 1 tsp. Cajun seasoning
- 1 tsp. maple syrup
- ¾ tsp. sea salt flakes
- ¼ tsp. red pepper flakes, crushed
- 1 tsp. onion powder
- 1 tsp. porcini powder
- ½ tsp. celery seeds
- 1 small-seized head of cabbage, shredded
- 1 cup mashed potatoes
- 1 small-sized brown onion, coarsely grated
- 1 tsp. garlic puree
- 1 medium whole egg, well whisked
- ½ tsp. table salt
- ½ tsp. ground black pepper
- 1 ½ tbsp. flour
- ¾ tsp. baking powder
- 1 heaped tbsp. cilantro
- 1 tbsp. sesame oil

Directions:
1. Pre-heat your Air Fryer to 390°F.
2. Pat the chicken wings dry. Place them in the fryer and cook for 25 - 30 minutes, ensuring they are cooked through.
3. Make the rub by combining the Cajun seasoning, maple syrup, sea salt flakes, red pepper, onion powder, porcini powder, and celery seeds.
4. Mix together the shredded cabbage, potato, onion, garlic puree, egg, table salt, black pepper, flour, baking powder and cilantro.
5. Separate the cabbage mixture into 4 portions and use your hands to mold each one into a cabbage-potato cake.
6. Douse each cake with the sesame oil.
7. Bake the cabbage-potato cakes in the fryer for 10 minutes, turning them once through the cooking time. You will need to do this in multiple batches.
8. Serve the cakes and the chicken wings together.

207.Peppery Lemon-chicken Breast

Servings:1
Cooking Time:
Ingredients:
- 1 chicken breast
- 1 teaspoon minced garlic
- 2 lemons, rinds and juice reserved
- Salt and pepper to taste

Directions:
1. Preheat the air fryer.
2. Place all ingredients in a baking dish that will fit in the air fryer.
3. Place in the air fryer basket.
4. Close and cook for 20 minutes at 400 °F.

208.Gourmet Chicken Omelet

Servings: 2
Cooking Time: 15 Minutes
Ingredients:
- 4 eggs, whisked
- 4 oz. ground chicken
- ½ cup scallions, finely chopped
- 2 cloves garlic, finely minced
- ½ tsp. salt
- ½ tsp. ground black pepper
- ½ tsp. paprika
- 1 tsp. dried thyme
- Dash of hot sauce

Directions:
1. Mix together all the ingredients in a bowl, ensuring to incorporate everything well.
2. Lightly grease two oven-safe ramekins with vegetable oil. Divide the mixture between them.
3. Transfer them to the Air Fryer, and air fry at 350°F for 13 minutes.
4. Ensure they are cooked through and serve immediately.

209.Lime And Mustard Marinated Chicken

Servings: 4
Cooking Time: 30 Minutes + Marinating Time
Ingredients:
- 1/2 teaspoon stone-ground mustard
- 1/2 teaspoon minced fresh oregano
- 1/3 cup freshly squeezed lime juice

- 2 small-sized chicken breasts, skin-on
- 1 teaspoon kosher salt
- 1teaspoon freshly cracked mixed peppercorns

Directions:
1. Preheat your Air Fryer to 345 degrees F.
2. Toss all of the above ingredients in a medium-sized mixing dish; allow it to marinate overnight.
3. Cook in the preheated Air Fryer for 26 minutes. Bon appétit!

210.Dijon Turkey Drumstick

Servings: 2
Cooking Time: 28 Minutes
Ingredients:
- 4 turkey drumsticks
- 1/3 tsp paprika
- 1/3 cup sherry wine
- 1/3 cup coconut milk
- 1/2 tbsp ginger, minced
- 2 tbsp Dijon mustard
- Pepper
- Salt

Directions:
1. Add all ingredients into the large bowl and stir to coat. Place in refrigerator for 2 hours.
2. Spray air fryer basket with cooking spray.
3. Place marinated turkey drumsticks into the air fryer basket and cook at 380 F for 28 minutes. Turn halfway through.
4. Serve and enjoy.

211.Paprika Duck And Eggplant Mix

Servings: 4
Cooking Time: 25 Minutes
Ingredients:
- 1 pound duck breasts, skinless, boneless and cubed
- 2 eggplants, cubed
- A pinch of salt and black pepper
- 2 tablespoons olive oil
- 1 tablespoon sweet paprika
- ½ cup keto tomato sauce

Directions:
1. Heat up a pan that fits your air fryer with the oil over medium heat, add the duck pieces and brown for 5 minutes. Add the rest of the ingredients, toss, introduce the pan in the fryer and cook at 370 degrees F for 20 minutes. Divide between plates and serve.

212.Holiday Colby Turkey Meatloaf

Servings:6
Cooking Time:50 Minutes
Ingredients:
- 1 pound turkey mince
- 1/2 cup scallions, finely chopped

- 2 garlic cloves, finely minced
- 1 teaspoon dried thyme
- 1/2 teaspoon dried basil
- 3/4 cup Colby cheese, shredded
- 3/4 cup crushed saltines
- 1 tablespoon tamari sauce
- Salt and black pepper, to your liking
- 1/4 cup roasted red pepper tomato sauce
- 1 teaspoon brown sugar
- 3/4 tablespoons olive oil
- 1 medium-sized egg, well beaten

Directions:
1. In a nonstick skillet, that is preheated over a moderate heat, sauté the turkey mince, scallions, garlic, thyme, and basil until just tender and fragrant.
2. Then set your Air Fryer to cook at 360 degrees. Combine sautéed mixture with the cheese, saltines and tamari sauce; then form the mixture into a loaf shape.
3. Mix the remaining items and pour them over the meatloaf. Cook in the Air Fryer baking pan for 45 to 47 minutes. Eat warm.

213.Ricotta Wraps & Spring Chicken

Servings: 12
Cooking Time: 20 Minutes
Ingredients:
- 2 large-sized chicken breasts, cooked and shredded
- ⅓ tsp. sea salt
- ¼ tsp. ground black pepper, or more to taste
- 2 spring onions, chopped
- ¼ cup soy sauce
- 1 tbsp. molasses
- 1 tbsp. rice vinegar
- 10 oz. Ricotta cheese
- 1 tsp. grated fresh ginger
- 50 wonton wrappers

Directions:
1. In a bowl, combine all of the ingredients, minus the wonton wrappers.
2. Unroll the wrappers and spritz with cooking spray.
3. Fill each of the wonton wrappers with equal amounts of the mixture.
4. Dampen the edges with a little water as an adhesive and roll up the wrappers, fully enclosing the filling.
5. Cook the rolls in the Air Fryer for 5 minutes at 375°F. You will need to do this step in batches.
6. Serve with your preferred sauce.

214.Creamy Duck And Lemon Sauce

Servings: 4
Cooking Time: 25 Minutes
Ingredients:

- 2 spring onions, chopped
- 2 tablespoons butter, melted
- 4 garlic cloves, minced
- 1 and ½ teaspoons coriander, ground
- Salt and black pepper to the taste
- 15 ounces tomatoes, crushed
- ¼ cup lemon juice
- 1 and ½ pounds duck breast, skinless, boneless and cubed
- ½ cup cilantro, chopped
- ½ cup chicken stock
- ½ cup heavy cream

Directions:
1. Heat up a pan that fits your air fryer with the butter over medium heat, add the duck pieces and cook for 5 minutes. Add the rest of the ingredients except the cilantro, toss, introduce the pan in the fryer and cook at 370 degrees F for 20 minutes. Divide between plates and serve.

215.Asain Chicken Wings

Servings: 2
Cooking Time: 30 Minutes
Ingredients:
- 4 chicken wings
- 3/4 tbsp Chinese spice
- 1 tbsp soy sauce
- 1 tsp mixed spice
- Pepper
- Salt

Directions:
1. Add chicken wings into the bowl. Add remaining ingredients and toss to coat.
2. Transfer chicken wings into the air fryer basket.
3. Cook at 350 f for 15 minutes.
4. Turn chicken to another side and cook for 15 minutes more.
5. Serve and enjoy.

216.Parmesan-crusted Chicken Fingers

Servings:2
Cooking Time: 30 Minutes
Ingredients:
- 1 tbsp salt
- 1 tbsp black pepper
- 2 cloves garlic, crushed
- 3 tbsp cornstarch
- 4 tbsp breadcrumbs, like flour bread
- 4 tbsp grated Parmesan cheese
- 2 eggs, beaten
- Cooking spray

Directions:
1. Mix salt, garlic, and pepper in a bowl. Add the chicken and stir to coat. Marinate for 1 hour in the fridge.
2. Mix the breadcrumbs with cheese evenly; set aside. Remove the chicken from the

fridge, lightly toss in cornstarch, dip in egg and coat them gently in the cheese mixture. Preheat the air fryer to 350 F. Lightly spray the air fryer basket with cooking spray and place the chicken inside; cook for 15 minutes, until nice and crispy. Serve the chicken with a side of vegetable fries and cheese dip. Yum!

217.Chicken Breasts With Tarragon

Servings:3
Cooking Time: 15 Minutes
Ingredients:
- ½ tbsp butter
- ¼ tbsp kosher salt
- ¼ cup dried tarragon
- ¼ tbsp black and fresh ground pepper

Directions:
1. Preheat the air fryer to 380 F and place each chicken breast on a 12x12 inches foil wrap. Top the chicken with tarragon and butter; season with salt and pepper to taste. Wrap the foil around the chicken breast in a loose way to create a flow of air. Cook the in the air fryer for 15 minutes. Carefully unwrap the chicken and serve.

218.Delicious Chicken Tenderloins

Servings: 6
Cooking Time: 15 Minutes
Ingredients:
- 1 egg, lightly beaten
- ¼ cup heavy whipping cream
- 8 oz chicken breast tenderloins
- 1 cup almond flour
- ¼ tsp garlic powder
- ¼ tsp onion powder
- 1 tsp pepper
- 1 tsp salt

Directions:
1. Whisk egg, with garlic powder, onion powder, cream, pepper, and salt in a bowl.
2. In a shallow dish, add the almond flour.
3. Dip chicken in egg mixture then coats with almond flour mixture.
4. Spray air fryer basket with cooking spray.
5. Place chicken into the air fryer basket and cook at 450 F for 15 minutes.
6. Serve and enjoy.

219.Crispy Chicken Thighs

Servings: 1
Cooking Time: 35 Minutes
Ingredients:
- 1 lb. chicken thighs
- Salt and pepper
- 2 cups roasted pecans
- 1 cup water
- 1 cup flour

Directions:
1. Pre-heat your fryer to 400°F.
2. Season the chicken with salt and pepper, then set aside.
3. Pulse the roasted pecans in a food processor until a flour-like consistency is achieved.
4. Fill a dish with the water, another with the flour, and a third with the pecans.
5. Coat the thighs with the flour. Mix the remaining flour with the processed pecans.
6. Dredge the thighs in the water and then press into the -pecan mix, ensuring the chicken is completely covered.
7. Cook the chicken in the fryer for twenty-two minutes, with an extra five minutes added if you would like the chicken a darker-brown color. Check the temperature has reached 165°F before serving.

220.Dry Rub Chicken Wings

Servings: 2
Cooking Time: 20 Minutes
Ingredients:
- 8 chicken wings
- ¼ tsp onion powder
- 1/2 tsp chili powder
- 1/2 tsp garlic powder
- 1/4 tsp pepper
- 1/4 tsp salt

Directions:
1. In a bowl, mix together chili powder, onion powder, garlic powder, pepper, and salt.
2. Add chicken wings to the bowl and coat well with spice mixture.
3. Add chicken wings into the air fryer basket and cook at 350 F for 20 minutes. Shake halfway through.
4. Serve and enjoy.

221.Thai Chicken With Bacon

Servings: 2
Cooking Time: 50 Minutes
Ingredients:
- 4 rashers smoked bacon
- 2 chicken filets
- 1/2 teaspoon coarse sea salt
- 1/4 teaspoon black pepper, preferably freshly ground
- 1 teaspoon garlic, minced
- 1 (2-inch) piece ginger, peeled and minced
- 1 teaspoon black mustard seeds
- 1 teaspoon mild curry powder
- 1/2 cup coconut milk
- 1/2 cup parmesan cheese, grated

Directions:
1. Start by preheating your Air Fryer to 400 degrees F. Add the smoked bacon and cook

in the preheated Air Fryer for 5 to 7 minutes. Reserve.
2. In a mixing bowl, place the chicken fillets, salt, black pepper, garlic, ginger, mustard seeds, curry powder, and milk. Let it marinate in your refrigerator about 30 minutes.
3. In another bowl, place the grated parmesan cheese.
4. Dredge the chicken fillets through the parmesan mixture and transfer them to the cooking basket. Reduce the temperature to 380 degrees F and cook the chicken for 6 minutes.
5. Turn them over and cook for a further 6 minutes. Repeat the process until you have run out of ingredients.
6. Serve with reserved bacon. Enjoy!

222.Parsley Duck

Servings: 4
Cooking Time: 25 Minutes
Ingredients:
- 4 duck breast fillets, boneless, skin-on and scored
- 2 tablespoons olive oil
- 2 tablespoons parsley, chopped
- Salt and black pepper to the taste
- 1 cup chicken stock
- 1 teaspoon balsamic vinegar

Directions:
1. Heat up a pan that fits your air fryer with the oil over medium heat, add the duck breasts skin side down and sear for 5 minutes. Add the rest of the ingredients, toss, put the pan in the fryer and cook at 380 degrees F for 20 minutes. Divide everything between plates and serve

223.Cajun Chicken Thighs

Servings:4
Cooking Time:25 Minutes
Ingredients:
- ½ cup all-purpose flour
- 1 egg
- 4 (4-ounces) skin-on chicken thighs
- 1½ tablespoons Cajun seasoning
- 1 teaspoon seasoning salt

Directions:
1. Preheat the Air fryer to 355 °F and grease an Air fryer basket.
2. Mix the flour, Cajun seasoning and salt in a bowl.
3. Whisk the egg in another bowl and coat the chicken thighs with the flour mixture.
4. Dip into the egg and dredge again into the flour mixture.

5. Arrange the chicken thighs into the Air Fryer basket, skin side down and cook for about 25 minutes.
6. Dish out the chicken thighs onto a serving platter and serve hot.

224.Nacho-fried Chicken Burgers

Servings: 4
Cooking Time: 25 Minutes
Ingredients:
- 1 palmful dried basil
- 1/3 cup parmesan cheese, grated
- 2 teaspoons dried marjoram
- 1/3 teaspoon ancho chili powder
- 2 teaspoons dried parsley flakes
- 1/2 teaspoon onion powder
- Toppings, to serve
- 1/3 teaspoon porcini powder
- 1 teaspoon sea salt flakes
- 1 pound chicken meat, ground
- 2 teaspoons cumin powder
- 1/3 teaspoon red pepper flakes, crushed
- 1 teaspoon freshly cracked black pepper

Directions:
1. Generously grease an Air Fryer cooking basket with a thin layer of vegetable oil.
2. In a mixing dish, combine chicken meat with all seasonings. Shape into 4 patties and coat them with grated parmesan cheese.
3. Cook chicken burgers in the preheated Air Fryer for 15 minutes at 345 degrees F, working in batches, flipping them once.
4. Serve with toppings of choice. Bon appétit!

225.Turkey Scotch Eggs

Servings:4
Cooking Time: 20 Minutes
Ingredients:
- 1 cup panko breadcrumbs
- 1 egg
- 1 pound ground turkey
- 1 tsp ground cumin
- 1 tbsp dried tarragon
- Salt and black pepper to taste

Directions:
1. Preheat the Air fryer to 400 F.
2. In a bowl, beat eggs with salt. In a separate bowl, mix panko breadcrumbs with tarragon. In a third bowl, pour the ground turkey and mix with cumin, salt, and pepper. Shape the mixture into 4 balls. Wrap the balls around the boiled eggs, so a bigger ball is formed, with the egg in the center.
3. Dip the wrapped eggs in egg and coat with breadcrumbs. Spray with cooking spray and place them in air fryer's basket and cook for 12 minutes, flipping once halfway through. Leave to cool before serving.

226.Chicken With Golden Roasted Cauliflower

Servings: 4
Cooking Time: 30 Minutes
Ingredients:
- 2 pounds chicken legs
- 2 tablespoons olive oil
- 1 teaspoon sea salt
- 1/2 teaspoon ground black pepper
- 1 teaspoon smoked paprika
- 1 teaspoon dried marjoram
- 1 (1-pound head cauliflower, broken into small florets
- 2 garlic cloves, minced
- 1/3 cup Pecorino Romano cheese, freshly grated
- 1/2 teaspoon dried thyme
- Salt, to taste

Directions:
1. Toss the chicken legs with the olive oil, salt, black pepper, paprika, and marjoram.
2. Cook in the preheated Air Fryer at 380 degrees F for 11 minutes. Flip the chicken legs and cook for a further 5 minutes.
3. Toss the cauliflower florets with garlic, cheese, thyme, and salt.
4. Increase the temperature to 400 degrees F; add the cauliflower florets and cook for 12 more minutes. Serve warm.

227.Sun-dried Tomatoes And Chicken Mix

Servings: 4
Cooking Time: 25 Minutes
Ingredients:
- 4 chicken thighs, skinless, boneless
- 1 tablespoon olive oil
- A pinch of salt and black pepper
- 1 tablespoon thyme, chopped
- 1 cup chicken stock
- 3 garlic cloves, minced
- ½ cup coconut cream
- 1 cup sun-dried tomatoes, chopped
- 4 tablespoons parmesan, grated

Directions:
1. Heat up a pan that fits the air fryer with the oil over medium-high heat, add the chicken, salt, pepper and the garlic, and brown for 2-3 minutes on each side. Add the rest of the ingredients except the parmesan, toss, put the pan in the air fryer and cook at 370 degrees F for 20 minutes. Sprinkle the parmesan on top, leave the mix aside for 5 minutes, divide everything between plates and serve.

228.Chicken Pizza Crusts

Servings: 1
Cooking Time: 35 Minutes

Ingredients:
- ½ cup mozzarella, shredded
- ¼ cup parmesan cheese, grated
- 1 lb. ground chicken

Directions:
1. In a large bowl, combine all the ingredients and then spread the mixture out, dividing it into four parts of equal size.
2. Cut a sheet of parchment paper into four circles, roughly six inches in diameter, and put some of the chicken mixture onto the center of each piece, flattening the mixture to fill out the circle.
3. Depending on the size of your fryer, cook either one or two circles at a time at 375°F for 25 minutes. Halfway through, turn the crust over to cook on the other side. Keep each batch warm while you move onto the next one.
4. Once all the crusts are cooked, top with cheese and the toppings of your choice. If desired, cook the topped crusts for an additional five minutes.
5. Serve hot, or freeze and save for later!

229.Ham & Cheese Chicken

Servings:4
Cooking Time: 25 Minutes
Ingredients:
- 4 slices ham
- 4 slices Swiss cheese
- 3 tbsp all-purpose flour
- 4 tbsp butter
- 1 tbsp paprika
- 1 tbsp chicken bouillon granules
- ½ cup dry white wine
- 1 cup heavy whipping cream
- 1 tbsp cornstarch

Directions:
1. Preheat the air fryer to 380 F. Pound the chicken breasts and put a slice of ham and cheese on each one. Fold the edges over the filling and seal the edges with toothpicks. In a medium bowl, combine the paprika and flour, and coat the chicken pieces. Transfer to the air fryer basket and cook for 15 minutes.
2. In a large skillet, melt the butter and add the bouillon and wine; reduce the heat to low. Remove the chicken to the skillet. Let simmer for around 5 minutes.

230.Barbecued Chicken Satay

Servings:4
Cooking Time: 15 Minutes
Ingredients:
- 4 cloves garlic, chopped
- 4 scallions, chopped
- 2 tbsp sesame seeds, toasted
- 1 tbsp fresh ginger, grated
- ½ cup pineapple juice
- ½ cup soy sauce
- ⅓ cup sesame oil
- A pinch of black pepper

Directions:
1. Skew each tender and trim any excess fat. Mix the other ingredients in a bowl. Add the skewered chicken and place in the fridge for 4 hours. Preheat the air fryer to 375°F. Transfer the marinated chicken to the air fryer basket and cook for 12 minutes.

231.Classic Chicken Nuggets

Servings: 4
Cooking Time: 20 Minutes
Ingredients:
- 1 ½ pounds chicken tenderloins, cut into small pieces
- 1/2 teaspoon garlic salt
- 1/2 teaspoon cayenne pepper
- 1/4 teaspoon black pepper, freshly cracked
- 4 tablespoons olive oil
- 2 scoops low-carb unflavored protein powder
- 4 tablespoons Parmesan cheese, freshly grated

Directions:
1. Start by preheating your Air Fryer to 390 degrees F.
2. Season each piece of the chicken with garlic salt, cayenne pepper, and black pepper.
3. In a mixing bowl, thoroughly combine the olive oil with protein powder and parmesan cheese. Dip each piece of chicken in the parmesan mixture.
4. Cook for 8 minutes, working in batches.
5. Later, if you want to warm the chicken nuggets, add them to the basket and cook for 1 minute more. Enjoy!

232.Garlic Chicken

Servings: 4
Cooking Time: 32 Minutes
Ingredients:
- 2 lbs chicken drumsticks
- 1 fresh lemon juice
- 9 garlic cloves, sliced
- 4 tbsp butter, melted
- 2 tbsp parsley, chopped
- 2 tbsp olive oil
- Pepper
- Salt

Directions:
1. Preheat the air fryer to 400 F.
2. Add all ingredients into the large mixing bowl and toss well.

3. Transfer chicken wings into the air fryer basket and cook for 32 minutes. Toss halfway through.
4. Serve and enjoy.

233.Spice Lime Chicken Tenders

Servings: 6
Cooking Time: 20 Minutes
Ingredients:
- 1 lime
- 2 pounds chicken tenderloins cut up
- 1 cup cornflakes, crushed
- 1/2 cup Parmesan cheese, grated
- 1 tablespoon olive oil
- Sea salt and ground black pepper, to taste
- 1 teaspoon cayenne pepper
- 1/3 teaspoon ground cumin
- 1 teaspoon chili powder
- 1 egg

Directions:
1. Squeeze the lime juice all over the chicken.
2. Spritz the cooking basket with a nonstick cooking spray.
3. In a mixing bowl, thoroughly combine the cornflakes, Parmesan, olive oil, salt, black pepper, cayenne pepper, cumin, and chili powder.
4. In another shallow bowl, whisk the egg until well beaten. Dip the chicken tenders in the egg, then in cornflakes mixture.
5. Transfer the breaded chicken to the prepared cooking basket. Cook in the preheated Air Fryer at 380 degrees F for 12 minutes. Turn them over halfway through the cooking time. Work in batches. Serve immediately.

234.Chicken Parmigiana With Fresh Rosemary

Servings:4
Cooking Time: 15 Minutes
Ingredients:
- 1 cup seasoned breadcrumbs
- ½ cup grated Parmesan cheese
- Salt and black pepper to taste
- 2 egg
- 2 sprigs rosemary, chopped

Directions:
1. Preheat your Air Fryer to 380 F. Spray the air fryer basket with cooking spray.
2. Put the chicken halves on a clean flat surface and cover with clingfilm. Gently pound them to become thinner using a rolling pin. Beat the eggs in a bowl and season with salt and black pepper. In a separate bowl, mix white breadcrumbs with Parmesan cheese.
3. Dip the chicken the eggs, then in the breadcrumb mixture. Spray with cooking

spray and place in the cooking basket. Cook for 6 minutes, Slide out the fryer basket and flip; cook for 6 more minutes. Sprinkle with rosemary and serve.

235.Dijon-garlic Thighs

Servings:6
Cooking Time: 25 Minutes
Ingredients:
- 1 tablespoon cider vinegar
- 1 tablespoon Dijon mustard
- 1-pound chicken thighs
- 2 tablespoon olive oil
- 2 teaspoons herbs de Provence
- Salt and pepper to taste

Directions:
1. Place all ingredients in a Ziploc bag.
2. Allow to marinate in the fridge for at least 2 hours.
3. Preheat the air fryer for 5 minutes.
4. Place the chicken in the fryer basket.
5. Cook for 25 minutes at 350 °F.

236.Thai Sticky Turkey Wings

Servings:4
Cooking Time:40 Minutes
Ingredients:
- 3/4 pound turkey wings, cut into pieces
- 1 teaspoon ginger powder
- 1 teaspoon garlic powder
- 3/4 teaspoon paprika
- 2 tablespoons soy sauce
- 1 handful minced lemongrass
- Sea salt flakes and ground black pepper, to savor
- 2 tablespoons rice wine vinegar
- 1/4 cup peanut butter
- 1 tablespoon sesame oil
- 1/2 cup Thai sweet chili sauce

Directions:
1. In a saucepan with boiling water, cook the turkey wings for 20 minutes.
2. Transfer the turkey wings to a large-sized mixing dish; toss with the remaining ingredients, without Thai sweet chili sauce.
3. Air-fry them for 20 minutes at 350 degrees F or until they are thoroughly cooked; make sure to flip them over during the cooking time.
4. Serve with Thai sweet chili sauce and lemon wedges. Bon appétit!

237.Crunchy Stuffed Chicken Breast

Servings:2
Cooking Time:45 Minutes
Ingredients:
- 1 medium eggplant, halved lengthwise
- ¼ cup pomegranate seeds

- 2 (4-ounce) chicken breasts, skinless and boneless
- 2 egg whites
- ¼ cup breadcrumbs
- Salt, to taste
- Freshly ground black pepper, to taste
- ½ tablespoon olive oil

Directions:
1. Preheat the Air fryer to 390 °F and grease an Air fryer basket.
2. Season the eggplant halves with some salt and keep aside for about 20 minutes.
3. Arrange the eggplant halves in the Air fryer basket, cut side up and cook for about 20 minutes.
4. Dish out and scoop out the flesh from each eggplant half.
5. Put the eggplant pulp and a pinch of salt and black pepper in the food processor and pulse until a puree is formed.
6. Dish out the eggplant puree into a bowl and stir in the pomegranate seeds.
7. Cut the chicken breasts lengthwise to make a pocket and stuff in the eggplant mixture.
8. Whisk together egg whites, a pinch of salt and black pepper in a shallow dish.
9. Mix breadcrumbs, thyme and olive oil in another dish.
10. Dip the chicken breasts in the egg white mixture and then coat with flour.
11. Set the Air fryer to 355 °F and transfer the chicken breasts into the Air fryer.
12. Cook for about 25 minutes and dish out to serve warm.

238. Turkey And Sausage Meatloaf With Herbs

Servings: 4
Cooking Time: 45 Minutes
Ingredients:
- 1/2 cup milk
- 4 bread slices, crustless
- 1 tablespoon olive oil
- 1 onion, finely chopped
- 1 garlic clove, minced
- 1/2 pound ground turkey
- 1/2 pound ground breakfast sausage
- 1 duck egg, whisked
- 1 teaspoon rosemary
- 1 teaspoon basil
- 1 teaspoon thyme
- 1 teaspoon cayenne pepper
- Kosher salt and ground black pepper, to taste
- 1/2 cup ketchup
- 2 tablespoons molasses
- 1 tablespoon brown mustard

Directions:

1. In a shallow bowl, pour the milk over the bread and let it soak in for 5 to 6 minutes.
2. Heat 1 tablespoon of oil over medium-high heat in a nonstick pan. Sauté the onions and garlic until tender and fragrant, about 2 minutes.
3. Add the turkey, sausage, egg, rosemary, basil, thyme, cayenne pepper, salt, and ground black pepper. Stir in the milk-soaked bread. Mix until everything is well incorporated.
4. Shape the mixture into a loaf and transfer it to a pan that is lightly greased with an olive oil mister.
5. Next, lower the pan onto the cooking basket.
6. In a mixing bowl, whisk the ketchup with molasses and mustard. Spread this mixture over the top of your meatloaf.
7. Cook approximately 27 minutes or until the meatloaf is no longer pink in the middle. Allow it to sit 10 minutes before slicing and serving. Bon appétit!

239. Tequila Glazed Chicken

Servings: 6
Cooking Time: 40 Minutes
Ingredients:
- 2 tablespoons whole coriander seeds
- Salt and pepper to taste
- 3 pounds chicken breasts
- 1/3 cup orange juice
- ¼ cup tequila
- 2 tablespoons brown sugar
- 2 tablespoons honey
- 3 cloves of garlic, minced
- 1 shallot, minced

Directions:
1. Place all ingredients in a Ziploc bag and allow to marinate for at least 2 hours in the fridge.
2. Preheat the air fryer at 375 °F.
3. Place the grill pan accessory in the air fryer.
4. Grill the chicken for at least 40 minutes.
5. Flip the chicken every 10 minutes for even cooking.
6. Meanwhile, pour the marinade in a saucepan and simmer until the sauce thickens.
7. Brush the chicken with the glaze before serving.

240. Gingered Chicken Drumsticks

Servings: 3
Cooking Time: 25 Minutes
Ingredients:
- ¼ cup full-fat coconut milk
- 3 (6-ounces) chicken drumsticks
- 2 teaspoons fresh ginger, minced
- 2 teaspoons galangal, minced

- 2 teaspoons ground turmeric
- Salt, to taste

Directions:
1. Preheat the Air fryer to 375 °F and grease an Air fryer basket.
2. Mix the coconut milk, galangal, ginger, and spices in a bowl.
3. Add the chicken drumsticks and coat generously with the marinade.
4. Refrigerate to marinate for at least 8 hours and transfer into the Air fryer basket.
5. Cook for about 25 minutes and dish out the chicken drumsticks onto a serving platter.

241.Chicken Breasts With Sweet Chili Adobo

Servings:3
Cooking Time: 20 Minutes
Ingredients:
- Salt to season
- ¼ cup sweet chili sauce
- 3 tbsp turmeric

Directions:
1. Preheat air fryer to 390 F. In a bowl, add salt, sweet chili sauce, and turmeric; mix with a spoon. Place the chicken on a clean flat surface and with a brush, apply the turmeric sauce lightly on the chicken.
2. Place in the fryer basket and grill for 18 minutes; turn them halfway through. Serve with a side of steamed greens.

242.Special Maple-glazed Chicken

Servings: 4
Cooking Time: 20 Minutes
Ingredients:
- 2 ½ tbsp. maple syrup
- 1 tbsp. tamari soy sauce
- 1 tbsp. oyster sauce
- 1 tsp. fresh lemon juice
- 1 tsp. minced fresh ginger
- 1 tsp. garlic puree
- Seasoned salt and freshly ground pepper, to taste
- 2 boneless, skinless chicken breasts

Directions:
1. In a bowl, combine the maple syrup, tamari sauce, oyster sauce, lemon juice, fresh ginger and garlic puree. This is your marinade.
2. Sprinkle the chicken breasts with salt and pepper.
3. Coat the chicken breasts with the marinade. Place some foil over the bowl and refrigerate for 3 hours, or overnight if possible.
4. Remove the chicken from the marinade. Place it in the Air Fryer and fry for 15

minutes at 365°F, flipping each one once or twice throughout.
5. In the meantime, add the remaining marinade to a pan over medium heat. Allow the marinade to simmer for 3 - 5 minutes until it has reduced by half.
6. Pour over the cooked chicken and serve.

243.Marjoram Chicken

Servings: 2
Cooking Time: 1 Hr.
Ingredients:
- 2 skinless, boneless small chicken breasts
- 2 tbsp. butter
- 1 tsp. sea salt
- ½ tsp. red pepper flakes, crushed
- 2 tsp. marjoram
- ¼ tsp. lemon pepper

Directions:
1. In a bowl, coat the chicken breasts with all of the other ingredients. Set aside to marinate for 30 – 60 minutes.
2. Pre-heat your Air Fryer to 390 degrees.
3. Cook for 20 minutes, turning halfway through cooking time.
4. Check for doneness using an instant-read thermometer. Serve over jasmine rice.

244.Sweet And Sour Chicken Thighs

Servings:2
Cooking Time:20 Minutes
Ingredients:
- 1 scallion, finely chopped
- 2 (4-ounces) skinless, boneless chicken thighs
- ½ cup corn flour
- 1 garlic clove, minced
- ½ tablespoon soy sauce
- ½ tablespoon rice vinegar
- 1 teaspoon sugar
- Salt and black pepper, as required

Directions:
1. Preheat the Air fryer to 390 °F and grease an Air fryer basket.
2. Mix all the ingredients except chicken and corn flour in a bowl.
3. Place the corn flour in another bowl.
4. Coat the chicken thighs into the marinade and then dredge into the corn flour.
5. Arrange the chicken thighs into the Air Fryer basket, skin side down and cook for about 10 minutes.
6. Set the Air fryer to 355 °F and cook for 10 more minutes.
7. Dish out the chicken thighs onto a serving platter and serve hot.

245.Marinated Duck Breasts

Servings:4

63

Cooking Time:16 Minutes
Ingredients:
- 1 teaspoon fresh rosemary, chopped
- 1 teaspoon fresh thyme, chopped
- 2 pounds
- ½ cup olive oil
- 1 teaspoon fresh lemon zest, duck breasts grated finely
- ¼ teaspoon sugar
- ¼ teaspoon red pepper flakes, crushed
- Salt and black pepper, to taste

Directions:
1. Preheat the Air fryer to 390 °F and grease an Air fryer basket.
2. Mix all the ingredients in a large bowl except duck breasts.
3. Stir in the duck breasts and refrigerate to marinate well for about 24 hours.
4. Transfer the duck breasts to the Air fryer and cook for about 16 minutes.
5. Dish out the duck breasts onto serving plates and serve hot.

246.Fried Herbed Chicken Wings

Servings: 4
Cooking Time: 11 Minutes
Ingredients:
- 1 tablespoon Emperor herbs chicken spices
- 8 chicken wings
- Cooking spray

Directions:
1. Generously sprinkle the chicken wings with Emperor herbs chicken spices and place in the preheated to 400F air fryer. Cook the chicken wings for 6 minutes from each side.

247.Indian Chicken Tenders

Servings: 4
Cooking Time: 15 Minutes
Ingredients:
- 1 lb chicken tenders, cut in half
- ¼ cup parsley, chopped
- 1/2 tbsp garlic, minced
- 1/2 tbsp ginger, minced
- ¼ cup yogurt
- 3/4 tsp paprika
- 1 tsp garam masala
- 1 tsp turmeric
- 1/2 tsp cayenne pepper
- 1 tsp salt

Directions:
1. Preheat the air fryer to 350 F.
2. Add all ingredients into the large bowl and mix well. Place in refrigerator for 30 minutes.
3. Spray air fryer basket with cooking spray.
4. Add marinated chicken into the air fryer basket and cook for 10 minutes.

5. Turn chicken to another side and cook for 5 minutes more.
6. Serve and enjoy.

248.Crispy Chicken Drumsticks

Servings:2
Cooking Time:20 Minutes
Ingredients:
- 4 (4-ounces) chicken drumsticks
- ½ cup buttermilk
- ½ cup all-purpose flour
- ½ cup panko breadcrumbs
- 3 tablespoons butter, melted
- ¼ teaspoon baking powder
- ¼ teaspoon dried oregano
- ¼ teaspoon dried thyme
- ¼ teaspoon celery salt
- ¼ teaspoon garlic powder
- ¼ teaspoon ground ginger
- ¼ teaspoon cayenne pepper
- ¼ teaspoon paprika
- Salt and ground black pepper, as required

Directions:
1. Preheat the Air fryer to 390 °F and grease an Air fryer basket.
2. Put the chicken drumsticks and buttermilk in a resealable plastic bag.
3. Seal the bag tightly and refrigerate for about 3 hours.
4. Mix the flour, breadcrumbs, baking powder, herbs and spices in a bowl.
5. Remove the chicken drumsticks from bag and coat chicken drumsticks evenly with the seasoned flour mixture.
6. Transfer the chicken drumsticks into the Air fryer basket and cook for about 20 minutes, flipping once in between.
7. Dish out and serve hot.

249.Turkey Wings With Butter Roasted Potatoes

Servings: 4
Cooking Time: 55 Minutes
Ingredients:
- 4 large-sized potatoes, peeled and cut into 1-inch chunks
- 1 tablespoon butter, melted
- 1 teaspoon rosemary
- 1 teaspoon garlic salt
- 1/2 teaspoon ground black pepper
- 1 ½ pounds turkey wings
- 2 tablespoons olive oil
- 2 garlic cloves, minced
- 1 tablespoon Dijon mustard
- 1/2 teaspoon cayenne pepper

Directions:
1. Add the potatoes, butter, rosemary, salt, and pepper to the cooking basket.

2. Cook at 400 degrees F for 12 minutes. Reserve the potatoes, keeping them warm.
3. Now, place the turkey wings in the cooking basket that is previously cleaned and greased with olive oil. Add the garlic, mustard, and cayenne pepper.
4. Cook in the preheated Air Fryer at 350 degrees f for 25 minutes. Turn them over and cook an additional 15 minutes.
5. Test for doneness with a meat thermometer. Serve with warm potatoes.

250.Mac's Chicken Nuggets

Servings: 4
Cooking Time: 40 Minutes
Ingredients:
- 2 slices friendly breadcrumbs
- 9 oz. chicken breast, chopped
- 1 tsp. garlic, minced
- 1 tsp. tomato ketchup
- 2 medium egg
- 1 tbsp. olive oil
- 1 tsp. paprika
- 1 tsp. parsley
- Salt and pepper to taste

Directions:
1. Combine the breadcrumbs, paprika, salt, pepper and oil into a thick batter.
2. Coat the chopped chicken with the parsley, one egg and ketchup.
3. Shape the mixture into several nuggets and dredge each one in the other egg. Roll the nuggets into the breadcrumbs.
4. Cook at 390°F for 10 minutes in the Air Fryer.
5. Serve the nuggets with a side of mayo dip if desired.

251.Quick 'n Easy Garlic Herb Wings

Servings:4
Cooking Time: 35 Minutes
Ingredients:
- ¼ cup chopped rosemary
- 2 pounds chicken wings
- 6 medium garlic cloves , grated
- Salt and pepper to taste

Directions:
1. Season the chicken with garlic, rosemary, salt and pepper.
2. Preheat the air fryer to 390 °F.
3. Place the grill pan accessory in the air fryer.
4. Grill for 35 minutes and make sure to flip the chicken every 10 minutes.

252.Non-fattening Breakfast Frittata

Servings:2
Cooking Time: 15 Minutes
Ingredients:
- ¼ cup sliced mushrooms

- ¼ cup sliced tomato
- 1 cup egg whites
- 2 Tbsp chopped fresh chives
- 2 Tbsp skim milk
- Salt and Black pepper, to taste

Directions:
1. Lightly grease baking pan of air fryer with cooking spray.
2. Spread mushrooms and tomato on bottom of pan.
3. In a bowl, whisk well egg whites, milk, chives, pepper and salt. Pour into baking pan.
4. For 15 minutes, cook on 330°F.
5. Remove basket and let it sit for a minute.
6. Serve and enjoy.

253.Cardamom And Almond Duck

Servings: 4
Cooking Time: 30 Minutes
Ingredients:
- 4 duck legs
- Juice of ½ lemon
- Zest of ½ lemon, grated
- 1 tablespoon cardamom, crushed
- ¼ teaspoon allspice
- 2 tablespoons almonds, toasted and chopped
- 2 tablespoons olive oil

Directions:
1. In a bowl, mix the duck legs with the remaining ingredients except the almonds and toss. Put the duck legs in your air fryer's basket and cook at 380 degrees F for 15 minutes on each side. Divide the duck legs between plates, sprinkle the almonds on top and serve with a side salad.

254.Herbed Chicken

Servings: 6
Cooking Time: 40 Minutes
Ingredients:
- 4 lb. chicken wings
- 6 tbsp. red wine vinegar
- 6 tbsp. lime juice
- 1 tsp. fresh ginger, minced
- 1 tbsp. sugar
- 1 tsp. thyme, chopped
- ½ tsp. white pepper
- ¼ tsp. ground cinnamon
- 1 habanero pepper, chopped
- 6 garlic cloves, chopped
- 2 tbsp. soy sauce
- 2 ½ tbsp. olive oil
- ¼ tsp. salt

Directions:
1. Place all of the ingredients in a bowl and combine well, ensuring to coat the chicken entirely.

2. Put the chicken in the refrigerator to marinate for 1 hour.
3. Pre-heat the Air Fryer to 390°F.
4. Put half of the marinated chicken in the fryer basket and cook for 15 minutes, shaking the basket once throughout the cooking process.
5. Repeat with the other half of the chicken.
6. Serve hot.

255.Chicken And Beer Mix

Servings: 4
Cooking Time: 30 Minutes
Ingredients:
- 1 yellow onion, minced
- 4 chicken drumsticks
- 1 tablespoon balsamic vinegar
- 1 chili pepper, chopped
- 15 ounces beer
- Salt and black pepper to taste
- 2 tablespoons olive oil

Directions:
1. Put the oil in a pan that fits your air fryer and heat up over medium heat.
2. Add the onion and the chili pepper, stir, and cook for 2 minutes.
3. Add the vinegar, beer, salt, and pepper; stir, and cook for 3 more minutes.
4. Add the chicken, toss, and put the pan in the fryer and cook at 370 degrees F for 20 minutes.
5. Divide everything between plates and serve.

BEEF,PORK & LAMB RECIPES

256.Monterey Jack'n Sausage Brekky Casserole

Servings:2
Cooking Time: 20 Minutes
Ingredients:
- ½ cup shredded Cheddar-Monterey Jack cheese blend
- 1 green onion, chopped
- 1 pinch cayenne pepper
- 1/4-lb breakfast sausage
- 2 tbsp red bell pepper, diced
- 4 eggs

Directions:
1. Lightly grease baking pan of air fryer with cooking spray.
2. Add sausage and for 8 minutes, cook on 390°F. Halfway through, crumble sausage and stir well.
3. Meanwhile, whisk eggs in a bowl and stir in bell pepper, green onion, and cayenne.
4. Remove basket and toss the mixture a bit. Evenly spread cheese and pour eggs on top.
5. Cook for another 12 minutes at 330°F or until eggs are set to desired doneness.
6. Serve and enjoy.

257.Simple Lamb Bbq With Herbed Salt

Servings:8
Cooking Time: 1 Hour 20 Minutes
Ingredients:
- 2 ½ tablespoons herb salt
- 2 tablespoons olive oil
- 4 pounds boneless leg of lamb, cut into 2-inch chunks

Directions:
1. Preheat the air fryer to 390 °F.
2. Place the grill pan accessory in the air fryer.
3. Season the meat with the herb salt and brush with olive oil.
4. Grill the meat for 20 minutes per batch.
5. Make sure to flip the meat every 10 minutes for even cooking.

258.Pork Stuffed With Gouda 'n Horseradish

Servings:2
Cooking Time: 15 Minutes
Ingredients:
- 1/4 teaspoon salt
- 1/8 teaspoon pepper
- 2 cups fresh baby spinach
- 2 pork sirloin cutlets (3 ounces each)
- 2 slices smoked Gouda cheese (about 2 ounces)
- 2 tablespoons grated Parmesan cheese
- 2 tablespoons horseradish mustard
- 3 tablespoons dry bread crumbs

Directions:
1. Mix well Parmesan and bread crumbs in a small bowl.
2. On a flat surface, season pork with pepper and salt. Add spinach and cheese on each cutlet and fold to enclose filling. With toothpicks secure pork.
3. Brush mustard all over pork and dip in crumb mixture.
4. Lightly grease baking pan of air fryer with cooking spray. Add pork.
5. For 15 minutes, cook on 330°F. Halfway through cooking time, turnover.
6. Serve and enjoy.

259.Grandma's Famous Pork Chops

Servings:4
Cooking Time:1 Hour 12 Minutes
Ingredients:
- 3 eggs, well-beaten
- 1 ½ cup crushed butter crackers
- 2 teaspoons mustard powder
- 1 ½ tablespoons olive oil
- 1/2 tablespoon soy sauce
- 2 tablespoons Worcestershire sauce
- ½ teaspoon dried rosemary
- 4 large-sized pork chops
- ½ teaspoon dried thyme
- 2 teaspoons fennel seeds
- Salt and freshly cracked black pepper, to taste
- 1 teaspoon red pepper flakes, crushed

Directions:
1. Add the pork chops along with olive oil, soy sauce, Worcestershire sauce, and seasonings to a resealable plastic bag. Allow pork chops to marinate for 50 minutes in your refrigerator.
2. Next step, dip the pork chops into the beaten eggs; then, coat the pork chops with the butter crackers on both sides.
3. Cook in the air fryer for 18 minutes at 405 degrees F, turning once. Bon appétit!

260.Lamb With Potatoes

Servings:2
Cooking Time:15 Minutes
Ingredients:
- ½ pound lamb meat
- 2 small potatoes, peeled and halved
- ½ small onion, peeled and halved
- ¼ cup frozen sweet potato fries
- 1 garlic clove, crushed
- ½ tablespoon dried rosemary, crushed
- 1 teaspoon olive oil

Directions:

1. Preheat the Air fryer to 355 °F and arrange a divider in the Air fryer.
2. Rub the lamb evenly with garlic and rosemary and place on one side of Air fryer divider.
3. Cook for about 20 minutes and meanwhile, microwave the potatoes for about 4 minutes.
4. Dish out the potatoes in a large bowl and stir in the olive oil and onions.
5. Transfer into the Air fryer divider and change the side of lamb ramp.
6. Cook for about 15 minutes, flipping once in between and dish out in a bowl.

261.Shepherd's Pie Made Of Ground Lamb

Servings:4
Cooking Time: 50 Minutes
Ingredients:
- 1-pound lean ground lamb
- 2 tablespoons and 2 teaspoons all-purpose flour
- salt and ground black pepper to taste
- 1 teaspoon minced fresh rosemary
- 2 tablespoons cream cheese
- 2 ounces Irish cheese (such as Dubliner®), shredded
- salt and ground black pepper to taste
- 1 tablespoon milk
- 1-1/2 teaspoons olive oil
- 1-1/2 teaspoons butter
- 1/2 onion, diced
- 1/2 teaspoon paprika
- 1-1/2 teaspoons ketchup
- 1-1/2 cloves garlic, minced
- 1/2 (12 ounce) package frozen peas and carrots, thawed
- 1-1/2 teaspoons butter
- 1/2 pinch ground cayenne pepper
- 1/2 egg yolk
- 1-1/4 cups water, or as needed
- 1-1/4 pounds Yukon Gold potatoes, peeled and halved
- 1/8 teaspoon ground cinnamon

Directions:
1. Bring a large pan of salted water to boil and add potatoes. Simmer for 15 minutes until tender.
2. Meanwhile, lightly grease baking pan of air fryer with butter. Melt for 2 minutes at 360°F.
3. Add ground lamb and onion. Cook for 10 minutes, stirring and crumbling halfway through cooking time.
4. Add garlic, ketchup, cinnamon, paprika, rosemary, black pepper, salt, and flour. Mix well and cook for 3 minutes.
5. Add water and deglaze pan. Continue cooking for 6 minutes.

6. Stir in carrots and peas. Evenly spread mixture in pan.
7. Once potatoes are done, drain well and transfer potatoes to a bowl. Mash potatoes and stir in Irish cheese, cream cheese, cayenne pepper, and butter. Mix well. Season with pepper and salt to taste.
8. In a small bowl, whisk well milk and egg yolk. Stir into mashed potatoes.
9. Top the ground lamb mixture with mashed potatoes.
10. Cook for another 15 minutes or until tops of potatoes are lightly browned.
11. Serve and enjoy.

262.Spicy Lamb Kebabs

Servings:6
Cooking Time:8 Minutes
Ingredients:
- 4 eggs, beaten
- 1 cup pistachios, chopped
- 1 pound ground lamb
- 4 tablespoons plain flour
- 4 tablespoons flat-leaf parsley, chopped
- 2 teaspoons chili flakes
- 4 garlic cloves, minced
- 2 tablespoons fresh lemon juice
- 2 teaspoons cumin seeds
- 1 teaspoon fennel seeds
- 2 teaspoons dried mint
- 2 teaspoons salt
- Olive oil
- 1 teaspoon coriander seeds
- 1 teaspoon freshly ground black pepper

Directions:
1. Preheat the Air fryer to 355 °F and grease an Air fryer basket.
2. Mix lamb, pistachios, eggs, lemon juice, chili flakes, flour, cumin seeds, fennel seeds, coriander seeds, mint, parsley, salt and black pepper in a large bowl.
3. Thread the lamb mixture onto metal skewers to form sausages and coat with olive oil.
4. Place the skewers in the Air fryer basket and cook for about 8 minutes.
5. Dish out in a platter and serve hot.

263.Spicy Pork Meatballs

Servings: 4
Cooking Time: 20 Minutes
Ingredients:
- 1 pound ground pork
- 1 cup scallions, finely chopped
- 2 cloves garlic, finely minced
- 1 ½ tablespoons Worcester sauce
- 1 tablespoon oyster sauce
- 1 teaspoon turmeric powder
- 1/2 teaspoon freshly grated ginger root

- 1 small sliced red chili, for garnish

Directions:
1. Mix all of the above ingredients, apart from the red chili. Knead with your hands to ensure an even mixture.
2. Roll into equal balls and transfer them to the Air Fryer cooking basket.
3. Set the timer for 15 minutes and push the power button. Air-fry at 350 degrees F. Sprinkle with sliced red chili; serve immediately with your favorite sauce for dipping. Enjoy!

264.Peppercorn Lamb With Rhubarb

Servings: 4
Cooking Time: 30 Minutes
Ingredients:
- 1 and ½ pound lamb ribs
- A pinch of salt and black pepper
- 1 tablespoon black peppercorns, ground
- 1 tablespoon white peppercorns, ground
- 1 tablespoon fennel seeds, ground
- 1 tablespoon coriander seeds, ground
- 4 rhubarb stalks, chopped
- ¼ cup balsamic vinegar
- 2 tablespoons olive oil

Directions:
1. Heat up a pan that fits your air fryer with the oil over medium heat, add the lamb and brown for 2 minutes. Add the rest of the ingredients, toss, bring to a simmer for 2 minutes and take off the heat. Put the pan in the fryer and cook at 380 degrees for 25 minutes. Divide everything into bowls and serve.

265.Orange Carne Asada

Servings: 4
Cooking Time: 14 Minutes
Ingredients:
- ¼ lime
- 2 tablespoons orange juice
- 1 teaspoon dried cilantro
- 1 chili pepper, chopped
- 1 tablespoon sesame oil
- 1 tablespoon apple cider vinegar
- ½ teaspoon chili paste
- ½ teaspoon ground cumin
- ½ teaspoon salt
- 1-pound beef skirt steak

Directions:
1. Chop the lime roughly and put it in the blender. Add orange juice, dried cilantro, chili pepper, sesame oil, apple cider vinegar, chili paste, ground cumin, and salt. Blend the mixture until smooth. Cut the skirt steak on 4 servings. Then brush every steak with blended lime mixture and leave for 10 minutes to marinate. Meanwhile, preheat the air fryer to 400F. Put the steaks in the air fryer in one layer and cook them for 7 minutes. Flip the meat on another side and cook it for 7 minutes more.

266.Adobo Oregano Beef

Servings: 4
Cooking Time: 30 Minutes
Ingredients:
- 1 pound beef roast, trimmed
- ½ teaspoon oregano, dried
- ¼ teaspoon garlic powder
- A pinch of salt and black pepper
- ½ teaspoon turmeric powder
- 1 tablespoon olive oil

Directions:
1. In a bowl, mix the roast with the rest of the ingredients, and rub well. Put the roast in the air fryer's basket and cook at 390 degrees F for 30 minutes. Slice the roast, divide it between plates and serve with a side salad.

267.Hot Pepper Lamb Mix

Servings: 4
Cooking Time: 35 Minutes
Ingredients:
- 1 pound lamb leg, boneless and sliced
- 2 tablespoons olive oil
- A pinch of salt and black pepper
- 2 garlic cloves, minced
- 1 tablespoon rosemary, chopped
- ½ cup walnuts, chopped
- ¼ teaspoon red pepper flakes
- ½ teaspoon mustard seeds
- ½ teaspoon Italian seasoning
- 1 tablespoon parsley, chopped

Directions:
1. In a bowl, mix the lamb with all the ingredients except the walnuts and parsley, rub well, put the slices your air fryer's basket and cook at 370 degrees F for 35 minutes, flipping the meat halfway. Divide between plates, sprinkle the parsley and walnuts on top and serve with a side salad.

268.Cajun Steak With Spicy Green Beans

Servings: 4
Cooking Time: 25 Minutes
Ingredients:
- 2 garlic cloves, smashed
- 2 teaspoons sunflower oil
- 1/2 teaspoon cayenne pepper
- 1 tablespoon Cajun seasoning
- 1 ½ pounds blade steak
- 2 cups green beans
- 1/2 teaspoon Tabasco pepper sauce
- Sea salt and ground black pepper, to taste

Directions:

1. Start by preheating your Air Fryer to 330 degrees F.
2. Mix the garlic, oil, cayenne pepper, and Cajun seasoning to make a paste. Rub it over both sides of the blade steak.
3. Cook for 13 minutes in the preheated Air Fryer. Now, flip the steak and cook an additional 8 minutes.
4. Heat the green beans in a saucepan. Add a few tablespoons of water, Tabasco, salt, and black pepper; heat until it wilts or about 10 minutes.
5. Serve the roasted blade steak with green beans on the side. Bon appétit!

269.Tangy Pork Chops With Vermouth

Servings: 5
Cooking Time: 34 Minutes
Ingredients:
- 5 pork chops
- 1/3 cup vermouth
- 1/2 teaspoon paprika
- 2 sprigs thyme, only leaves, crushed
- 1/2 teaspoon dried oregano
- Fresh parsley, to serve
- 1 teaspoon garlic salt
- ½ lemon, cut into wedges
- 1 teaspoon freshly cracked black pepper
- 3 tablespoons lemon juice
- 3 cloves garlic, minced
- 2 tablespoons canola oil

Directions:
1. Firstly, heat the canola oil in a sauté pan over a moderate heat. Now, sweat the garlic until just fragrant.
2. Remove the pan from the heat and pour in the lemon juice and vermouth. Now, throw in the seasonings. Dump the sauce into a baking dish, along with the pork chops.
3. Tuck the lemon wedges among the pork chops and air-fry for 27 minutes at 345 degrees F. Bon appétit!

270.Steak With Bell Peppers

Servings:4
Cooking Time:22 Minutes
Ingredients:
- 1¼ pounds beef steak, cut into thin strips
- 2 green bell peppers, seeded and cubed
- 1 red bell pepper, seeded and cubed
- 1 red onion, sliced
- 1 teaspoon dried oregano, crushed
- 1 teaspoon onion powder
- 1 teaspoon garlic powder
- 1 teaspoon red chili powder
- 1 teaspoon paprika
- Salt, to taste
- 2 tablespoons olive oil

Directions:

1. Preheat the Air fryer to 390 °F and grease an Air fryer basket.
2. Mix the oregano and spices in a bowl.
3. Add bell peppers, onion, oil, and beef strips and mix until well combined.
4. Transfer half of the steak strips in the Air fryer basket and cook for about 11 minutes, flipping once in between.
5. Repeat with the remaining mixture and dish out to serve hot.

271.Cilantro-mint Pork Bbq Thai Style

Servings:3
Cooking Time: 15 Minutes
Ingredients:
- 1 minced hot chile
- 1 minced shallot
- 1-pound ground pork
- 2 tablespoons fish sauce
- 2 tablespoons lime juice
- 3 tablespoons basil
- 3 tablespoons chopped mint
- 3 tablespoons cilantro

Directions:
1. In a shallow dish, mix well all Ingredients with hands. Form into 1-inch ovals.
2. Thread ovals in skewers. Place on skewer rack in air fryer.
3. For 15 minutes, cook on 360°F. Halfway through cooking time, turnover skewers. If needed, cook in batches.
4. Serve and enjoy.

272.Filling Pork Chops

Servings:2
Cooking Time:12 Minutes
Ingredients:
- 2 (1-inch thick) pork chops
- ½ tablespoon fresh cilantro, chopped
- ½ tablespoon fresh rosemary, chopped
- ½ tablespoon fresh parsley, chopped
- 2 garlic cloves, minced
- 2 tablespoons olive oil
- ¾ tablespoon Dijon mustard
- 1 tablespoon ground coriander
- 1 teaspoon sugar
- Salt, to taste

Directions:
1. Preheat the Air fryer to 390 °F and grease an Air fryer basket.
2. Mix all the ingredients in a large bowl except the chops.
3. Coat the pork chops with marinade generously and cover to refrigerate for about 3 hours.
4. Keep the pork chops at room temperature for about 30 minutes and transfer into the Air fryer basket.

5. Cook for about 12 minutes, flipping once in between and dish out to serve hot.

273.Wine Marinated Flank Steak

Servings: 4
Cooking Time: 20 Minutes + Marinating Time
Ingredients:
- 1 ½ pounds flank steak
- 1/2 cup red wine
- 1/2 cup apple cider vinegar
- 2 tablespoons soy sauce
- Salt, to taste
- 1/2 teaspoon ground black pepper
- 1/2 teaspoon red pepper flakes, crushed
- 1/2 teaspoon dried basil
- 1 teaspoon thyme

Directions:
1. Add all ingredients to a large ceramic bowl. Cover and let it marinate for 3 hours in your refrigerator.
2. Transfer the flank steak to the Air Fryer basket that is previously greased with nonstick cooking oil.
3. Cook in the preheated Air Fryer at 400 degrees F for 12 minutes, flipping over halfway through the cooking time. Bon appétit!

274.Fried Sausage And Mushrooms Recipe

Servings: 6
Cooking Time:50 Minutes
Ingredients:
- 3 red bell peppers; chopped
- 2 sweet onions; chopped.
- 1 tbsp. brown sugar
- 1 tsp. olive oil
- 2 lbs. pork sausage; sliced
- Salt and black pepper to the taste
- 2 lbs. Portobello mushrooms; sliced

Directions:
1. In a baking dish that fits your air fryer, mix sausage slices with oil, salt, pepper, bell pepper, mushrooms, onion and sugar, toss, introduce in your air fryer and cook at 300 °F, for 40 minutes. Divide among plates and serve right away.

275.Rosemary Steaks

Servings: 4
Cooking Time: 24 Minutes
Ingredients:
- 4 rib eye steaks
- A pinch of salt and black pepper
- 1 tablespoon olive oil
- 1 teaspoon sweet paprika
- 1 teaspoon cumin, ground
- 1 teaspoon rosemary, chopped

Directions:

1. In a bowl, mix the steaks with the rest of the ingredients, toss and put them in your air fryer's basket. Cook at 380 degrees F for 12 minutes on each side, divide between plates and serve.

276.Boozy Pork Loin Chops

Servings: 6
Cooking Time: 22 Minutes
Ingredients:
- 2 tablespoons vermouth
- 6 center-cut loin pork chops
- 1/2 tablespoon fresh basil, minced
- 1/3 teaspoon freshly ground black pepper, or more to taste
- 2 tablespoons whole grain mustard
- 1 teaspoon fine kosher salt

Directions:
1. Toss pork chops with other ingredients until they are well coated on both sides.
2. Air-fry your chops for 18 minutes at 405 degrees F, turning once or twice.
3. Mound your favorite salad on a serving plate; top with pork chops and enjoy.

277.Pork Belly With Lime Aromatics

Servings: 4
Cooking Time: 1 Hour 15 Minutes + Marinating Time
Ingredients:
- 1 pound pork belly
- 2 garlic cloves, halved
- 1 teaspoon shallot powder
- 1 teaspoon sea salt
- 1 teaspoon dried basil
- 1 teaspoon dried oregano
- 1 teaspoon dried thyme
- 1 teaspoon dried marjoram
- 1 teaspoon ground black pepper
- 1 lime, juiced

Directions:
1. Blanch the pork belly in a pot of boiling water for 10 to 13 minutes.
2. Pat it dry with a kitchen towel. Now, poke holes all over the skin by using a fork.
3. Then, mix the remaining ingredients to make the rub. Massage the rub all over the pork belly. Drizzle lime juice all over the meat; place the pork belly in the refrigerator for 3 hours.
4. Preheat your Air Fryer to 320 degrees F. Cook the pork belly for 35 minutes.
5. Turn up the temperature to 360 degrees F and continue cooking for 20 minutes longer. Serve warm. Bon appétit!

278.Garlic-rosemary Rubbed Beef Rib Roast

Servings:14
Cooking Time: 2 Hours

Ingredients:
- 1 cup dried porcini mushrooms
- 1 medium shallot, chopped
- 2 cloves of garlic, minced
- 2 cups water
- 3 tablespoons unsalted pepper
- 3 tablespoons vegetable oil
- 4 sprigs of thyme
- 6 ribs, beef rib roast
- Salt and pepper to taste

Directions:
1. Preheat the air fryer for 5 minutes.
2. Place all ingredients in a baking dish that will fit in the air fryer.
3. Place the dish in the air fryer and cook for 2 hours at 325 °F.

279.Hickory Smoked Beef Jerky

Servings:2
Cooking Time: 1 Hour
Ingredients:
- ¼ cup Worcestershire sauce
- ½ cup brown sugar
- ½ cup soy sauce
- ½ teaspoon black pepper
- ½ teaspoon smoked paprika
- 1 tablespoon chili pepper sauce
- 1 tablespoon liquid smoke, hickory
- 1 teaspoon garlic powder
- 1 teaspoon onion powder
- 1-pound ground beef, sliced thinly

Directions:
1. Combine all Ingredients in a mixing bowl or Ziploc bag.
2. Marinate in the fridge overnight.
3. Preheat the air fryer to 330 °F.
4. Place the beef slices on the double layer rack.
5. Cook for one hour until the beef jerky is very dry.

280.Roast Beef With Buttered Garlic-celery

Servings:8
Cooking Time: 1 Hour
Ingredients:
- 1 bulb of garlic, peeled and crushed
- 1 tablespoon butter
- 2 medium onions, chopped
- 2 pounds topside of beef
- 2 sticks of celery, sliced
- 3 tablespoons olive oil
- A bunch of fresh herbs of your choice
- Salt and pepper to taste

Directions:
1. Preheat the air fryer for 5 minutes.
2. In a baking dish that will fit in the air fryer, place all the ingredients and give a good stir.

3. Place the dish in the air fryer and bake for 1 hour at 350 °F.

281.Perfect Skirt Steak

Servings:4
Cooking Time:30 Minutes
Ingredients:
- 1 cup fresh parsley leaves, chopped finely
- 3 tablespoons fresh oregano, chopped finely
- 3 tablespoons fresh mint leaves, chopped finely
- 2 (8-ounce) skirt steaks
- 3 garlic cloves, minced
- 1 tablespoon ground cumin
- 2 teaspoons smoked paprika
- 1 teaspoon cayenne pepper
- 1 teaspoon red pepper flakes, crushed
- Salt and freshly ground black pepper, to taste
- ¾ cup olive oil
- 3 tablespoons red wine vinegar

Directions:
1. Preheat the Air fryer to 390 °F and grease an Air fryer basket.
2. Season the steaks with a little salt and black pepper.
3. Mix all the ingredients in a large bowl except the steaks.
4. Put ¼ cup of the herb mixture and steaks in a resealable bag and shake well.
5. Refrigerate for about 24 hours and reserve the remaining herb mixture.
6. Keep the steaks at room temperature for about 30 minutes and transfer into the Air fryer basket.
7. Cook for about 10 minutes and sprinkle with remaining herb mixture to serve.

282.Authentic Pakistani Seekh Kebabs

Servings: 3
Cooking Time: 25 Minutes
Ingredients:
- 1 pound lean pork, ground
- 1 onion, chopped
- 1 garlic clove, smashed
- 1 Thai bird chili, deveined and finely chopped
- 1 teaspoon mustard
- 1 teaspoon coriander seed, ground
- 1/2 teaspoon cumin powder
- Salt and ground black pepper, to taste
- 6 tablespoons parmesan cheese, grated

Directions:
1. Mix all ingredients using your hands. Knead until everything is well incorporated.
2. Shape the meat mixture around flat skewers (sausage shapes).

3. Cook at 365 degrees F for 11 to 12 minutes, turning them over once or twice. Work in batches. Serve!

283.Beef And Thyme Cabbage Mix

Servings: 4
Cooking Time: 25 Minutes
Ingredients:
- 2 pounds beef, cubed
- ½ pound bacon, chopped
- 2 shallots, chopped
- 1 napa cabbage, shredded
- 2 garlic cloves, minced
- A pinch of salt and black pepper
- 2 tablespoons olive oil
- 1 teaspoon thyme, dried
- 1 cup beef stock

Directions:
1. Heat up a pan that fits the air fryer with the oil over medium-high heat, add the beef and brown for 3 minutes. Add the bacon, shallots and garlic and cook for 2 minutes more. Add the rest of the ingredients, toss, put the pan in the air fryer and cook at 390 degrees F for 20 minutes. Divide between plates and serve.

284.Grilled Spicy Carne Asada

Servings:2
Cooking Time: 50 Minutes
Ingredients:
- 1 chipotle pepper, chopped
- 1 dried ancho chilies, chopped
- 1 tablespoon coriander seeds
- 1 tablespoon cumin
- 1 tablespoons soy sauce
- 2 slices skirt steak
- 2 tablespoons Asian fish sauce
- 2 tablespoons brown sugar
- 2 tablespoons of fresh lemon juice
- 2 tablespoons olive oil
- 3 cloves of garlic, minced

Directions:
1. Place all ingredients in a Ziploc bag and marinate in the fridge for 2 hours.
2. Preheat the air fryer to 390 °F.
3. Place the grill pan accessory in the air fryer.
4. Grill the skirt steak for 20 minutes.
5. Flip the steak every 10 minutes for even grilling.

285.German Sausage With Sauerkraut

Servings: 4
Cooking Time: 35 Minutes
Ingredients:
- 4 pork sausages, smoked
- 2 tablespoons canola oil
- 2 garlic cloves, minced
- 1 pound sauerkraut
- 1 teaspoon cayenne pepper
- 1/2 teaspoon black peppercorns
- 2 bay leaves

Directions:
1. Start by preheating your Air Fryer to 360 degrees F.
2. Prick holes into the sausages using a fork and transfer them to the cooking basket. Cook approximately 14 minutes, shaking the basket a couple of times. Set aside.
3. Now, heat the canola oil in a baking pan at 380 degrees F. Add the garlic and cook for 1 minute. Immediately stir in the sauerkraut, cayenne pepper, peppercorns, and bay leaves.
4. Let it cook for 15 minutes, stirring every 5 minutes. Serve in individual bowls with warm sausages on the side!

286.Cilantro Steak

Servings: 4
Cooking Time: 25 Minutes
Ingredients:
- 1-pound flank steak
- 1 oz fresh cilantro, chopped
- 1 garlic clove, diced
- 1 oz fresh parsley, chopped
- 1 egg, hard-boiled, peeled
- ½ green bell pepper, chopped
- 1 tablespoon avocado oil
- ½ teaspoon salt
- ½ teaspoon ground black pepper
- 1 teaspoon peanut oil

Directions:
1. In the mixing bowl, mix up fresh cilantro, diced garlic, parsley, and avocado oil. Then slice the flank steak in one big fillet (square) and brush it with a cilantro mixture. Then chop the egg roughly and put it on the steak. Add chopped bell pepper. After this, roll the meat and secure it with the kitchen thread. Carefully rub the meat roll with salt and ground black pepper. Then sprinkle the meat roll with peanut oil. Preheat the air fryer to 400F. Put the meat in the air fryer basket and cook it for 25 minutes.

287.Beef And Spring Onions

Servings: 2
Cooking Time: 15 Minutes
Ingredients:
- 2 cups corned beef, cooked and shredded
- 2 garlic cloves, minced
- 1 pound radishes, quartered
- 2 spring onions, chopped
- A pinch of salt and black pepper

Directions:
1. In a pan that fits your air fryer, mix the beef with the rest of the ingredients, toss, put the

pan in the fryer and cook at 390 degrees F for 15 minutes. Divide everything into bowls and serve.

288.Pork Shoulder With Pineapple Sauce

Servings:3
Cooking Time: 24 Minutes
Ingredients:
- For Pork:
- 10½ ounces pork shoulder, cut into bite-sized pieces
- 2 pinches of Maggi seasoning
- 1 teaspoon light soy sauce
- Dash of sesame oil
- 1 egg
- ¼ cup plain flour
- For Sauce:
- 1 teaspoon olive oil
- 1 medium onion, sliced
- 1 tablespoon garlic, minced
- 1 large pineapple slice, cubed
- 1 medium tomato, chopped
- 2 tablespoons tomato sauce
- 2 tablespoons oyster sauce
- 1 tablespoon Worcestershire sauce
- 1 teaspoon sugar
- 1 tablespoon water
- ½ tablespoon corn flour

Directions:
1. For pork: in a large bowl, mix together the Maggi seasoning, soy sauce, and sesame oil.
2. Add the pork cubes and generously mix with the mixture.
3. Refrigerate to marinate for about 4-6 hours.
4. In a shallow dish, beat the egg.
5. In another dish, place the plain flour.
6. Dip the cubed pork in beaten egg and then, coat evenly with the flour.
7. Set the temperature of air fryer to 248 degrees F. Grease an air fryer basket.
8. Arrange pork cubes into the prepared air fryer basket in a single layer.
9. Air fry for about 20 minutes.
10. Meanwhile, for the sauce: in a skillet, heat oil over medium heat and sauté the onion and garlic for about 1 minute.
11. Add the pineapple, and tomato and cook for about 1 minute.
12. Add the tomato sauce, oyster sauce, Worcestershire sauce, and sugar and stir to combine.
13. Meanwhile, in a bowl, mix together the water and corn flour.
14. Add the corn flour mixture into the sauce, stirring continuously.
15. Cook until the sauce is thicken enough, stirring continuously.
16. Remove pork cubes from air fryer and add into the sauce.

17. Cook for about 1-2 minutes or until coated completely.
18. Remove from the heat and serve hot.

289.Spiced Chops

Servings: 3
Cooking Time: 12 Minutes
Ingredients:
- 10 oz pork chops, bone-in (3 pork chops)
- 1 teaspoon Erythritol
- 1 teaspoon ground black pepper
- 1 teaspoon ground paprika
- ½ teaspoon onion powder
- ¼ teaspoon garlic powder
- 2 teaspoons olive oil

Directions:
1. In the mixing bowl mix up Erythritol, ground black pepper, ground paprika, onion powder, and garlic powder. Then rub the pork chops with the spice mixture from both sides. After this, sprinkle the meat with olive oil. Leave the meat for 5-10 minutes to marinate. Preheat the air fryer to 400F. Put the pork chops in the air fryer and cook them for 6 minutes. Then flip the meat on another side and cook it for 6 minutes more.

290.Beef Schnitzel

Servings: 1
Cooking Time: 30 Minutes
Ingredients:
- 1 egg
- 1 thin beef schnitzel
- 3 tbsp. friendly bread crumbs
- 2 tbsp. olive oil
- 1 parsley, roughly chopped
- ½ lemon, cut in wedges

Directions:
1. Pre-heat your Air Fryer to the 360°F.
2. In a bowl combine the bread crumbs and olive oil to form a loose, crumbly mixture.
3. Beat the egg with a whisk.
4. Coat the schnitzel first in the egg and then in the bread crumbs, ensuring to cover it fully.
5. Place the schnitzel in the Air Fryer and cook for 12 – 14 minutes. Garnish the schnitzel with the lemon wedges and parsley before serving.

291.Moroccan Beef Kebab

Servings: 4
Cooking Time: 30 Minutes
Ingredients:
- 1/2 cup leeks, chopped
- 2 garlic cloves, smashed
- 2 pounds ground chuck
- Salt, to taste

- 1/4 teaspoon ground black pepper, or more to taste
- 1 teaspoon cayenne pepper
- 1/2 teaspoon ground sumac
- 3 saffron threads
- 2 tablespoons loosely packed fresh continental parsley leaves
- 4 tablespoons tahini sauce
- 4 ounces baby arugula
- 1 tomato, cut into slices

Directions:
1. In a bowl, mix the chopped leeks, garlic, ground chuck, and spices; knead with your hands until everything is well incorporated.
2. Now, mound the beef mixture around a wooden skewer into a pointed-ended sausage.
3. Cook in the preheated Air Fryer at 360 degrees F for 25 minutes.
4. Serve your kebab with the tahini sauce baby arugula and tomato. Enjoy!

292.Paprika Burgers With Blue Cheese

Servings: 6
Cooking Time: 44 Minutes
Ingredients:
- 1 cup blue cheese, sliced
- 2 teaspoons dried basil
- 1 teaspoon smoked paprika
- 2 pounds ground pork
- 2 tablespoons tomato puree
- 2 small-sized onions, peeled and chopped
- 1/2 teaspoon ground black pepper
- 3 garlic cloves, minced
- 1 teaspoon fine sea salt

Directions:
1. Start by preheating your Air Fryer to 385 degrees F.
2. In a mixing dish, combine the pork, onion, garlic, tomato puree, and seasonings; mix to combine well.
3. Form the pork mixture into six patties; cook the burgers for 23 minutes. Pause the machine, turn the temperature to 365 degrees F and cook for 18 more minutes.
4. Place the prepared burgers on a serving platter; top with blue cheese and serve warm.

293.Pork With Padrón Peppers And Green Olives

Servings: 4
Cooking Time: 30 Minutes
Ingredients:
- 1 tablespoon olive oil
- 8 ounces Padrón peppers
- 2 pounds pork loin, sliced
- 1 teaspoon Celtic salt
- 1 teaspoon paprika

- 1 heaped tablespoon capers, drained
- 8 green olives, pitted and halved

Directions:
1. Drizzle olive oil all over the Padrón peppers; cook them in the preheated Air Fryer at 400 degrees F for 10 minutes, turning occasionally, until well blistered all over and tender-crisp.
2. Then, turn the temperature to 360 degrees F.
3. Season the pork loin with salt and paprika. Add the capers and cook for 16 minutes, turning them over halfway through the cooking time.
4. Serve with olives and the reserved Padrón peppers. Bon appétit!

294.Oregano And Rosemary Lamb Skewers

Servings: 4
Cooking Time: 20 Minutes
Ingredients:
- 2 pounds lamb meat, cubed
- ¼ cup olive oil
- 1 tablespoon garlic, minced
- 1 tablespoon oregano, dried
- ½ teaspoon rosemary, dried
- 2 tablespoons lemon juice
- A pinch of salt and black pepper
- 1 tablespoon red vinegar
- 2 red bell peppers, cut into medium pieces

Directions:
1. In a bowl, mix all the ingredients and toss them well. Thread the lamb and bell peppers on skewers, place them in your air fryer's basket and cook at 380 degrees F for 10 minutes on each side. Divide between plates and serve with a side salad.

295.Sausage Meatballs

Servings:4
Cooking Time:15 Minutes
Ingredients:
- 3½-ounce sausage, casing removed
- ½ medium onion, minced finely
- 1 teaspoon fresh sage, chopped finely
- 3 tablespoons Italian breadcrumbs
- ½ teaspoon garlic, minced
- Salt and black pepper, to taste

Directions:
1. Preheat the Air fryer to 355 °F and grease an Air fryer basket.
2. Mix all the ingredients in a bowl until well combined.
3. Shape the mixture into equal-sized balls and arrange the balls in the Air fryer basket.
4. Cook for about 15 minutes and dish out to serve warm.

296.Cocoa Ribs

Servings: 4
Cooking Time: 45 Minutes
Ingredients:
- 2 tablespoons cocoa powder
- ½ teaspoon cinnamon powder
- ½ teaspoon chili powder
- 1 tablespoon coriander, chopped
- ½ teaspoon cumin, ground
- 2 racks of ribs
- A pinch of salt and black pepper
- Cooking spray

Directions:
1. Grease the ribs with the cooking spray, mix with the other ingredients and rub very well. Put the ribs in your air fryer's basket and cook at 390 degrees F for 45 minutes. Divide between plates and serve with a side salad.

297.Beef & Mushroom Meatloaf

Servings:4
Cooking Time: 25 Minutes
Ingredients:
- 1 pound lean ground beef
- 1 small onion, finely chopped
- 1 tablespoon fresh thyme, finely chopped
- 3 tablespoons dry breadcrumbs
- 1 egg, lightly beaten
- Salt and ground black pepper, as required
- 2 mushrooms, thickly sliced
- 1 tablespoon olive oil

Directions:
1. In a bowl, add the beef, onion, thyme, breadcrumbs, egg, salt, and black pepper. With your hands, mix until well combined.
2. Put the beef mixture into a lightly greased baking pan and with the back of spoon, smooth the top surface.
3. Arrange the mushroom slices on top and gently, press each inside the meatloaf.
4. Coat the meatloaf with oil.
5. Set the temperature of Air Fryer to 392 degrees F.
6. Arrange the pan of meatloaf into the Air Fryer basket.
7. Air Fry for about 25 minutes or until meatloaf becomes golden brown.
8. Remove from Air Fryer and place the pan onto a wire rack for about 10 minutes before serving.
9. Cut into desired size wedges and serve.

298.Hot Paprika Beef

Servings: 4
Cooking Time: 20 Minutes
Ingredients:
- 1 tablespoon hot paprika
- 4 beef steaks

- Salt and black pepper to the taste
- 1 tablespoon butter, melted

Directions:
1. In a bowl, mix the beef with the rest of the ingredients, rub well, transfer the steaks to your air fryer's basket and cook at 390 degrees F for 10 minutes on each side. Divide the steaks between plates and serve with a side salad.

299.Beef Roast In Worcestershire-rosemary

Servings:6
Cooking Time: 2 Hours
Ingredients:
- 1 onion, chopped
- 1 tablespoon butter
- 1 tablespoon Worcestershire sauce
- 1 teaspoon rosemary
- 1 teaspoon thyme
- 1-pound beef chuck roast
- 2 cloves of garlic, minced
- 2 tablespoons olive oil
- 3 cups water
- 3 stalks of celery, sliced

Directions:
1. Preheat the air fryer for 5 minutes.
2. Place all ingredients in a deep baking dish that will fit in the air fryer.
3. Bake for 2 hours at 350 °F.
4. Braise the meat with its sauce every 30 minutes until cooked.

300.Beef Roast

Servings:6
Cooking Time:50 Minutes
Ingredients:
- 2½ pounds beef eye of round roast, trimmed
- 2 tablespoons olive oil
- ½ teaspoon onion powder
- ½ teaspoon garlic powder
- ½ teaspoon cayenne pepper
- ½ teaspoon ground black pepper
- Salt, to taste

Directions:
1. Preheat the Air fryer to 360 °F and grease an Air fryer basket.
2. Rub the roast generously with all the spices and coat with olive oil.
3. Arrange the roast in the Air fryer basket and cook for about 50 minutes.
4. Dish out the roast and cover with foil.
5. Cut into desired size slices and serve.

301.Beef And Zucchini Sauté

Servings: 4
Cooking Time: 25 Minutes
Ingredients:

- 1 pound beef meat, cut into thin strips
- 1 zucchini, roughly cubed
- 2 tablespoons coconut aminos
- 2 garlic cloves, minced
- ¼ cup cilantro, chopped
- 2 tablespoons avocado oil

Directions:
1. Heat up a pan that fits your air fryer with the oil over medium heat, add the meat and brown for 5 minutes. Add the rest of the ingredients, toss, put the pan in the fryer and cook at 380 degrees F for 20 minutes. Divide everything into bowls and serve.

302.Pork Butt With Herb-garlic Sauce

Servings: 4
Cooking Time: 35 Minutes + Marinating Time
Ingredients:
- 1 pound pork butt, cut into pieces 2-inches long
- 1 teaspoon golden flaxseed meal
- 1 egg white, well whisked
- Salt and ground black pepper, to taste
- 1 tablespoon olive oil
- 1 tablespoon coconut aminos
- 1 teaspoon lemon juice, preferably freshly squeezed
- For the Coriander-Garlic Sauce:
- 3 garlic cloves, peeled
- 1/3 cup fresh parsley leaves
- 1/3 cup fresh coriander leaves
- 1/2 tablespoon salt
- 1 teaspoon lemon juice
- 1/3 cup extra-virgin olive oil

Directions:
1. Combine the pork strips with the flaxseed meal, egg white, salt, pepper, olive oil, coconut aminos, and lemon juice. Cover and refrigerate for 30 to 45 minutes.
2. After that, spritz the pork strips with a nonstick cooking spray.
3. Set your Air Fryer to cook at 380 degrees F. Press the power button and air-fry for 15 minutes; pause the machine, shake the basket and cook for 15 more minutes.
4. Meanwhile, puree the garlic in a food processor until finely minced. Now, puree the parsley, coriander, salt, and lemon juice. With the machine running, carefully pour in the olive oil.
5. Serve the pork with well-chilled sauce with and enjoy!

303.Cornbread, Ham 'n Eggs Frittata

Servings:3
Cooking Time: 45 Minutes
Ingredients:
- 1 stalk celery, diced
- 1/2 (14.5 ounce) can chicken broth

- 1/2 (14-ounce) package seasoned cornbread stuffing mix
- 1/2 cup chopped onion
- 1/4 cup butter
- 1/4 cup water
- 1/4 teaspoon paprika, for garnish
- 2 cups diced cooked ham
- 3 eggs
- 3/4 cup shredded Cheddar cheese

Directions:
1. Lightly grease baking pan of air fryer with cooking spray. Add celery and onions.
2. For 5 minutes, cook at 360°F. Open and stir in ham. Cook for another 5 minutes.
3. Open and stir in butter, water, and chicken broth. Mix well and continue cooking for another 5 minutes.
4. Toss in stuffing mix and toss well to coat. Cover pan with foil.
5. Cook for another 15 minutes.
6. Remove foil and make 3 indentation in the stuffing to hold an egg. Break an egg in each hole.
7. Cook uncovered for another 10 minutes or until egg is cooked to desired doneness.
8. Sprinkle with cheese and paprika. Let it stand in air fryer for another 5 minutes.
9. Serve and enjoy.

304.Tasty Stuffed Gyoza

Servings:4
Cooking Time: 20 Minutes
Ingredients:
- ¼ cup chopped onion
- ¼ teaspoon ground cumin
- ¼ teaspoon paprika
- ½ cup chopped tomatoes
- 1 egg, beaten
- 1 tablespoon olive oil
- 1/8 teaspoon ground cinnamon
- 2 teaspoons chopped garlic
- 3 ounces chopped cremini mushrooms
- 3 ounces lean ground beef
- 6 pitted green olives, chopped
- 8 gyoza wrappers

Directions:
1. Heat oil in a skillet over medium flame and stir in the beef for 3 minutes. Add the onions and garlic until fragrant. Stir in the mushrooms, olives, paprika, cumin, cinnamon, and tomatoes.
2. Close the lid and allow to simmer for 5 minutes. Allow to cool before making the empanada.
3. Place the meat mixture in the middle of the gyoza wrapper. Fold the gyoza wrapper and seal the edges by brushing with the egg mixture.
4. Preheat the air fryer to 390 °F.

5. Place the grill pan accessory.
6. Place the prepared empanada on the grill pan accessory.
7. Cook for 10 minutes.
8. Flip the empanadas halfway through the cooking time.

305.Cumin-sichuan Lamb Bbq With Dip

Servings:4
Cooking Time: 25 Minutes
Directions:
1. In a food processor, process cumin seeds, peppercorns, caraway seeds, pepper flakes, and sugar until smooth.
2. Thread lamb pieces into skewers. Season with salt. Rub paste all over meat pieces.
3. Place on skewer rack.
4. Cook for 5 minutes at 390°F or to desired doneness.
5. Meanwhile, in a medium bowl whisk well dip Ingredients and set aside.
6. Serve and enjoy with dip.

306.Classic Cube Steak With Sauce

Servings: 4
Cooking Time: 20 Minutes

Ingredients:
- 1 ½ pounds cube steak
- Salt, to taste
- 1/4 teaspoon ground black pepper, or more to taste
- 4 ounces butter
- 2 garlic cloves, finely chopped
- 2 scallions, finely chopped
- 2 tablespoon fresh parsley, finely chopped
- 1 tablespoon fresh horseradish, grated
- 1 teaspoon cayenne pepper

Directions:
1. Pat dry the cube steak and season it with salt and black pepper. Spritz the Air Fryer basket with cooking oil. Add the meat to the basket.
2. Cook in the preheated Air Fryer at 400 degrees F for 14 minutes.
3. Meanwhile, melt the butter in a skillet over a moderate heat. Add the remaining ingredients and simmer until the sauce has thickened and reduced slightly.
4. Top the warm cube steaks with Cowboy sauce and serve immediately.

FISH & SEAFOOD RECIPES

307.Lemony Salmon

Servings:2
Cooking Time: 20 Minutes
Ingredients:
- Cooking spray
- Salt, to taste
- Zest of a lemon

Directions:
1. Spray the fillets with olive oil and rub them with salt and lemon zest. Line baking paper in your air fryer's basket to avoid sticking. Cook the fillets for 10 minutes at 360 F, turning once halfway through. Serve with steamed asparagus and a drizzle of lemon juice.

308.Jumbo Shrimp

Servings: 4
Cooking Time: 10 Minutes
Ingredients:
- 12 jumbo shrimps
- ½ tsp. garlic salt
- ¼ tsp. freshly cracked mixed peppercorns
- For the Sauce:
- 1 tsp. Dijon mustard
- 4 tbsp. mayonnaise
- 1 tsp. lemon zest
- 1 tsp. chipotle powder
- ½ tsp. cumin powder

Directions:
1. Sprinkle the garlic salt over the shrimp and coat with the cracked peppercorns.
2. Fry the shrimp in the cooking basket at 395°F for 5 minutes.
3. Turn the shrimp over and allow to cook for a further 2 minutes.
4. In the meantime, mix together all ingredients for the sauce with a whisk.
5. Serve over the shrimp.

309.Italian Sardinas Fritas

Servings: 4
Cooking Time: 1 Hour 15 Minutes
Ingredients:
- 1 ½ pounds sardines, cleaned and rinsed
- Salt and ground black pepper, to savor
- 1 tablespoon Italian seasoning mix
- 1 tablespoon lemon juice
- 1 tablespoon soy sauce
- 2 tablespoons olive oil

Directions:
1. Firstly, pat the sardines dry with a kitchen towel. Add salt, black pepper, Italian seasoning mix, lemon juice, soy sauce, and olive oil; marinate them for 30 minutes.

2. Air-fry the sardines at 350 degrees F for approximately 5 minutes. Increase the temperature to 385 degrees F and air-fry them for further 7 to 8 minutes.
3. Then, place the sardines in a nice serving platter. Bon appétit!

310.Tartar Sauce 'n Crispy Cod Nuggets

Servings:3
Cooking Time: 10 Minutes
Ingredients:
- ½ cup flour
- ½ cup non-fat mayonnaise
- ½ teaspoon Worcestershire sauce
- 1 ½ pounds cod fillet
- 1 cup cracker crumbs
- 1 egg, beaten
- 1 tablespoon sweet pickle relish
- 1 tablespoon vegetable oil
- 1 teaspoon honey
- Juice from half a lemon
- Salt and pepper to taste
- Zest from half of a lemon

Directions:
1. Preheat the air fryer to 390 °F.
2. Season the cods with salt and pepper.
3. Dredge the fish on flour and dip in the beaten egg before dredging on the cracker crumbs. Brush with oil.
4. Place the fish on the double layer rack and cook for 10 minutes.
5. Meanwhile, prepare the sauce by mixing all ingredients in a bowl.
6. Serve the fish with the sauce.

311.Sunday's Salmon

Servings: 3
Cooking Time: 20 Minutes
Ingredients:
- ½ lb. salmon fillet, chopped
- 2 egg whites
- 2 tbsp. chives, chopped
- 2 tbsp. garlic, minced
- ½ cup onion, chopped
- 2/3 cup carrots, grated
- 2/3 cup potato, grated
- ½ cup friendly bread crumbs
- ¼ cup flour
- Pepper and salt

Directions:
1. In a shallow dish, combine the bread crumbs with the pepper and salt.
2. Pour the flour into another dish.
3. In a third dish, add the egg whites.
4. Put all of the other ingredients in a large mixing bowl and stir together to combine.

5. Using your hands, shape equal amounts of the mixture into small balls. Roll each ball in the flour before dredging it in the egg and lastly covering it with bread crumbs. Transfer all the coated croquettes to the Air Fryer basket and air fry at 320°F for 6 minutes.
6. Reduce the heat to 350°F and allow to cook for another 4 minutes.
7. Serve hot.

312.Great Cat Fish

Servings:4
Cooking Time: 25 Minutes
Ingredients:
- ¼ cup seasoned fish fry
- 1 tbsp olive oil
- 1 tbsp parsley, chopped

Directions:
1. Preheat your air fryer to 400 F, and add seasoned fish fry, and fillets in a large Ziploc bag; massage well to coat. Place the fillets in your air fryer's cooking basket and cook for 10 minutes. Flip the fish and cook for 2-3 more minutes. Top with parsley and serve.

313.Halibut And Capers Mix

Servings: 4
Cooking Time: 18 Minutes
Ingredients:
- 4 halibut fillets, boneless
- A pinch of salt and black pepper
- 1 shallot, chopped
- 2 garlic cloves, minced
- 1 cup parsley, chopped
- 1 tablespoon chives, chopped
- 1 tablespoon lemon zest, grated
- 1 tablespoon capers, drained and chopped
- 1 tablespoon lemon juice
- 1 tablespoon olive oil
- 1 tablespoon butter, melted

Directions:
1. Heat up a pan that fits your air fryer with the oil and the butter over medium-high heat, add the shallot and the garlic and sauté for 2 minutes. Add the rest of the ingredients except the fish, toss and sauté for 3 minutes more. Add the fish, sear for 1 minute on each side, toss it gently with the herbed mix, place the pan in the air fryer and cook at 380 degrees F for 12 minutes. Divide everything between plates and serve.

314.Paprika Prawns

Servings: 5
Cooking Time: 5 Minutes
Ingredients:
- 3-pound prawns, peeled
- 1 tablespoon ground turmeric

- 1 teaspoon smoked paprika
- 1 tablespoon coconut milk
- 1 teaspoon avocado oil
- ½ teaspoon salt

Directions:
1. Put the prawns in the bowl and sprinkle them with ground turmeric, smoked paprika, and salt. Then add coconut milk and leave them for 10 minutes to marinate. Meanwhile, preheat the air fryer to 400F. Put the marinated prawns in the air fryer basket and sprinkle with avocado oil. Cook the prawns for 3 minutes. Then shake them well and cook for 2 minutes more.

315.Grilled Shrimp With Chipotle-orange Seasoning

Servings:2
Cooking Time: 24 Minutes
Ingredients:
- 3 tablespoons minced chipotles in adobo sauce
- salt
- ½-pound large shrimps
- juice of 1/2 orange
- 1/4 cup barbecue sauce

Directions:
1. In a small shallow dish, mix well all Ingredients except for shrimp. Save ¼ of the mixture for basting.
2. Add shrimp in dish and toss well to coat. Marinate for at least 10 minutes.
3. Thread shrimps in skewers. Place on skewer rack in air fryer.
4. For 12 minutes, cook on 360°F. Halfway through cooking time, turnover skewers and baste with sauce. If needed, cook in batches.
5. Serve and enjoy.

316.Grilled Shrimp With Butter

Servings:4
Cooking Time: 15 Minutes
Ingredients:
- 6 tablespoons unsalted butter
- ½ cup red onion, chopped
- 1 ½ teaspoon red pepper
- 1 teaspoon shrimp paste or fish sauce
- 1 ½ teaspoon lime juice
- Salt and pepper to taste
- 24 large shrimps, shelled and deveined

Directions:
1. Preheat the air fryer at 390 °F.
2. Place the grill pan accessory in the air fryer.
3. Place all ingredients in a Ziploc bag and give a good shake.
4. Skewer the shrimps through a bamboo skewer and place on the grill pan.
5. Cook for 15 minutes.

6. Flip the shrimps halfway through the cooking time.

317. Spicy Shrimp

Servings: 2
Cooking Time: 6 Minutes
Ingredients:
- 1/2 lb shrimp, peeled and deveined
- 1/2 tsp old bay seasoning
- 1 tsp cayenne pepper
- 1 tbsp olive oil
- 1/4 tsp paprika
- 1/8 tsp salt

Directions:
1. Preheat the air fryer to 390 F.
2. Add all ingredients into the bowl and toss well.
3. Transfer shrimp into the air fryer basket and cook for 6 minutes.
4. Serve and enjoy.

318. Crumbed Fish Fillets With Tarragon

Servings: 4
Cooking Time: 25 Minutes
Ingredients:
- 2 eggs, beaten
- 1/2 teaspoon tarragon
- 4 fish fillets, halved
- 2 tablespoons dry white wine
- 1/3 cup parmesan cheese, grated
- 1 teaspoon seasoned salt
- 1/3 teaspoon mixed peppercorns
- 1/2 teaspoon fennel seed

Directions:
1. Add the parmesan cheese, salt, peppercorns, fennel seeds, and tarragon to your food processor; blitz for about 20 seconds.
2. Drizzle fish fillets with dry white wine. Dump the egg into a shallow dish.
3. Now, coat the fish fillets with the beaten egg on all sides; then, coat them with the seasoned cracker mix.
4. Air-fry at 345 degrees F for about 17 minutes. Bon appétit!

319. Fisherman's Fish Fingers

Servings: 4
Cooking Time: 40 Minutes
Ingredients:
- ¾ lb. fish, cut into fingers
- 1 cup friendly bread crumbs
- 2 tsp. mixed herbs
- ¼ tsp. baking soda
- 2 eggs, beaten
- 3 tsp. flour
- 2 tbsp. Maida
- 1 tsp. garlic ginger puree
- ½ tsp. black pepper
- 2 tsp. garlic powder

- ½ tsp. red chili flakes
- ½ tsp. turmeric powder
- 2 tbsp. lemon juice
- ½ tsp. salt

Directions:
1. Put the fish, garlic ginger puree, garlic powder, red chili flakes, turmeric powder, lemon juice, 1 teaspoon of the mixed herbs, and salt in a bowl and combine well.
2. In a separate bowl, combine the flour, Maida, and baking soda.
3. In a third bowl pour in the beaten eggs.
4. In a fourth bowl, stir together the bread crumbs, black pepper, and another teaspoon of mixed herbs.
5. Pre-heat the Air Fryer to 350°F.
6. Coat the fish fingers in the flour. Dredge in the egg, then roll in the breadcrumb mixture.
7. Put the fish fingers in the fryer's basket and allow to cook for 10 minutes, ensuring they crisp up nicely.

320. Lemon-garlic On Buttered Shrimp Fry

Servings: 4
Cooking Time: 15 Minutes
Ingredients:
- 1 tablespoon chopped chives or 1 teaspoon dried chives
- 1 tablespoon lemon juice
- 1 tablespoon minced basil leaves plus more for sprinkling or 1 teaspoon dried basil
- 1 tablespoon minced garlic
- 1-lb defrosted shrimp (21-25 count)
- 2 tablespoons chicken stock (or white wine)
- 2 teaspoons red pepper flakes
- 4 tablespoons butter

Directions:
1. Lightly grease baking pan of air fryer with cooking spray. Melt butter for 2 minutes at 330°F. Stir in red pepper flakes and garlic. Cook for 3 minutes.
2. Add remaining Ingredients in pan and toss well to coat.
3. Cook for 5 minutes at 330°F. Stir and let it stand for another 5 minutes.
4. Serve and enjoy.

321. Halibut With Thai Lemongrass Marinade

Servings: 2
Cooking Time: 45 Minutes
Ingredients:
- 2 tablespoons tamari sauce
- 2 tablespoons fresh lime juice
- 2 tablespoons olive oil
- 1 teaspoon Thai curry paste
- 1/2 inch lemongrass, finely chopped
- 1 teaspoon basil

- 2 cloves garlic, minced
- 2 tablespoons shallot, minced
- Sea salt and ground black pepper, to taste
- 2 halibut steaks

Directions:
1. Place all ingredients in a ceramic dish; let it marinate for 30 minutes.
2. Place the halibut steaks in the lightly greased cooking basket.
3. Bake in the preheated Air Fryer at 400 degrees F for 9 to 10 minutes, basting with the reserved marinade and flipping them halfway through the cooking time. Bon appétit!

322.Cajun Seasoned Salmon Filet

Servings:1
Cooking Time: 15 Minutes
Ingredients:
- 1 salmon fillet
- 1 teaspoon juice from lemon, freshly squeezed
- 3 tablespoons extra virgin olive oil
- A dash of Cajun seasoning mix
- Salt and pepper to taste

Directions:
1. Preheat the air fryer for 5 minutes.
2. Place all ingredients in a bowl and toss to coat.
3. Place the fish fillet in the air fryer basket.
4. Bake for 15 minutes at 325 °F.
5. Once cooked drizzle with olive oil

323.Sesame Seeds Coated Haddock

Servings:4
Cooking Time:14 Minutes
Ingredients:
- 4 tablespoons plain flour
- 2 eggs
- ½ cup sesame seeds, toasted
- ½ cup breadcrumbs
- 4 (6-ounces) frozen haddock fillets
- 1/8 teaspoon dried rosemary, crushed
- Salt and ground black pepper, as required
- 3 tablespoons olive oil

Directions:
1. Preheat the Air fryer to 390 °F and grease an Air fryer basket.
2. Place the flour in a shallow bowl and whisk the eggs in a second bowl.
3. Mix sesame seeds, breadcrumbs, rosemary, salt, black pepper and olive oil in a third bowl until a crumbly mixture is formed.
4. Coat each fillet with flour, dip into whisked eggs and finally, dredge into the breadcrumb mixture
5. Arrange haddock fillets into the Air fryer basket in a single layer and cook for about 14 minutes, flipping once in between.

6. Dish out the haddock fillets onto serving plates and serve hot.

324.Thyme Scallops

Servings: 1
Cooking Time: 12 Minutes
Ingredients:
- 1 lb. scallops
- Salt and pepper
- ½ tbsp. butter
- ½ cup thyme, chopped

Directions:
1. Wash the scallops and dry them completely. Season with pepper and salt, then set aside while you prepare the pan.
2. Grease a foil pan in several spots with the butter and cover the bottom with the thyme. Place the scallops on top.
3. Pre-heat the fryer at 400°F and set the rack inside.
4. Place the foil pan on the rack and allow to cook for seven minutes.
5. Take care when removing the pan from the fryer and transfer the scallops to a serving dish. Spoon any remaining butter in the pan over the fish and enjoy.

325.Almond Flour Coated Crispy Shrimps

Servings:4
Cooking Time: 10 Minutes
Ingredients:
- ½ cup almond flour
- 1 tablespoon yellow mustard
- 1-pound raw shrimps, peeled and deveined
- 3 tablespoons olive oil
- Salt and pepper to taste

Directions:
1. Place all ingredients in a Ziploc bag and give a good shake.
2. Place in the air fryer and cook for 10 minutes at 400 °F.

326.Tilapia Bowls

Servings: 4
Cooking Time: 10 Minutes
Ingredients:
- 7 oz tilapia fillet or flathead fish
- 1 teaspoon arrowroot powder
- 1 teaspoon ground paprika
- ½ teaspoon salt
- ½ teaspoon ground black pepper
- ¼ teaspoon ground cumin
- ½ teaspoon garlic powder
- 1 teaspoon lemon juice
- 4 oz purple cabbage, shredded
- 1 jalapeno, sliced
- 1 tablespoon heavy cream
- ½ teaspoon minced garlic
- Cooking spray

Directions:
1. Sprinkle the tilapia fillet with arrowroot powder, ground paprika, salt, ground black pepper, ground cumin, and garlic powder. Preheat the air fryer to 385F. Spray the tilapia fillet with cooking spray and place it in the air fryer. Cook the fish for 10 minutes. Meanwhile, in the bowl mix up shredded cabbage, jalapeno pepper, and lemon juice. When the tilapia fillet is cooked, chop it roughly. Put the shredded cabbage mixture in the serving bowls. Top them with chopped tilapia. After this, in the shallow bowl mix up minced garlic and heavy cream. Sprinkle the meal with a heavy cream mixture.

327.Lemon And Oregano Tilapia Mix

Servings: 4
Cooking Time: 20 Minutes
Ingredients:
- 4 tilapia fillets, boneless and halved
- Salt and black pepper to the taste
- 1 cup roasted peppers, chopped
- ¼ cup keto tomato sauce
- 1 cup tomatoes, cubed
- 1 tablespoon lemon juice
- 2 tablespoons olive oil
- 1 teaspoon garlic powder
- 1 teaspoon oregano, dried

Directions:
1. In a baking dish that fits your air fryer, mix the fish with all the other ingredients, toss, introduce in your air fryer and cook at 380 degrees F for 20 minutes. Divide into bowls and serve.

328.Shrimp And Pine Nuts Mix

Servings: 4
Cooking Time: 12 Minutes
Ingredients:
- ½ cup parsley leaves
- ½ cup basil leaves
- 2 tablespoons lemon juice
- 1/3 cup pine nuts
- ¼ cup parmesan, grated
- A pinch of salt and black pepper
- ½ cup olive oil
- 1 and ½ pounds shrimp, peeled and deveined
- ¼ teaspoon lemon zest, grated

Directions:
1. In a blender, combine all the ingredients except the shrimp and pulse well. In a bowl, mix the shrimp with the pesto and toss. Put the shrimp in your air fryer's basket and cook at 360 degrees F for 12 minutes, flipping the shrimp halfway. Divide the shrimp into bowls and serve.

329.Lemon-pepper Red Mullet Fry

Servings:4
Cooking Time: 15 Minutes
Ingredients:
- 1 tablespoon olive oil
- 4 whole red mullets, gutted and scales removed
- Juice from 1 lemon
- Salt and pepper to taste

Directions:
1. Preheat the air fryer to 390 °F.
2. Place the grill pan accessory in the air fryer.
3. Season the red mullet with salt, pepper, and lemon juice.
4. Brush with olive oil.
5. Grill for 15 minutes per batch.

330.Turmeric Salmon

Servings: 2
Cooking Time: 7 Minutes
Ingredients:
- 8 oz salmon fillet
- 2 tablespoons coconut flakes
- 1 tablespoon coconut cream
- ½ teaspoon salt
- ½ teaspoon ground turmeric
- ½ teaspoon onion powder
- 1 teaspoon nut oil

Directions:
1. Cut the salmon fillet into halves and sprinkle with salt, ground turmeric, and onion powder. After this, dip the fish fillets in the coconut cream and coat in the coconut flakes. Sprinkle the salmon fillets with nut oil. Preheat the air fryer to 380F. Arrange the salmon fillets in the air fryer basket and cook for 7 minutes.

331.Hot Tilapia

Servings: 2
Cooking Time: 9 Minutes
Ingredients:
- 1 chili pepper, chopped
- 1 teaspoon chili flakes
- 1 tablespoon sesame oil
- ½ teaspoon salt
- 10 oz tilapia fillet
- ¼ teaspoon onion powder

Directions:
1. In the shallow bowl mix up chili pepper, chili flakes, salt, and onion powder. Gently churn the mixture and add sesame oil. After this, slice the tilapia fillet and sprinkle with chili mixture. Massage the fish with the help of the fingertips gently and leave for 10 minutes to marinate. Preheat the air fryer to 390F. Put the tilapia fillets in the air fryer basket and cook for 5 minutes. Then flip the

fish on another side and cook for 4 minutes more.

332.Oregano & Cumin Flavored Salmon Grill

Servings:4
Cooking Time: 15 Minutes
Ingredients:
- 1 1/2 pounds skinless salmon fillet (preferably wild), cut into 1" pieces
- 1 teaspoon ground cumin
- 1 teaspoon kosher salt
- 1/4 teaspoon crushed red pepper flakes
- 2 lemons, very thinly sliced into rounds
- 2 tablespoons chopped fresh oregano
- 2 tablespoons olive oil
- 2 teaspoons sesame seeds

Directions:
1. In a small bowl, mix well oregano, sesame seeds, cumin, salt, and pepper flakes.
2. Thread salmon and folded lemon slices in a skewer. Brush with oil and sprinkle with spice.
3. Place skewers on air fryer skewer rack.
4. For 5 minutes, cook on 360°F. If needed, cook in batches.
5. Serve and enjoy.

333.Tarragon And Spring Onions Salmon

Servings: 4
Cooking Time: 15 Minutes
Ingredients:
- 12 oz salmon fillet
- 2 spring onions, chopped
- 1 tablespoon ghee, melted
- 1 teaspoon peppercorns
- ½ teaspoon salt
- ½ teaspoon ground black pepper
- 1 teaspoon tarragon
- ½ teaspoon dried cilantro

Directions:
1. Cut the salmon fillet on 4 servings. Then make the parchment pockets and place the fish fillets in the parchment pockets. Sprinkle the salmon with salt, ground black pepper, tarragon, and dried cilantro. After this, top the fish with spring onions, peppercorns, and ghee. Preheat the air fryer to 385F. Arrange the salmon pockets in the air fryer in one layer and cook them for 15 minutes.

334.Paprika Cod And Endives

Servings: 4
Cooking Time: 20 Minutes
Ingredients:
- 2 endives, shredded
- 2 tablespoons olive oil
- Salt and back pepper to the taste

- 4 salmon fillets, boneless
- ½ teaspoon sweet paprika

Directions:
1. In a pan that fits the air fryer, combine the fish with the rest of the ingredients, toss, introduce in the fryer and cook at 350 degrees F for 20 minutes, flipping the fish halfway. Divide between plates and serve right away.

335.Cajun Spiced Veggie-shrimp Bake

Servings:4
Cooking Time: 20 Minutes
Ingredients:
- 1 Bag of Frozen Mixed Vegetables
- 1 Tbsp Gluten Free Cajun Seasoning
- Olive Oil Spray
- Season with salt and pepper
- Small Shrimp Peeled & Deveined (Regular Size Bag about 50-80 Small Shrimp)

Directions:
1. Lightly grease baking pan of air fryer with cooking spray. Add all Ingredients and toss well to coat. Season with pepper and salt, generously.
2. For 10 minutes, cook on 330°F. Halfway through cooking time, stir.
3. Cook for 10 minutes at 330°F.
4. Serve and enjoy.

336.Tuna-stuffed Potato Boats

Servings:4
Cooking Time:16 Minutes
Ingredients:
- 4 starchy potatoes, soaked for about 30 minutes and drain
- 1 (6-ounce) can tuna, drained
- 2 tablespoons plain Greek yogurt
- 1 scallion, chopped and divided
- 1 tablespoon capers
- ½ tablespoon olive oil
- 1 teaspoon red chili powder
- Salt and black pepper, to taste

Directions:
1. Preheat the Air fryer to 355 °F and grease an Air fryer basket.
2. Arrange the potatoes in the Air fryer basket and cook for about 30 minutes.
3. Meanwhile, mix tuna, yogurt, red chili powder, salt, black pepper and half of scallion in a bowl and mash the mixture well.
4. Remove the potatoes from the Air fryer and halve the potatoes lengthwise carefully.
5. Stuff in the tuna mixture in the potatoes and top with capers and remaining scallion.
6. Dish out in a platter and serve immediately.

337.Miso Fish

Servings: 2
Cooking Time: 10 Minutes
Ingredients:
- 2 cod fish fillets
- 1 tbsp garlic, chopped
- 2 tsp swerve
- 2 tbsp miso

Directions:
1. Add all ingredients to the zip-lock bag. Shake well place in the refrigerator for overnight.
2. Place marinated fish fillets into the air fryer basket and cook at 350 F for 10 minutes.
3. Serve and enjoy.

338.Fish Fillets

Servings: 4
Cooking Time: 25 Minutes
Ingredients:
- 4 fish fillets
- 1 egg, beaten
- 1 cup bread crumbs
- 4 tbsp. olive oil
- Pepper and salt to taste

Directions:
1. Pre-heat the Air Fryer at 350°F.
2. In a shallow dish, combine together the bread crumbs, oil, pepper, and salt.
3. Pour the beaten egg into a second dish.
4. Dredge each fish fillet in the egg before rolling them in the bread crumbs. Place in the Air Fryer basket.
5. Allow to cook in the Air Fryer for 12 minutes.

339.Lemon And Thyme Sea Bass

Servings: 3
Cooking Time: 15 Minutes
Ingredients:
- 8 oz sea bass, trimmed, peeled
- 4 lemon slices
- 1 tablespoon thyme
- 2 teaspoons sesame oil
- 1 teaspoon salt

Directions:
1. Fill the sea bass with lemon slices and rub with thyme, salt, and sesame oil. Then preheat the air fryer to 385F and put the fish in the air fryer basket. Cook it for 12 minutes. Then flip the fish on another side and cook it for 3 minutes more.

340.Lemony-sage On Grilled Swordfish

Servings:2
Cooking Time: 16 Minutes
Ingredients:
- ½ lemon, sliced thinly in rounds
- 1 tbsp lemon juice
- 1 tsp parsley
- 1 zucchini, peeled and then thinly sliced in lengths
- 1/2-pound swordfish, sliced into 2-inch chunks
- 2 tbsp olive oil
- 6-8 sage leaves
- salt and pepper to taste

Directions:
1. In a shallow dish, mix well lemon juice, parsley, and sliced swordfish. Toss well to coat and generously season with pepper and salt. Marinate for at least 10 minutes.
2. Place one length of zucchini on a flat surface. Add one piece of fish and sage leaf. Roll zucchini and then thread into a skewer. Repeat process to remaining Ingredients.
3. Brush with oil and place on skewer rack in air fryer.
4. For 8 minutes, cook on 390°F. If needed, cook in batches.
5. Serve and enjoy with lemon slices.

341.Rice In Crab Shell

Servings:2
Cooking Time:8 Minutes
Ingredients:
- 1 bowl cooked rice
- 4 tablespoons crab meat
- 2 tablespoons butter
- 2 tablespoons Parmesan cheese, shredded
- 2 crab shells
- Paprika, to taste

Directions:
1. Preheat the Air fryer to 390 °F and grease an Air fryer basket.
2. Mix rice, crab meat, butter and paprika in a bowl.
3. Fill crab shell with rice mixture and top with Parmesan cheese.
4. Arrange the crab shell in the Air fryer basket and cook for about 8 minutes.
5. Sprinkle with more paprika and serve hot.

342.Easy Bacon Shrimp

Servings: 4
Cooking Time: 7 Minutes
Ingredients:
- 16 shrimp, deveined
- 1/4 tsp pepper
- 16 bacon slices

Directions:
1. Preheat the air fryer to 390 F.
2. Spray air fryer basket with cooking spray.
3. Wrap shrimp with bacon slice and place into the air fryer basket and cook for 5 minutes.
4. Turn shrimp to another side and cook for 2 minutes more. Season shrimp with pepper.

5. Serve and enjoy.

343.Mustard Cod

Servings: 4
Cooking Time: 14 Minutes
Ingredients:
- 1 cup parmesan, grated
- 4 cod fillets, boneless
- Salt and black pepper to the taste
- 1 tablespoon mustard

Directions:
1. In a bowl, mix the parmesan with salt, pepper and the mustard and stir. Spread this over the cod, arrange the fish in the air fryer's basket and cook at 370 degrees F for 7 minutes on each side. Divide between plates and serve with a side salad.

344.Amazing Salmon Fillets

Servings:2
Cooking Time:7 Minutes
Ingredients:
- 2 (7-ounce) (¾-inch thick) salmon fillets
- 1 tablespoon Italian seasoning
- 1 tablespoon fresh lemon juice

Directions:
1. Preheat the Air fryer to 355 °F and grease an Air fryer grill pan.
2. Rub the salmon evenly with Italian seasoning and transfer into the Air fryer grill pan, skin-side up.
3. Cook for about 7 minutes and squeeze lemon juice on it to serve.

345.Pesto Sauce Over Fish Filet

Servings:3
Cooking Time: 20 Minutes
Ingredients:
- 1 bunch fresh basil
- 1 cup olive oil
- 1 tablespoon parmesan cheese, grated
- 2 cloves of garlic,
- 2 tablespoons pine nuts
- 3 white fish fillets
- Salt and pepper to taste

Directions:
1. In a food processor, combine all ingredients except for the fish fillets.
2. Pulse until smooth.
3. Place the fish in a baking dish and pour over the pesto sauce.
4. Place in the air fryer and cook for 20 minutes at 400 °F.

346.Original Trout Frittata

Servings:6
Cooking Time: 12 Minutes
Ingredients:
- 1 onion, sliced

- 1 egg, beaten
- 6 tbsp crème fraiche
- ½ tbsp horseradish sauce
- 2 trout fillet, hot and smoked
- A handful of fresh dill

Directions:
1. Heat oil in a frying pan over medium heat. Add onion and stir-fry until tender; season the onions well. Preheat your air fryer to 320 F, and in a bowl, mix egg, crème Fraiche, and horseradish. Add cooked onion and trout, and mix well. Place the mixture in your fryer's cooking basket and cook for 20 minutes.

347.Crunchy Topped Fish Bake

Servings: 4
Cooking Time: 20 Minutes
Ingredients:
- 1 tablespoon butter, melted
- 1 medium-sized leek, thinly sliced
- 1 tablespoon chicken stock
- 1 tablespoon dry white wine
- 1 pound tuna
- 1/2 teaspoon red pepper flakes, crushed
- Sea salt and ground black pepper, to taste
- 1/2 teaspoon dried rosemary
- 1/2 teaspoon dried basil
- 1/2 teaspoon dried thyme
- 2 ripe tomatoes, pureed
- 1/4 cup breadcrumbs
- 1/4 cup Parmesan cheese, grated

Directions:
1. Melt 1/2 tablespoon of butter in a sauté pan over medium-high heat. Now, cook the leek and garlic until tender and aromatic. Add the stock and wine to deglaze the pan.
2. Preheat your Air Fryer to 370 degrees F.
3. Grease a casserole dish with the remaining 1/2 tablespoon of melted butter. Place the fish in the casserole dish. Add the seasonings. Top with the sautéed leek mixture.
4. Add the tomato puree. Cook for 10 minutes in the preheated Air Fryer. Top with the breadcrumbs and cheese; cook an additional 7 minutes until the crumbs are golden. Bon appétit!

348.Beer Battered Cod Filet

Servings:2
Cooking Time: 15 Minutes
Ingredients:
- ½ cup all-purpose flour
- ¾ teaspoon baking powder
- 1 ¼ cup lager beer
- 2 cod fillets
- 2 eggs, beaten
- Salt and pepper to taste

Directions:
1. Preheat the air fryer to 390 °F.
2. Pat the fish fillets dry then set aside.
3. In a bowl, combine the rest of the Ingredients to create a batter.
4. Dip the fillets on the batter and place on the double layer rack.
5. Cook for 15 minutes.

349.Sweet-chili Sauce Dip 'n Shrimp Rolls

Servings:8
Cooking Time: 9 Minutes
Ingredients:
- ¼ teaspoon crushed red pepper
- ½ cup sweet chili sauce
- ¾ cup snow peas, julienned
- 1 cup carrots, julienned
- 1 cup red bell pepper, seeded and julienned
- 2 ½ tablespoons sesame oil, divided
- 2 cups cabbage, shredded
- 2 teaspoons fish sauce
- 4 ounces raw shrimps, deveined and chopped
- 8 spring roll wrappers

Directions:
1. Heat sesame oil in a skillet over medium flame and stir in the cabbage, carrots, and bell pepper for 2 minutes. Set aside and allow to cool.
2. Once cooled, Add shrimps and snow peas. Season with fish sauce and red pepper.
3. Lay spring roll wrapper on a flat surface and place a tablespoon or two of the vegetable mixtures in the middle of the spring roll wrapper. Fold the wrapper and seal the edges with water.
4. Preheat the air fryer to 390 °F.
5. Place the spring rolls in the double layer rack accessory. Spray with cooking oil.
6. Cook for 7 minutes.
7. Serve with chili sauce.

350.Smoked Halibut And Eggs In Brioche

Servings: 4
Cooking Time: 25 Minutes
Ingredients:
- 4 brioche rolls
- 1 pound smoked halibut, chopped
- 4 eggs
- 1 teaspoon dried thyme
- 1 teaspoon dried basil
- Salt and black pepper, to taste

Directions:
1. Cut off the top of each brioche; then, scoop out the insides to make the shells.
2. Lay the prepared brioche shells in the lightly greased cooking basket.
3. Spritz with cooking oil; add the halibut. Crack an egg into each brioche shell;

sprinkle with thyme, basil, salt, and black pepper.
4. Bake in the preheated Air Fryer at 325 degrees F for 20 minutes. Bon appétit!

351.Saltine Fish Fillets

Servings: 4
Cooking Time: 15 Minutes
Ingredients:
- 1 cup crushed saltines
- ¼ cup extra-virgin olive oil
- 1 tsp. garlic powder
- ½ tsp. shallot powder
- 1 egg, well whisked
- 4 white fish fillets
- Salt and ground black pepper to taste
- Fresh Italian parsley to serve

Directions:
1. In a shallow bowl, combine the crushed saltines and olive oil.
2. In a separate bowl, mix together the garlic powder, shallot powder, and the beaten egg.
3. Sprinkle a good amount of salt and pepper over the fish, before dipping each fillet into the egg mixture.
4. Coat the fillets with the crumb mixture.
5. Air fry the fish at 370°F for 10 - 12 minutes.
6. Serve with fresh parsley.

352.Easy Prawns Alla Parmigiana

Servings: 4
Cooking Time: 20 Minutes
Ingredients:
- 2 egg whites
- 1 cup all-purpose flour
- 1 cup Parmigiano-Reggiano, grated
- 1/2 cup fine breadcrumbs
- 1/2 teaspoon celery seeds
- 1/2 teaspoon porcini powder
- 1/2 teaspoon onion powder
- 1 teaspoon garlic powder
- 1/2 teaspoon dried rosemary
- 1/2 teaspoon sea salt
- 1/2 teaspoon ground black pepper
- 1 ½ pounds prawns, deveined

Directions:
1. To make a breading station, whisk the egg whites in a shallow dish. In a separate dish, place the all-purpose flour.
2. In a third dish, thoroughly combine the Parmigiano-Reggiano, breadcrumbs, and seasonings; mix to combine well.
3. Dip the prawns in the flour, then, into the egg whites; lastly, dip them in the parm/breadcrumb mixture. Roll until they are covered on all sides.
4. Cook in the preheated Air Fryer at 390 degrees F for 5 to 7 minutes or until golden

brown. Work in batches. Serve with lemon wedges if desired.

353.Grilled Salmon Fillets

Servings: 2
Cooking Time: 20 Minutes
Ingredients:
- 2 salmon fillets
- ⅓ cup of water
- ⅓ cup of light soy sauce
- ⅓ cup sugar
- 2 tbsp. olive oil
- Black pepper and salt to taste
- Garlic powder [optional]

Directions:
1. 1 Sprinkle some salt and pepper on top of the salmon fillets. Season with some garlic powder if desired.
2. 2 In a medium bowl, mix together the remaining ingredients with a whisk and use this mixture to coat the salmon fillets. Leave to marinate for 2 hours.
3. 3 Pre-heat the Air Fryer at 355°F.
4. 4 Remove any excess liquid from the salmon fillets and transfer to the fryer. Cook for 8 minutes before serving warm.

354.Shrimp And Scallions

Servings: 4
Cooking Time: 10 Minutes
Ingredients:
- 1 pound shrimp, peeled and deveined
- 2 tablespoons olive oil
- 1 tablespoon scallions, chopped
- 1 cup chicken stock

Directions:
1. In a pan that fits your air fryer, mix the shrimp with the oil, onion and the stock, introduce the pan in the fryer and cook at 380 degrees F for 10 minutes. Divide into bowls and serve.

355.Salmon And Garlic Sauce

Servings: 4
Cooking Time: 15 Minutes
Ingredients:
- 3 tablespoons parsley, chopped
- 4 salmon fillets, boneless
- ¼ cup ghee, melted
- 2 garlic cloves, minced

- 4 shallots, chopped
- Salt and black pepper to the taste

Directions:
1. Heat up a pan that fits the air fryer with the ghee over medium-high heat, add the garlic, shallots, salt, pepper and the parsley, stir and cook for 5 minutes. Add the salmon fillets, toss gently, introduce the pan in the air fryer and cook at 380 degrees F for 15 minutes. Divide between plates and serve.

356.Butter Flounder Fillets

Servings: 4
Cooking Time: 20 Minutes
Ingredients:
- 4 flounder fillets, boneless
- A pinch of salt and black pepper
- 1 cup parmesan, grated
- 4 tablespoons butter, melted
- 2 tablespoons olive oil

Directions:
1. In a bowl, mix the parmesan with salt, pepper, butter and the oil and stir well. Arrange the fish in a pan that fits the air fryer, spread the parmesan mix all over, introduce in the fryer and cook at 400 degrees F for 20 minutes. Divide between plates and serve with a side salad.

357.Paprika Tilapia

Servings: 4
Cooking Time: 20 Minutes
Ingredients:
- 4 tilapia fillets, boneless
- 3 tablespoons ghee, melted
- A pinch of salt and black pepper
- 2 tablespoons capers
- 1 teaspoon garlic powder
- ½ teaspoon smoked paprika
- ½ teaspoon oregano, dried
- 2 tablespoons lemon juice

Directions:
1. In a bowl, mix all the ingredients except the fish and toss. Arrange the fish in a pan that fits the air fryer, pour the capers mix all over, put the pan in the air fryer and cook 360 degrees F for 20 minutes, shaking halfway. Divide between plates and serve hot.

358.Cucumber Sushi

Servings:10
Cooking Time: 10 Minutes
Ingredients:
- 10 bacon slices
- 2 tablespoons cream cheese
- 1 cucumber

Directions:
1. Place the bacon slices in the air fryer in one layer and cook for 10 minutes at 400F. Meanwhile, cut the cucumber into small wedges. When the bacon is cooked, cool it to the room temperature and spread with cream cheese. Then place the cucumber wedges over the cream cheese and roll the bacon into the sushi.

359.Healthy Tofu Steaks

Servings: 4
Cooking Time: 35 Minutes
Ingredients:
- 1 package tofu, press and remove excess liquid
- 1/4 tsp dried thyme
- 1/4 cup lemon juice
- 2 tbsp lemon zest
- 3 garlic cloves, minced
- 1/4 cup olive oil
- Pepper
- Salt

Directions:
1. Cut tofu into eight pieces.
2. In a bowl, mix together olive oil, thyme, lemon juice, lemon zest, garlic, pepper, and salt.
3. Add tofu into the bowl and coat well and place in the refrigerator for overnight.
4. Spray air fryer basket with cooking spray.
5. Place marinated tofu into the air fryer basket and cook at 350 F for 30-35 minutes. Turn halfway through.
6. Serve and enjoy.

360.Coconut Chicken Bites

Servings: 4
Cooking Time: 20 Minutes
Ingredients:
- 2 teaspoons garlic powder
- 2 eggs
- Salt and black pepper to the taste
- ¾ cup coconut flakes
- Cooking spray
- 1 pound chicken breasts, skinless, boneless and cubed

Directions:

1. Put the coconut in a bowl and mix the eggs with garlic powder, salt and pepper in a second one. Dredge the chicken cubes in eggs and then in coconut and arrange them all in your air fryer's basket. Grease with cooking spray, cook at 370 degrees F for 20 minutes. Arrange the chicken bites on a platter and serve as an appetizer.

361.Cheesy Brussels Sprouts

Servings: 2
Cooking Time: 5 Minutes
Ingredients:
- 1 cup Brussels sprouts, halved
- 1/4 cup mozzarella cheese, shredded
- 1 tbsp olive oil
- 1/4 tsp salt

Directions:
1. Toss Brussels sprouts with oil and season with salt.
2. Preheat the air fryer to 375 F.
3. Transfer Brussels sprouts into the air fryer basket and top with shredded cheese.
4. Cook for 5 minutes.
5. Serve and enjoy.

362.Jalapeño Guacamole

Servings: 4
Cooking Time: 30 Minutes
Ingredients:
- 2 Hass avocados, ripe
- ¼ red onion
- 1 jalapeño
- 1 tbsp fresh lime juice
- Sea salt

Directions:
1. Spoon the avocado innings into a bowl.
2. Dice the jalapeño and onion.
3. Mash the avocado to the desired consistency.
4. Add in the onion, jalapeño and lime juice.
5. Sprinkle with salt.

363.Southern Cheese Straws

Servings: 6
Cooking Time: 30 Minutes
Ingredients:
- 1 cup all-purpose flour
- Sea salt and ground black pepper, to taste
- 1/4 teaspoon smoked paprika
- 1/2 teaspoon celery seeds
- 4 ounces mature Cheddar, cold, freshly grated
- 1 sticks butter

Directions:

1. Start by preheating your air Fryer to 330 degrees F. Line the Air Fryer basket with parchment paper.
2. In a mixing bowl, thoroughly combine the flour, salt, black pepper, paprika, and celery seeds.
3. Then, combine the cheese and butter in the bowl of a stand mixer. Slowly stir in the flour mixture and mix to combine well.
4. Then, pack the dough into a cookie press fitted with a star disk. Pipe the long ribbons of dough across the parchment paper. Then cut into six-inch lengths.
5. Bake in the preheated Air Fryer for 15 minutes.
6. Repeat with the remaining dough. Let the cheese straws cool on a rack. You can store them between sheets of parchment in an airtight container. Bon appétit!

364.Veggie Pastries

Servings:8
Cooking Time: 37 Minutes
Ingredients:
- 2 large potatoes, peeled
- 1 tablespoon olive oil
- ½ cup carrot, peeled and chopped
- ½ cup onion, chopped
- 2 garlic cloves, minced
- 2 tablespoons fresh ginger, minced
- ½ cup green peas, shelled
- Salt and ground black pepper, as needed
- 3 puff pastry sheets

Directions:
1. In the pan of a boiling water, put the potatoes and cook for about 15-20 minutes.
2. Drain the potatoes well and with a potato masher, mash the potatoes.
3. In a skillet, heat the oil over medium heat and sauté the carrot, onion, ginger, and garlic for about 4-5 minutes.
4. Drain all the fat from the skillet.
5. Stir in the mashed potatoes, peas, salt, and black pepper. Cook for about 1-2 minutes.
6. Once done, remove the potato mixture from heat and set aside to cool completely.
7. Put the puff pastry onto a smooth surface.
8. Cut each puff pastry sheet into four pieces and then cut each piece in a round shape.
9. Add about two tablespoons of veggie filling over each pastry round.
10. Moisten the edges using your wet fingers.
11. Fold each pastry round in half to seal the filling.
12. Using a fork, firmly press the edges.
13. Set the temperature of Air Fryer to 390 degrees F.
14. Add the pastries in an Air Fryer basket in a single layer in 2 batches.
15. Air Fry for about 5 minutes.

16. Serve.

365.Crispy Zucchini Fries

Servings: 4
Cooking Time: 10 Minutes
Ingredients:
- 2 medium zucchinis, cut into fries shape
- 1/2 tsp garlic powder
- 1 tsp Italian seasoning
- 1/2 cup parmesan cheese, grated
- 1/2 cup almond flour
- 1 egg, lightly beaten
- Pepper
- Salt

Directions:
1. Add egg in a bowl and whisk well.
2. In a shallow bowl, mix together almond flour, spices, parmesan cheese, pepper, and salt.
3. Spray air fryer basket with cooking spray.
4. Dip zucchini fries in egg then coat with almond flour mixture and place in the air fryer basket.
5. Cook zucchini fries for 10 minutes at 400 F.
6. Serve and enjoy.

366.Crunchy Spicy Chickpeas

Servings:4
Cooking Time:20 Minutes
Ingredients:
- 1 (15-ounce) can chickpeas, rinsed and drained
- 1 tablespoon olive oil
- ½ teaspoon ground cumin
- ½ teaspoon cayenne pepper
- ½ teaspoon smoked paprika
- Salt, taste

Directions:
1. Preheat the Air fryer to 390 °F and grease an Air fryer basket.
2. Mix together all the ingredients in a bowl and toss to coat well.
3. Place half of the chickpeas in the Air fryer basket and cook for about 10 minutes.
4. Repeat with the remaining chickpeas and dish out to serve warm.

367.Pickled Fries

Servings:4
Cooking Time: 8 Minutes
Ingredients:
- 2 pickles, sliced
- 1 tablespoon dried dill
- 1 egg, beaten
- 2 tablespoons flax meal

Directions:
1. Dip the sliced pickles in the egg and then sprinkle with dried ill and flax meal. Place

them in the air fryer basket in one layer and cook at 400F for 8 minutes.

368.Dill Pickle Fries

Servings:12
Cooking Time:28 Minutes
Ingredients:
- 1½ (16-ounces) jars spicy dill pickle spears, drained and pat dried
- 1 cup all-purpose flour
- 1 egg, beaten
- ¼ cup milk
- 1 cup panko breadcrumbs
- ½ teaspoon paprika

Directions:
1. Preheat the Air fryer to 440 °F and grease an Air fryer basket.
2. Place flour and paprika in a shallow dish and whisk the egg with milk in a second dish.
3. Place the breadcrumbs in a third shallow dish.
4. Coat the pickle spears evenly in flour and dip in the egg mixture.
5. Roll into the breadcrumbs evenly and arrange half of the pickle spears in an Air fryer basket.
6. Cook for about 14 minutes, flipping once in between.
7. Repeat with the remaining pickle spears and dish out to serve warm.

369.Vegetable Pastries

Servings:8
Cooking Time:10 Minutes
Ingredients:
- 2 large potatoes, boiled and mashed
- ½ cup carrot, peeled and chopped
- ½ cup onion, chopped
- ½ cup green peas, shelled
- 3 puff pastry sheets, each cut into 4 round pieces
- 1 tablespoon olive oil
- Salt and black pepper, to taste
- 2 garlic cloves, minced
- 1 tablespoon curry powder
- 2 tablespoons fresh ginger, minced

Directions:
1. Preheat the Air fryer to 390 °F and grease an Air fryer basket.
2. Heat olive oil on medium heat in a skillet and add carrot, onion, ginger and garlic.
3. Sauté for about 5 minutes and stir in the mashed potatoes, peas, curry powder, salt and black pepper.
4. Cook for about 2 minutes and dish out in a bowl.
5. Put about 2 tablespoons of vegetable filling mixture over each pastry round.

6. Fold each pastry round into half-circle and press the edges firmly with a fork.
7. Place half of the pastries in the Air fryer basket and cook for about 5 minutes.
8. Dish out in a platter and serve warm.

370.The Best Calamari Appetizer

Servings: 6
Cooking Time: 20 Minutes
Ingredients:
- 1 ½ pounds calamari tubes, cleaned, cut into rings
- Sea salt and ground black pepper, to taste
- 2 tablespoons lemon juice
- 1 cup cornmeal
- 1 cup all-purpose flour
- 1 teaspoon paprika
- 1 egg, whisked
- 1/4 cup buttermilk

Directions:
1. Preheat your Air Fryer to 390 degrees F. Rinse the calamari and pat it dry. Season with salt and black pepper. Drizzle lemon juice all over the calamari.
2. Now, combine the cornmeal, flour, and paprika in a bowl; add the whisked egg and buttermilk.
3. Dredge the calamari in the egg/flour mixture.
4. Arrange them in the cooking basket. Spritz with cooking oil and cook for 9 to 12 minutes, shaking the basket occasionally. Work in batches.
5. Serve with toothpicks. Bon appétit!

371.Grilled Tomatoes

Servings: 2
Cooking Time: 25 Minutes
Ingredients:
- 2 tomatoes, medium to large
- Herbs of your choice, to taste
- Pepper to taste
- High quality cooking spray

Directions:
1. 1 Wash and dry the tomatoes, before chopping them in half.
2. 2 Lightly spritz them all over with cooking spray.
3. 3 Season each half with herbs (oregano, basil, parsley, rosemary, thyme, sage, etc.) as desired and black pepper.
4. 4 Put the halves in the tray of your Air Fryer. Cook for 20 minutes at 320°F, or longer if necessary. Larger tomatoes will take longer to cook.

372.Spicy Dip

Servings: 6
Cooking Time: 5 Minutes

Ingredients:

- 12 oz hot peppers, chopped
- 1 1/2 cups apple cider vinegar
- Pepper
- Salt

Directions:

1. Add all ingredients into the air fryer baking dish and stir well.
2. Place dish in the air fryer and cook at 380 F for 5 minutes.
3. Transfer pepper mixture into the blender and blend until smooth.
4. Serve and enjoy.

373.Tomato Salad

Servings: 6
Cooking Time: 12 Minutes
Ingredients:

- 1 pound tomatoes, sliced
- 1 tablespoon balsamic vinegar
- 1 tablespoon ginger, grated
- ½ teaspoon coriander, ground
- 1 teaspoon sweet paprika
- 1 teaspoon chili powder
- 1 cup mozzarella, shredded

Directions:

1. In a pan that fits your air fryer, mix all the ingredients except the mozzarella, toss, introduce the pan in the air fryer and cook at 360 degrees F for 12 minutes. Divide into bowls and serve cold as an appetizer with the mozzarella sprinkled all over.

374.Aromatic Kale Chips

Servings: 4
Cooking Time: 5 Minutes
Ingredients:

- 2 ½ tablespoons olive oil
- 1 ½ teaspoons garlic powder
- 1 bunch of kale, torn into small pieces
- 2 tablespoons lemon juice
- 1 1/2 teaspoons seasoned salt

Directions:

1. Toss your kale with the other ingredients.
2. Cook at 195 degrees F for 4 to 5 minutes, tossing kale halfway through.
3. Serve with your favorite dipping sauce.

375.Chicken, Mushroom & Spinach Pizza

Servings: 4
Cooking Time: 25 Minutes
Ingredients:

- 10 ½ oz. minced chicken
- 1 tsp. garlic powder
- 1 tsp. black pepper
- 2 tbsp. tomato basil sauce
- 5 button mushrooms, sliced thinly
- Handful of spinach

Directions:

1. 1 Pre-heat your Air Fryer at 450°F.
2. 2 Add parchment paper onto your baking tray.
3. 3 In a large bowl add the chicken with the black pepper and garlic powder.
4. 4 Add one spoonful of the chicken mix onto your baking tray.
5. 5 Flatten them into 7-inch rounds.
6. 6 Bake in the Air Fryer for about 10 minutes.
7. 7 Take out off the Air Fryer and add the tomato basil sauce onto each round.
8. 8 Add the mushroom on top. Bake again for 5 minutes.
9. 9 Serve immediately.

376.Cajun Spiced Snack

Servings: 5
Cooking Time: 30 Minutes
Ingredients:

- 2 tbsp. Cajun or Creole seasoning
- ½ cup butter, melted
- 2 cups peanut
- 2 cups mini wheat thin crackers
- 2 cups mini pretzels
- 2 tsp. salt
- 1 tsp. cayenne pepper
- 4 cups plain popcorn
- 1 tsp. paprika
- 1 tsp. garlic
- ½ tsp. thyme
- ½ tsp. oregano
- 1 tsp. black pepper
- ½ tsp. onion powder

Directions:

1. Pre-heat the Air Fryer to 370°F.
2. In a bowl, combine the Cajun spice with the melted butter.
3. In a separate bowl, stir together the peanuts, crackers, popcorn and pretzels. Coat the snacks with the butter mixture.
4. Place in the fryer and fry for 8 - 10 minutes, shaking the basket frequently during the cooking time. You will have to complete this step in two batches.
5. Put the snack mix on a cookie sheet and leave to cool.
6. The snacks can be kept in an airtight container for up to one week.

377.Garlic Avocado Balls

Servings: 4
Cooking Time: 5 Minutes
Ingredients:

- 1 avocado, peeled, pitted and mashed
- ¼ cup ghee, melted
- 2 garlic cloves, minced
- 2 spring onions, minced
- 1 chili pepper, chopped
- 1 tablespoon lime juice

- 2 tablespoons cilantro
- A pinch of salt and black pepper
- 4 bacon slices, cooked and crumbled
- Cooking spray

Directions:
1. In a bowl, mix all the ingredients except the cooking spray, stir well and shape medium balls out of this mix. Place them in your air fryer's basket, grease with cooking spray and cook at 370 degrees F for 5 minutes. Serve as a snack.

378.Lemon Biscuits

Servings:10
Cooking Time: 5 Minutes
Ingredients:
- 8½ ounces self-rising flour
- 3½ ounces caster sugar
- 3½ ounces cold butter
- 1 small egg
- 1 teaspoon fresh lemon zest, finely grated
- 2 tablespoons fresh lemon juice
- 1 teaspoon vanilla extract

Directions:
1. In a bowl, mix together the flour, and sugar.
2. Using two forks, cut in the butter until coarse crumb forms.
3. Add in the egg, vanilla extract, lemon juice, and zest. Mix until a soft dough forms.
4. Then, take out the dough from bowl and put onto a floured surface.
5. Now, roll it into an even thickness. (½ inch)
6. Cut the dough into medium-sized biscuits using a cookie cutter.
7. Set the temperature of Air Fryer to 355 degrees F.
8. Place the biscuits in a baking sheet in a single layer.
9. Put the baking sheet in an Air Fryer basket.
10. Air Fry for about 5 minutes or until golden brown.
11. Enjoy!

379.Beef Jerky

Servings: 4
Cooking Time: 250 Minutes
Ingredients:
- ¼ tsp. garlic powder
- ¼ tsp. onion powder
- ¼ cup soy sauce
- 2 tsp. Worcestershire sauce
- 1 lb. flat iron steak, thinly sliced

Directions:
1. In a bowl, combine the garlic powder, onion powder, soy sauce, and Worcestershire sauce. Marinade the beef slices with the mixture in an airtight bag, shaking it well to ensure the beef is well-coated. Leave to marinate for at least two hours

2. Place the meat in the basket of your air fryer, making sure it is evenly spaced. Cook the beef slices in more than one batch if necessary.
3. Cook for four hours at 160°F.
4. Allow to cool before serving. You can keep the jerky in an airtight container for up to a week, if you can resist it that long.

380.Paprika Zucchini Bombs With Goat Cheese

Servings: 4
Cooking Time: 20 Minutes
Ingredients:
- 1 cup zucchini, grated, juice squeezed out
- 1 egg
- 1 garlic clove, minced
- 1/2 cup all-purpose flour
- 1/2 cup cornbread crumbs
- 1/2 cup parmesan cheese, grated
- 1/2 cup goat cheese, grated
- Salt and black pepper, to taste
- 1 teaspoon paprika

Directions:
1. Start by preheating your Air Fryer to 330 degrees F. Spritz the cooking basket with nonstick cooking oil.
2. Mix all ingredients until everything is well incorporated. Shape the zucchini mixture into golf sized balls and place them in the cooking basket.
3. Cook in the preheated Air Fryer for 15 to 18 minutes, shaking the basket periodically to ensure even cooking.
4. Garnish with some extra paprika if desired and serve at room temperature. Bon appétit!

381.Baked Potatoes

Servings: 3
Cooking Time: 45 Minutes
Ingredients:
- 3 Idaho or russet baking potatoes, washed
- 2 cloves garlic, crushed
- 1 tbsp. olive oil
- 1 tbsp. sea salt
- Parsley, roughly chopped
- Sour cream to taste

Directions:
1. Pierce each potato several times with a fork.
2. Sprinkle the potatoes with salt and coat with the garlic puree and olive oil.
3. Place the potatoes in the Air Fryer basket and cook at 390°F for 35 - 40 minutes until soft. Serve with parsley and sour cream, or whatever toppings you desire.

382.Old-fashioned Onion Rings

Servings:4
Cooking Time:10 Minutes

Ingredients:

- 1 large onion, cut into rings
- 1¼ cups all-purpose flour
- 1 cup milk
- 1 egg
- ¾ cup dry bread crumbs
- Salt, to taste

Directions:

1. Preheat the Air fryer to 360 °F and grease the Air fryer basket.
2. Mix together flour and salt in a dish.
3. Whisk egg with milk in a second dish until well mixed.
4. Place the breadcrumbs in a third dish.
5. Coat the onion rings with the flour mixture and dip into the egg mixture.
6. Lastly dredge in the breadcrumbs and transfer the onion rings in the Air fryer basket.
7. Cook for about 10 minutes and dish out to serve warm.

383. Bacon Butter

Servings: 5
Cooking Time: 2 Minutes
Ingredients:

- ½ cup butter
- 3 oz bacon, chopped

Directions:

1. Preheat the air fryer to 400F and put the bacon inside. Cook it for 8 minutes. Stir the bacon every 2 minutes. Meanwhile, soften the butter in the oven and put it in the butter mold. Add cooked bacon and churn the butter. Refrigerate the butter for 30 minutes.

384. Asparagus

Servings: 4
Cooking Time: 15 Minutes
Ingredients:

- 10 asparagus spears, woody end cut off
- 1 clove garlic, minced
- 4 tbsp. olive oil
- Pepper to taste
- Salt to taste

Directions:

1. Set the Air Fryer to 400°F and allow to heat for 5 minutes.
2. In a bowl, combine the garlic and oil.
3. Cover the asparagus with this mixture and put it in the fryer basket. Sprinkle over some pepper and salt.
4. Cook for 10 minutes and serve hot.

385. Bacon And Onion Fat Bombs

Servings: 6
Cooking Time: 15 Minutes
Ingredients:

- 2 onions, sliced
- 1 cup bacon, finely chopped
- 1/2 cup Colby cheese, shredded
- 8 ounces soft cheese
- 2 ½ tablespoons canola oil
- 2 eggs

Directions:

1. Combine all the ingredients in a mixing dish. Roll the mixture into bite-sized balls.
2. Air-fry them at 390 degrees F for 5 minutes. Work in batches.
3. Serve with toothpicks and enjoy!

386. Portabella Pizza Treat

Servings: 2
Cooking Time: 6 Minutes
Ingredients:

- 2 Portabella caps, stemmed
- 2 tablespoons canned tomatoes with basil
- 2 tablespoons mozzarella cheese, shredded
- 4 pepperoni slices
- 2 tablespoons Parmesan cheese, grated freshly
- 2 tablespoon olive oil
- 1/8 teaspoon dried Italian seasonings
- Salt, to taste
- 1 teaspoon red pepper flakes, crushed

Directions:

1. Preheat the Air fryer to 320 °F and grease an Air fryer basket.
2. Drizzle olive oil on both sides of portabella cap and season salt, red pepper flakes and Italian seasonings.
3. Top canned tomatoes on the mushrooms, followed by mozzarella cheese.
4. Place portabella caps in the Air fryer basket and cook for about 2 minutes.
5. Top with pepperoni slices and cook for about 4 minutes.
6. Sprinkle with Parmesan cheese and dish out to serve warm.

387. Healthy Vegetable Kabobs

Servings: 4
Cooking Time: 10 Minutes
Ingredients:

- 1/2 onion
- 1 zucchini
- 1 eggplant
- 2 bell peppers
- Pepper
- Salt

Directions:

1. Cut all vegetables into 1-inch pieces.
2. Thread vegetables onto the soaked wooden skewers and season with pepper and salt.
3. Place skewers into the air fryer basket and cook for 10 minutes at 390 F. Turn halfway through.

4. Serve and enjoy.

388.Sweet Potato Wedges

Servings: 2
Cooking Time: 25 Minutes
Ingredients:
- 2 large sweet potatoes, cut into wedges
- 1 tbsp. olive oil
- 1 tsp. chili powder
- 1 tsp. mustard powder
- 1 tsp. cumin
- 1 tbsp. Mexican seasoning
- Pepper to taste
- Salt to taste

Directions:
1. Pre-heat the Air Fryer at 350°F.
2. Place all of the ingredients into a bowl and combine well to coat the sweet potatoes entirely.
3. Place the wedges in the Air Fryer basket and air fry for 20 minutes, shaking the basket at 5-minute intervals.

389.Italian-style Tomato-parmesan Crisps

Servings: 4
Cooking Time: 20 Minutes
Ingredients:
- 4 Roma tomatoes, sliced
- 2 tablespoons olive oil
- Sea salt and white pepper, to taste
- 1 teaspoon Italian seasoning mix
- 4 tablespoons Parmesan cheese, grated

Directions:
1. Start by preheating your Air Fryer to 350 degrees F. Generously grease the Air Fryer basket with nonstick cooking oil.
2. Toss the sliced tomatoes with the remaining ingredients. Transfer them to the cooking basket without overlapping.
3. Cook in the preheated Air Fryer for 5 minutes. Shake the cooking basket and cook an additional 5 minutes. Work in batches.
4. Serve with Mediterranean aioli for dipping, if desired. Bon appétit!

390.Bacon-wrapped Shrimp

Servings:6
Cooking Time:7 Minutes
Ingredients:
- 1 pound bacon, sliced thinly
- 1 pound shrimp, peeled and deveined
- Salt, to taste

Directions:
1. Preheat the Air fryer to 390 °F and grease an Air fryer basket.
2. Wrap 1 shrimp with a bacon slices, covering completely.
3. Repeat with the remaining shrimp and bacon slices.

4. Arrange the bacon wrapped shrimps in a baking dish and freeze for about 15 minutes.
5. Place the shrimps in an Air fryer basket and cook for about 7 minutes.
6. Dish out and serve warm.

391.Turkey Sausage Patties

Servings: 6
Cooking Time: 20 Minutes
Ingredients:
- 1 lb. lean ground turkey
- 1 tsp. olive oil
- 1 tbsp. chopped chives
- 1 small onion, diced
- 1 large garlic clove, chopped
- ¾ tsp. paprika
- Kosher salt and pepper to taste
- Pinch of raw sugar
- 1 tbsp. vinegar
- 1 tsp. fennel seed
- Pinch of nutmeg

Directions:
1. 1 Pre-heat the Air Fryer to 375°F.
2. 2 Add a half-teaspoon of the oil to the fryer, along with the onion and garlic. Air fry for 30 seconds before adding in the fennel. Place everything on a plate.
3. 3 In a bowl, combine the ground turkey with the sugar, paprika, nutmeg, vinegar, chives and the onion mixture. Divide into equal portions and shape each one into a patty.
4. 4 Add another teaspoon of oil to the fryer. Put the patties in the fryer and cook for roughly 3 minutes.
5. 5 Serve with salad or on hamburger buns.

392.Zucchini Fries

Servings:4
Cooking Time: 20 Minutes
Ingredients:
- 1 pound zucchini, sliced into 2½-inch sticks
- Salt, as required
- 2 tablespoons olive oil
- ¾ cup panko breadcrumbs

Directions:
1. In a colander, add the zucchini and sprinkle with salt. Set aside for about 10 minutes.
2. Set the temperature of Air Fryer to 390 degrees F.
3. Gently pat dry the zucchini sticks with the paper towels and coat with oil.
4. In a shallow dish, add the breadcrumbs.
5. Coat the zucchini sticks evenly with breadcrumbs.
6. Place the zucchini sticks in an Air Fryer basket in a single layer in 2 batches.

7. Now, set the temperature of Air Fryer to 425 degrees F and Air Fry for about 10 minutes.
8. Serve.

393.Chili Kale Chips

Servings:4
Cooking Time: 5 Minutes
Ingredients:
- 1 teaspoon nutritional yeast
- 1 teaspoon salt
- 2 cups kale, chopped
- ½ teaspoon chili flakes
- 1 teaspoon sesame oil

Directions:
1. Mix up kale leaves with nutritional yeast, salt, chili flakes, and sesame oil. Shake the greens well. Preheat the air fryer to 400F and put the kale leaves in the air fryer basket. Cook them for 3 minutes and then give a good shake. Cook the kale leaves for 2 minutes more.

394.Ranch Kale Chips

Servings: 4
Cooking Time: 5 Minutes
Ingredients:
- 4 cups kale, stemmed
- 1 tbsp nutritional yeast flakes
- 2 tsp ranch seasoning
- 2 tbsp olive oil
- 1/4 tsp salt

Directions:
1. Add all ingredients into the large mixing bowl and toss well.
2. Spray air fryer basket with cooking spray.
3. Add kale in air fryer basket and cook for 4-5 minutes at 370 F. Shake halfway through.
4. Serve and enjoy.

395.Crispy Onion Rings

Servings: 3
Cooking Time: 10 Minutes
Ingredients:
- 1 egg, lightly beaten
- 1 onion, cut into slices
- 3/4 cup pork rind, crushed
- 1 cup coconut milk
- 1 tbsp baking powder
- 1 1/2 cups almond flour
- Pepper
- Salt

Directions:
1. Preheat the air fryer to 360 F.
2. In a bowl, mix together almond flour, baking powder, pepper, and salt.
3. In another bowl, whisk the egg with milk. Pour egg mixture into the almond flour mixture and stir to combine.

4. In a shallow dish, add crushed pork rinds.
5. Spray air fryer basket with cooking spray.
6. Dip onion ring in egg batter and coat with pork rind and place into the air fryer basket.
7. Cook onion rings for 10 minutes at 360 F.
8. Serve and enjoy.

396.Country Style Chard

Servings: 2
Cooking Time: 5 Minutes
Ingredients:
- 4 slices bacon, chopped
- 2 tbsp butter
- 2 tbsp fresh lemon juice
- ½ tsp garlic paste
- 1 bunch Swiss chard, stems removed, leaves cut into 1-inch pieces

Directions:
1. On a medium heat, cook the bacon in a skillet until the fat begins to brown.
2. Melt the butter in the skillet and add the lemon juice and garlic paste.
3. Add the chard leaves and cook until they begin to wilt.
4. Cover and turn up the heat to high.
5. Cook for 3 minutes.
6. Mix well, sprinkle with salt and serve.

397.Beer Battered Vidalia Rings

Servings: 4
Cooking Time: 30 Minutes
Ingredients:
- 1/2 pound Vidalia onions, sliced into rings
- 1/2 cup all-purpose flour
- 1/4 cup cornmeal
- 1/2 teaspoon baking powder
- Sea salt and freshly cracked black pepper, to taste
- 1/4 teaspoon garlic powder
- 2 eggs, beaten
- 1/2 cup lager-style beer
- 1 cup plain breadcrumbs
- 2 tablespoons peanut oil

Directions:
1. Place the onion rings in the bowl with icy cold water; let them soak approximately 20 minutes; drain the onion rings and pat them dry.
2. In a shallow bowl, mix the flour, cornmeal, baking powder, salt, and black pepper. Add the garlic powder, eggs and beer; mix well to combine.
3. In another shallow bowl, mix the breadcrumbs with the peanut oil. Dip the onion rings in the flour/egg mixture; then, dredge in the breadcrumb mixture. Roll to coat them evenly.

4. Spritz the Air Fryer basket with cooking spray; arrange the breaded onion rings in the basket.
5. Cook in the preheated Air Fryer at 400 degrees F for 4 to 5 minutes, turning them over halfway through the cooking time. Bon appétit!

398.Bell Pepper Chips

Servings: 4
Cooking Time: 20 Minutes
Ingredients:
- 1 egg, beaten
- 1/2 cup parmesan, grated
- 1 teaspoon sea salt
- 1/2 teaspoon red pepper flakes, crushed
- 3/4 pound bell peppers, deveined and cut to 1/4-inch strips
- 2 tablespoons grapeseed oil

Directions:
1. In a mixing bowl, combine together the egg, parmesan, salt, and red pepper flakes; mix to combine well.
2. Dip bell peppers into the batter and transfer them to the cooking basket. Brush with the grapeseed oil.
3. Cook in the preheated Air Fryer at 390 degrees F for 4 minutes. Shake the basket and cook for a further 3 minutes. Work in batches.
4. Taste, adjust the seasonings and serve. Bon appétit!

399.Steak Nuggets

Servings: 4
Cooking Time: 15 Minutes
Ingredients:
- 1 lb beef steak, cut into chunks
- 1 large egg, lightly beaten
- 1/2 cup pork rind, crushed
- 1/2 cup parmesan cheese, grated
- 1/2 tsp salt

Directions:
1. Add egg in a small bowl.
2. In a shallow bowl, mix together pork rind, cheese, and salt.
3. Dip each steak chunk in egg then coat with pork rind mixture and place on a plate. Place in refrigerator for 30 minutes.
4. Spray air fryer basket with cooking spray.
5. Preheat the air fryer to 400 F.
6. Place steak nuggets in air fryer basket and cook for 15-18 minutes or until cooked. Shake after every 4 minutes.
7. Serve and enjoy.

400.Mushroom Bites

Servings: 6
Cooking Time: 12 Minutes

Ingredients:
- Salt and black pepper to the taste
- 1 and ¼ cups coconut flour
- 2 garlic clove, minced
- 2 tablespoons basil, minced
- ½ pound mushrooms, minced
- 1 egg, whisked

Directions:
1. In a bowl, mix all the ingredients except the cooking spray, stir well and shape medium balls out of this mix. Arrange the balls in your air fryer's basket, grease them with cooking spray and bake at 350 degrees F for 6 minutes on each side. Serve as an appetizer.

401.Spinach Melts With Parsley Yogurt Dip

Servings: 4
Cooking Time: 20 Minutes
Ingredients:
- Spinach Melts:
- 2 cups spinach, torn into pieces
- 1 ½ cups cauliflower
- 1 tablespoon sesame oil
- 1/2 cup scallions, chopped
- 2 garlic cloves, minced
- 1/2 cup almond flour
- 1/4 cup coconut flour
- 1 teaspoon baking powder
- 1/2 teaspoon sea salt
- 1/2 teaspoon ground black pepper
- 1/4 teaspoon dried dill
- 1/2 teaspoon dried basil
- 1 cup cheddar cheese, shredded
- Parsley Yogurt Dip:
- 1/2 cup Greek-Style yoghurt
- 2 tablespoons mayonnaise
- 2 tablespoons fresh parsley, chopped
- 1 tablespoon fresh lemon juice
- 1/2 teaspoon garlic, smashed

Directions:
1. Place spinach in a mixing dish; pour in hot water. Drain and rinse well.
2. Add cauliflower to the steamer basket; steam until the cauliflower is tender about 5 minutes.
3. Mash the cauliflower; add the remaining ingredients for Spinach Melts and mix to combine well. Shape the mixture into patties and transfer them to the lightly greased cooking basket.
4. Bake at 330 degrees F for 14 minutes or until thoroughly heated.
5. Meanwhile, make your dipping sauce by whisking the remaining ingredients. Place in your refrigerator until ready to serve.
6. Serve the Spinach Melts with the chilled sauce on the side. Enjoy!

402.Eggplant Chips

Servings: 4
Cooking Time: 45 Minutes
Ingredients:
- 2 eggplants, peeled and thinly sliced
- Salt
- ½ cup tapioca starch
- ¼ cup canola oil
- ½ cup water
- 1 tsp. garlic powder
- ½ tsp. dried dill weed
- ½ tsp. ground black pepper, to taste

Directions:
1. 1 Season the eggplant slices with salt and leave for half an hour.
2. 2 Run them under cold water to rinse off any excess salt.
3. 3 In a bowl, coat the eggplant slices with all of the other ingredients.
4. 4 Cook at 390°F for 13 minutes. You may need to do this in batches.
5. 5 Serve with the dipping sauce of your choice.

403.Pita Bread Cheese Pizza

Servings:4
Cooking Time:6 Minutes
Ingredients:
- 1 pita bread
- ¼ cup Mozzarella cheese
- 7 slices pepperoni
- ¼ cup sausage
- 1 tablespoon yellow onion, sliced thinly
- 1 tablespoon pizza sauce
- 1 drizzle extra-virgin olive oil
- ½ teaspoon fresh garlic, minced

Directions:
1. Preheat the Air fryer to 350 °F and grease an Air fryer basket.
2. Spread pizza sauce on the pita bread and add sausages, pepperoni, onions, garlic and cheese.
3. Drizzle with olive oil and place it in the Air fryer basket.
4. Cook for about 6 minutes and dish out to serve warm.

404.Feta Triangles

Servings: 5
Cooking Time: 55 Minutes
Ingredients:
- 1 egg yolk, beaten
- 4 oz. feta cheese
- 2 tbsp. flat-leafed parsley, finely chopped
- 1 scallion, finely chopped
- 2 sheets of frozen filo pastry, defrosted
- 2 tbsp. olive oil ground black pepper to taste

Directions:
1. 1 In a bowl, combine the beaten egg yolk with the feta, parsley and scallion. Sprinkle on some pepper to taste.
2. 2 Slice each sheet of filo dough into three strips.
3. 3 Place a teaspoonful of the feta mixture on each strip of pastry.
4. 4 Pinch the tip of the pastry and fold it up to enclose the filling and create a triangle. Continue folding the strip in zig-zags until the filling is wrapped in a triangle. Repeat with all of the strips of pastry.
5. 5 Pre-heat the Air Fryer to 390°F.
6. 6 Coat the pastry with a light coating of oil and arrange in the cooking basket.
7. 7 Place the basket in the Air Fryer and cook for 3 minutes.
8. 8 Lower the heat to 360°F and cook for a further 2 minutes or until a golden brown color is achieved

405.Masala Cashew

Servings: 3
Cooking Time: 20 Minutes
Ingredients:
- ½ lb. cashew nuts
- ½ tsp. garam masala powder
- 1 tsp. coriander powder
- 1 tsp. ghee
- 1 tsp. red chili powder
- ½ tsp. black pepper
- 2 tsp. dry mango powder
- 1 tsp. sea salt

Directions:
1. 1 Put all the ingredients in a large bowl and toss together well.
2. 2 Arrange the cashew nuts in the basket of your Air Fryer.
3. 3 Cook at 250°F for 15 minutes until the nuts are brown and crispy.
4. 4 Let the nuts cool before serving or transferring to an airtight container to be stored for up to 2 weeks.

406.Paprika Bacon Shrimp

Servings: 10
Cooking Time: 45 Minutes
Ingredients:
- 1 ¼ pounds shrimp, peeled and deveined
- 1 teaspoon paprika
- 1/2 teaspoon ground black pepper
- 1/2 teaspoon red pepper flakes, crushed
- 1 tablespoon salt
- 1 teaspoon chili powder
- 1 tablespoon shallot powder
- 1/4 teaspoon cumin powder
- 1 ¼ pounds thin bacon slices

Directions:

1. Toss the shrimps with all the seasoning until they are coated well.
2. Next, wrap a slice of bacon around the shrimps, securing with a toothpick; repeat with the remaining ingredients; chill for 30 minutes.
3. Air-fry them at 360 degrees F for 7 to 8 minutes, working in batches. Serve with cocktail sticks if desired. Enjoy!

407.Carrots & Rhubarb

Servings: 4
Cooking Time: 35 Minutes
Ingredients:
- 1 lb. heritage carrots
- 1 lb. rhubarb
- 1 medium orange
- ½ cup walnuts, halved
- 2 tsp. walnut oil
- ½ tsp. sugar or a few drops of sugar extract

Directions:
1. 1 Rinse the carrots to wash. Dry and chop them into 1-inch pieces.
2. 2 Transfer them to the Air Fryer basket and drizzle over the walnut oil.
3. 3 Cook at 320°F for about 20 minutes.
4. 4 In the meantime, wash the rhubarb and chop it into ½-inch pieces.
5. 5 Coarsely dice the walnuts.

6. 6 Wash the orange and grate its skin into a small bowl. Peel the rest of the orange and cut it up into wedges.
7. 7 Place the rhubarb, walnuts and sugar in the fryer and allow to cook for an additional 5 minutes.
8. 8 Add in 2 tbsp. of the orange zest, along with the orange wedges. Serve immediately.

408.Cheesy Garlic Bread

Servings: 2
Cooking Time: 20 Minutes
Ingredients:
- 1 friendly baguette
- 4 tsp. butter, melted
- 3 chopped garlic cloves
- 5 tsp. sundried tomato pesto
- 1 cup mozzarella cheese, grated

Directions:
1. 1 Cut your baguette into 5 thick round slices.
2. 2 Add the garlic cloves to the melted butter and brush onto each slice of bread.
3. 3 Spread a teaspoon of sun dried tomato pesto onto each slice.
4. 4 Top each slice with the grated mozzarella.
5. 5 Transfer the bread slices to the Air Fryer and cook them at 180°F for 6 – 8 minutes.
6. 6 Top with some freshly chopped basil leaves, chili flakes and oregano if desired.

DESSERTS RECIPES

409.Grandma's Butter Cookies

Servings: 4
Cooking Time: 25 Minutes
Ingredients:
- 8 ounces all-purpose flour
- 2 ½ ounces sugar
- 1 teaspoon baking powder
- A pinch of grated nutmeg
- A pinch of coarse salt
- 1 large egg, room temperature.
- 1 stick butter, room temperature
- 1 teaspoon vanilla extract

Directions:
1. Mix the flour, sugar, baking powder, grated nutmeg, and salt in a bowl. In a separate bowl, whisk the egg, butter, and vanilla extract.
2. Stir the egg mixture into the flour mixture; mix to combine well or until it forms a nice, soft dough.
3. Roll your dough out and cut out with a cookie cutter of your choice.
4. Bake in the preheated Air Fryer at 350 degrees F for 10 minutes. Decrease the temperature to 330 degrees F and cook for 10 minutes longer. Bon appétit!

410.Cherries 'n Almond Flour Bars

Servings:12
Cooking Time: 35 Minutes
Ingredients:
- ¼ cup water
- ½ cup butter, softened
- ½ teaspoon salt
- ½ teaspoon vanilla
- 1 ½ cups almond flour
- 1 cup erythritol
- 1 cup fresh cherries, pitted
- 1 tablespoon xanthan gum
- 2 eggs

Directions:
1. In a mixing bowl, combine the first 6 ingredients until you form a dough.
2. Press the dough in a baking dish that will fit in the air fryer.
3. Place in the air fryer and bake for 10 minutes at 375 °F.
4. Meanwhile, mix the cherries, water, and xanthan gum in a bowl.
5. Take the dough out and pour over the cherry mixture.
6. Return to the air fryer and cook for 25 minutes more at 375 °F.

411.Air Fryer Chocolate Cake

Servings:6

Cooking Time:25 Minutes
Ingredients:
- 3 eggs
- 1 cup almond flour
- 1 stick butter, room temperature
- 1/3 cup cocoa powder
- 1½ teaspoons baking powder
- ½ cup sour cream
- 2/3 cup swerve
- 2 teaspoons vanilla

Directions:
1. Preheat the Air fryer to 360 °F and grease a cake pan lightly.
2. Mix all the ingredients in a bowl and beat well.
3. Pour the batter in the cake pan and transfer into the Air fryer basket.
4. Cook for about 25 minutes and cut into slices to serve.

412.Vanilla Coconut Cheese Cookies

Servings: 15
Cooking Time: 12 Minutes
Ingredients:
- 1 egg
- 1/2 tsp baking powder
- 1 tsp vanilla
- 1/2 cup swerve
- 1/2 cup butter, softened
- 3 tbsp cream cheese, softened
- 1/2 cup coconut flour
- Pinch of salt

Directions:
1. In a bowl, beat together butter, sweetener, and cream cheese.
2. Add egg and vanilla and beat until smooth and creamy.
3. Add coconut flour, salt, and baking powder and beat until combined. Cover and place in the fridge for 1 hour.
4. Preheat the air fryer to 325 F.
5. Make cookies from dough and place into the air fryer and cook for 12 minutes.
6. Serve and enjoy.

413.Berry Layer Cake

Servings: 1
Cooking Time: 8 Minutes
Ingredients:
- ¼ lemon pound cake
- ¼ cup whipping cream
- ½ tsp Truvia
- 1/8 tsp orange flavor
- 1 cup of mixed berries

Directions:
1. Using a sharp knife, divide the lemon cake into small cubes.

2. Dice the strawberries.
3. Combine the whipping cream, Truvia, and orange flavor.
4. Layer the fruit, cake and cream in a glass.
5. Serve!

414.Crispy Fruit Tacos

Servings:2
Cooking Time:5 Minutes
Ingredients:
- 2 soft shell tortillas
- 4 tablespoons strawberry jelly
- ¼ cup blueberries
- ¼ cup raspberries
- 2 tablespoons powdered sugar

Directions:
1. Preheat the Air fryer to 300 °F and grease an Air fryer basket.
2. Put 2 tablespoons of strawberry jelly over each tortilla and top with blueberries and raspberries.
3. Sprinkle with powdered sugar and transfer into the Air fryer basket.
4. Cook for about 5 minutes until crispy and serve.

415.Creamy Pudding

Servings: 6
Cooking Time: 25 Minutes
Ingredients:
- 2 cups fresh cream
- 6 egg yolks, whisked
- 6 tablespoons white sugar
- Zest of 1 orange

Directions:
1. Combine all ingredients in a bowl and whisk well.
2. Divide the mixture between 6 small ramekins.
3. Place the ramekins in your air fryer and cook at 340 degrees F for 25 minutes.
4. Place in the fridge for 1 hour before serving.

416.Perfect Apple Pie

Servings:6
Cooking Time:30 Minutes
Ingredients:
- 1 frozen pie crust, thawed
- 1 large apple, peeled, cored and chopped
- 1 tablespoon butter, chopped
- 1 egg, beaten
- 3 tablespoons sugar, divided
- 1 tablespoon ground cinnamon
- 2 teaspoons fresh lemon juice
- ½ teaspoon vanilla extract

Directions:
1. Preheat the Air fryer to 320 °F and grease a pie pan lightly.

2. Cut 2 crusts, first about 1/8-inch larger than pie pan and second, a little smaller than first one.
3. Arrange the large crust in the bottom of pie pan.
4. Mix apple, 2 tablespoons of sugar, cinnamon, lemon juice and vanilla extract in a large bowl.
5. Put the apple mixture evenly over the bottom crust and top with butter.
6. Arrange the second crust on top and seal the edges.
7. Cut 4 slits in the top crust carefully and brush with egg.
8. Sprinkle with sugar and arrange the pie pan in the Air fryer basket.
9. Cook for about 30 minutes and dish out to serve.

417.Cashew Pie

Servings: 8
Cooking Time: 18 Minutes
Ingredients:
- 1 egg
- 2 oz cashews, crushed
- ½ tsp baking soda
- 1/3 cup heavy cream
- 1 oz dark chocolate, melted
- 1 tbsp butter
- 1 tsp vinegar
- 1 cup coconut flour

Directions:
1. Add egg in a bowl and beat using a hand mixer. Add coconut flour and stir well.
2. Add butter, vinegar, baking soda, heavy cream, and melted chocolate and stir well.
3. Add cashews and mix well.
4. Preheat the air fryer to 350 F.
5. Add prepared dough in air fryer baking dish and flatten it into a pie shape.
6. Cook for 18 minutes.
7. Slice and serve.

418.Avocado Walnut Bread

Servings:6
Cooking Time:35 Minutes
Ingredients:
- ¾ cup (3 oz.) almond flour, white
- ¼ teaspoon baking soda
- 2 ripe avocados, cored, peeled and mashed
- 2 large eggs, beaten
- 2 tablespoons (3/4 oz.) Toasted walnuts, chopped roughly
- 1 teaspoon cinnamon ground
- ½ teaspoon kosher salt
- 2 tablespoons vegetable oil
- ½ cup granulated swerve
- 1 teaspoon vanilla extract

Directions:

1. Preheat the Air fryer to 310 °F and line a 6-inch baking pan with parchment paper.
2. Mix almond flour, salt, baking soda, and cinnamon in a bowl.
3. Whisk eggs with avocado mash, yogurt, swerve, oil, and vanilla in a bowl.
4. Stir in the almond flour mixture and mix until well combined.
5. Pour the batter evenly into the pan and top with the walnuts.
6. Place the baking pan into the Air fryer basket and cook for about 35 minutes.
7. Dish out in a platter and cut into slices to serve.

419.Walnut Brownies

Servings:8
Cooking Time:22 Minutes
Ingredients:
- ½ cup chocolate, chopped roughly
- 1/3 cup butter
- 1 large egg, beaten
- 5 tablespoons self-rising flour
- ¼ cup walnuts, chopped
- 5 tablespoons sugar
- 1 teaspoon vanilla extract
- Pinch of salt

Directions:
1. Preheat the Air fryer to 355 °F and line a baking pan with greased parchment paper.
2. Microwave chocolate and butter on high for about 2 minutes.
3. Mix sugar, egg, vanilla extract, salt and chocolate mixture in a bowl until well combined.
4. Stir in the flour mixture slowly and fold in the walnuts.
5. Pour this mixture into the baking pan and smooth the top surface of mixture with the back of spatula.
6. Transfer the baking pan into the Air fryer basket and cook for about 20 minutes.
7. Dish out and cut into 8 equal sized squares to serve.

420.Apple Pastry Pouch

Servings:2
Cooking Time: 25 Minutes
Ingredients:
- 1 tablespoon brown sugar
- 2 tablespoons raisins
- 2 small apples, peeled and cored
- 2 puff pastry sheets
- 2 tablespoons butter, melted

Directions:
1. In a bowl, mix together the sugar and raisins.
2. Fill the core of each apple with raisins mixture.

3. Place one apple in the center of each pastry sheet and fold dough to cover the apple completely.
4. Then, pinch the edges to seal.
5. Coat each apple evenly with butter.
6. Set the temperature of air fryer to 355 degrees F. Lightly, grease an air fryer basket.
7. Arrange apple pouches into the prepared air fryer basket in a single layer.
8. Air fry for about 25 minutes.
9. Remove from air fryer and transfer the apple pouches onto a platter.
10. Serve warm.

421.Cream Cheese Cupcakes

Servings:10
Cooking Time:20 Minutes
Ingredients:
- 4½-ounce self-rising flour
- ½-ounce cream cheese, softened
- 4¾-ounce butter, softened
- 2 eggs
- ½ cup fresh raspberries
- Pinch of salt
- 4¼-ounce caster sugar
- 2 teaspoons fresh lemon juice

Directions:
1. Preheat the Air fryer to 365 °F and grease 10 silicon cups.
2. Mix flour, baking powder and salt in a bowl.
3. Combine cream cheese, sugar, eggs and butter in another bowl.
4. Mix the flour mixture with the cream cheese mixture and squeeze in the lemon juice.
5. Transfer the mixture into 10 silicon cups and top each cup with 2 raspberries.
6. Place the silicon cups in the Air fryer basket and cook for about 20 minutes.
7. Dish out and serve to enjoy.

422.All-star Banana Fritters

Servings:5
Cooking Time: 15 Minutes
Ingredients:
- 5 bananas, sliced
- 1 tsp salt
- 3 tbsp sesame seeds
- 1 cup water
- 2 eggs, beaten
- 1 tsp baking powder
- ½ tbsp sugar

Directions:
1. Preheat the air fryer to 340 F.
2. In a bowl, mix salt, sesame seeds, flour, baking powder, eggs, sugar, and water.
3. Coat sliced bananas with the flour mixture; place the prepared slices in the air fryer basket; cook for 8 minutes.

423.New England Pumpkin Cake

Servings: 4
Cooking Time: 50 Minutes
Ingredients:
- 1 large egg
- ½ cup skimmed milk
- 7 oz. flour
- 2 tbsp. sugar
- 5 oz. pumpkin puree
- Pinch of salt
- Pinch of cinnamon [if desired]
- Cooking spray

Directions:
1. Stir together the pumpkin puree and sugar in a bowl. Crack in the egg and combine using a whisk until smooth.
2. Add in the flour and salt, stirring constantly. Pour in the milk, ensuring to combine everything well.
3. Spritz a baking tin with cooking spray.
4. Transfer the batter to the baking tin.
5. Pre-heat the Air Fryer to 350°F.
6. Put the tin in the Air Fryer basket and bake for 15 minutes.

424.Cheesecake

Servings: 6
Cooking Time: 28 Minutes
Ingredients:
- For crust:
- 2 tbsp butter, melted
- ¼ tsp cinnamon
- 1 tbsp swerve
- ½ cup almond flour
- Pinch of salt
- For Cheesecake:
- 1 egg
- ½ tsp vanilla
- ½ cup swerve
- 8 oz cream cheese

Directions:
1. Preheat the air fryer to 280 F.
2. Spray air fryer baking dish with cooking spray.
3. Add all crust ingredients into the bowl and mix until combined. Transfer crust mixture into the prepared baking dish and press down into the bottom of the dish.
4. Place dish in the air fryer and cook for 12 minutes.
5. In a large bowl, beat cream cheese using a hand mixer until smooth.
6. Add egg, vanilla, and salt and stir to combine.
7. Pour cream cheese mixture over cooked crust and cook for 16 minutes.
8. Allow to cool completely.
9. Slice and serve.

425.Cherry-choco Bars

Servings:8
Cooking Time: 15 Minutes
Ingredients:
- ¼ teaspoon salt
- ½ cup almonds, sliced
- ½ cup chia seeds
- ½ cup dark chocolate, chopped
- ½ cup dried cherries, chopped
- ½ cup prunes, pureed
- ½ cup quinoa, cooked
- ¾ cup almond butter
- 1/3 cup honey
- 2 cups old-fashioned oats
- 2 tablespoon coconut oil

Directions:
1. Preheat the air fryer to 375 °F.
2. In a mixing bowl, combine the oats, quinoa, chia seeds, almond, cherries, and chocolate.
3. In a saucepan, heat the almond butter, honey, and coconut oil.
4. Pour the butter mixture over the dry mixture. Add salt and prunes.
5. Mix until well combined.
6. Pour over a baking dish that can fit inside the air fryer.
7. Cook for 15 minutes.
8. Let it cool for an hour before slicing into bars.

426.Fruity Crumble

Servings:4
Cooking Time:20 Minutes
Ingredients:
- ½ pound fresh apricots, pitted and cubed
- 1 cup fresh blackberries
- 7/8 cup flour
- 1 tablespoon cold water
- ¼ cup chilled butter, cubed
- 1/3 cup sugar, divided
- 1 tablespoon fresh lemon juice
- Pinch of salt

Directions:
1. Preheat the Air fryer to 390 °F and grease a baking pan lightly.
2. Mix apricots, blackberries, 2 tablespoons of sugar and lemon juice in a bowl.
3. Combine the remaining ingredients in a bowl and mix until a crumbly mixture is formed.
4. Pour the apricot mixture in the baking pan and top with the crumbly mixture.
5. Transfer the baking pan in the Air fryer basket and cook for about 20 minutes.
6. Dish out in a bowl and serve warm.

427.White Chocolate Chip Cookies

Servings:8
Cooking Time: 30 Minutes

Ingredients:
- 3 oz brown sugar
- 2 oz white chocolate chips
- 1 tbsp honey
- 1 ½ tbsp milk
- 4 oz butter

Directions:
1. Preheat the air fryer to 350 F, and beat the butter and sugar until fluffy. Beat in the honey, milk, and flour. Gently fold in the chocolate cookies. Drop spoonfuls of the mixture onto a prepared cookie sheet. Cook for 18 minutes.

428.Lusciously Easy Brownies

Servings:8
Cooking Time: 20 Minutes
Ingredients:
- 1 egg
- 2 tablespoons and 2 teaspoons unsweetened cocoa powder
- 1/2 cup white sugar
- 1/2 teaspoon vanilla extract
- 1/4 cup butter
- 1/4 cup all-purpose flour
- 1/8 teaspoon salt
- 1/8 teaspoon baking powder
- Frosting Ingredients
- 1 tablespoon and 1-1/2 teaspoons butter, softened
- 1 tablespoon and 1-1/2 teaspoons unsweetened cocoa powder
- 1-1/2 teaspoons honey
- 1/2 teaspoon vanilla extract
- 1/2 cup confectioners' sugar

Directions:
1. Lightly grease baking pan of air fryer with cooking spray. Melt ¼ cup butter for 3 minutes. Stir in vanilla, eggs, and sugar. Mix well.
2. Stir in baking powder, salt, flour, and cocoa mix well. Evenly spread.
3. For 20 minutes, cook on 300°F.
4. In a small bowl, make the frosting by mixing well all Ingredients. Frost brownies while still warm.
5. Serve and enjoy.

429.Chocolate Brownies & Caramel Sauce

Servings: 4
Cooking Time: 45 Minutes
Ingredients:
- ½ cup butter, plus more for greasing the pan
- 1 ¾ oz. unsweetened chocolate
- 1 cup sugar
- 2 medium eggs, beaten
- 1 cup flour
- 2 tsp. vanilla

- 2 tbsp. water
- 2/3 cup milk

Directions:
1. In a saucepan over a medium heat, melt the butter and chocolate together.
2. Take the saucepan off the heat and stir in the sugar, eggs, flour, and vanilla, combining everything well.
3. Pre-heat your Air Fryer to 350°F.
4. Coat the inside of a baking dish with a little butter. Transfer the batter to the dish and place inside the fryer.
5. Bake for 15 minutes.
6. In the meantime, prepare the caramel sauce. In a small saucepan, slowly bring the water to a boil. Cook for around 3 minutes, until the mixture turns light brown.
7. Lower the heat and allow to cook for another two minutes. Gradually add in the rest of the butter. Take the saucepan off the heat and allow the caramel to cool.
8. When the brownies are ready, slice them into squares. Pour the caramel sauce on top and add on some sliced banana if desired before serving.

430.Mixed Berry Puffed Pastry

Servings: 3
Cooking Time: 20 Minutes
Ingredients:
- 3 pastry dough sheets
- ½ cup mixed berries, mashed
- 1 tbsp. honey
- 2 tbsp. cream cheese
- 3 tbsp. chopped walnuts
- ¼ tsp. vanilla extract

Directions:
1. Pre-heat your Air Fryer to 375°F.
2. Roll out the pastry sheets and spread the cream cheese over each one.
3. In a bowl, combine the berries, vanilla extract and honey.
4. Cover a baking sheet with parchment paper.
5. Spoon equal amounts of the berry mixture into the center of each sheet of pastry. Scatter the chopped walnuts on top.
6. Fold up the pastry around the filling and press down the edges with the back of a fork to seal them.
7. Transfer the baking sheet to the Air Fryer and cook for approximately 15 minutes.

431.Nana's Famous Apple Fritters

Servings: 4
Cooking Time: 20 Minutes
Ingredients:
- 2/3 cup all-purpose flour
- 3 tablespoons granulated sugar
- A pinch of sea salt

- A pinch of freshly grated nutmeg
- 1 teaspoon baking powder
- 2 eggs, whisked
- 1/4 cup milk
- 2 apples, peeled, cored and diced
- 1/2 cup powdered sugar

Directions:
1. Mix the flour, sugar, salt, nutmeg and baking powder.
2. In a separate bowl whisk the eggs with the milk; add this wet mixture into the dry ingredients; mix to combine well.
3. Add the apple pieces and mix again.
4. Cook in the preheated Air Fryer at 370 degrees for 3 minutes, flipping them halfway through the cooking time. Repeat with the remaining batter.
5. Dust with powdered sugar and serve at room temperature. Bon appétit!

432.Cinnamon Ginger Cookies

Servings: 8
Cooking Time: 12 Minutes
Ingredients:
- 1 egg
- 1/2 tsp vanilla
- 1/8 tsp ground cloves
- 1 tsp baking powder
- 3/4 cup erythritol
- 2/4 cup butter, melted
- 1 1/2 cups almond flour
- 1/4 tsp ground nutmeg
- 1/4 tsp ground cinnamon
- 1/2 tsp ground ginger
- Pinch of salt

Directions:
1. In a large bowl, mix together all dry ingredients.
2. In a separate bowl, mix together all wet ingredients.
3. Add dry ingredients to the wet ingredients and mix until dough is formed. Cover and place in the fridge for 30 minutes.
4. Preheat the air fryer to 325 F.
5. Make cookies from dough and place into the air fryer and cook for 12 minutes.
6. Serve and enjoy.

433.Apple-toffee Upside-down Cake

Servings:9
Cooking Time: 30 Minutes
Ingredients:
- ¼ cup almond butter
- ¼ cup sunflower oil
- ½ cup walnuts, chopped
- ¾ cup + 3 tablespoon coconut sugar
- ¾ cup water
- 1 ½ teaspoon mixed spice
- 1 cup plain flour

- 1 lemon, zest
- 1 teaspoon baking soda
- 1 teaspoon vinegar
- 3 baking apples, cored and sliced

Directions:
1. Preheat the air fryer to 390 °F.
2. In a skillet, melt the almond butter and 3 tablespoons sugar. Pour the mixture over a baking dish that will fit in the air fryer. Arrange the slices of apples on top. Set aside.
3. In a mixing bowl, combine flour, ¾ cup sugar, and baking soda. Add the mixed spice.
4. In another bowl, mix the oil, water, vinegar, and lemon zest. Stir in the chopped walnuts.
5. Combine the wet ingredients to the dry ingredients until well combined.
6. Pour over the tin with apple slices.
7. Bake for 30 minutes or until a toothpick inserted comes out clean.

434.Almond Chocolate Cupcakes

Servings: 6
Cooking Time: 20 Minutes
Ingredients:
- 3/4 cup self-raising flour
- 1 cup powdered sugar
- 1/4 teaspoon salt
- 1/4 teaspoon nutmeg, preferably freshly grated
- 1 tablespoon cocoa powder
- 2 ounces butter, softened
- 1 egg, whisked
- 2 tablespoons almond milk
- 1/2 teaspoon vanilla extract
- 1 ½ ounces dark chocolate chunks
- 1/2 cup almonds, chopped

Directions:
1. In a mixing bowl, combine the flour, sugar, salt, nutmeg, and cocoa powder. Mix to combine well.
2. In another mixing bowl, whisk the butter, egg, almond milk, and vanilla.
3. Now, add the wet egg mixture to the dry ingredients. Then, carefully fold in the chocolate chunks and almonds; gently stir to combine.
4. Scrape the batter mixture into muffin cups. Bake your cupcakes at 350 degrees F for 12 minutes until a toothpick comes out clean.
5. Decorate with chocolate sprinkles if desired. Serve and enjoy!

435.Sage Cream

Servings: 4
Cooking Time: 30 Minutes
Ingredients:
- 7 cups red currants
- 1 cup swerve
- 1 cup water

- 6 sage leaves

Directions:
1. In a pan that fits your air fryer, mix all the ingredients, toss, put the pan in the fryer and cook at 330 degrees F for 30 minutes. Discard sage leaves, divide into cups and serve cold.

436.Apple Pie In Air Fryer

Servings:4
Cooking Time: 35 Minutes
Ingredients:
- ½ teaspoon vanilla extract
- 1 beaten egg
- 1 large apple, chopped
- 1 Pillsbury Refrigerator pie crust
- 1 tablespoon butter
- 1 tablespoon ground cinnamon
- 1 tablespoon raw sugar
- 2 tablespoon sugar
- 2 teaspoons lemon juice
- Baking spray

Directions:
1. Lightly grease baking pan of air fryer with cooking spray. Spread pie crust on bottom of pan up to the sides.
2. In a bowl, mix vanilla, sugar, cinnamon, lemon juice, and apples. Pour on top of pie crust. Top apples with butter slices.
3. Cover apples with the other pie crust. Pierce with knife the tops of pie.
4. Spread beaten egg on top of crust and sprinkle sugar.
5. Cover with foil.
6. For 25 minutes, cook on 390°F.
7. Remove foil cook for 10 minutes at 330°F until tops are browned.
8. Serve and enjoy.

437.Blueberry & Lemon Cake

Servings:4
Cooking Time: 17 Minutes
Ingredients:
- 2 eggs
- 1 cup blueberries
- zest from 1 lemon
- juice from 1 lemon
- 1 tsp. vanilla
- brown sugar for topping (a little sprinkling on top of each muffin-less than a teaspoon)
- 2 1/2 cups self-rising flour
- 1/2 cup Monk Fruit (or use your preferred sugar)
- 1/2 cup cream
- 1/4 cup avocado oil (any light cooking oil)

Directions:
1. In mixing bowl, beat well wet Ingredients. Stir in dry ingredients and mix thoroughly.

2. Lightly grease baking pan of air fryer with cooking spray. Pour in batter.
3. For 12 minutes, cook on 330°F.
4. Let it stand in air fryer for 5 minutes.
5. Serve and enjoy.

438.Luscious Cheesecake

Servings:8
Cooking Time:25 Minutes
Ingredients:
- 17.6-ounce ricotta cheese
- 3 eggs
- 3 tablespoons corn starch
- ¾ cup sugar
- 1 tablespoon fresh lemon juice
- 2 teaspoons vanilla extract
- 1 teaspoon fresh lemon zest, grated finely

Directions:
1. Preheat the Air fryer to 320 °F and grease a baking dish lightly.
2. Mix all the ingredients in a bowl and transfer the mixture into the baking dish.
3. Place the baking dish in the Air fryer basket and cook for 25 about minutes.
4. Dish out and serve immediately.

439.Fluffy Butter Cake

Servings: 8
Cooking Time: 35 Minutes
Ingredients:
- 6 egg yolks
- 3 cups almond flour
- 2 tsp vanilla
- 1 egg, lightly beaten
- ¼ cup erythritol
- 1 cup butter
- Pinch of salt

Directions:
1. Preheat the air fryer to 350 F.
2. In a bowl, beat butter and sweetener until fluffy.
3. Add vanilla, egg yolks and beat until well combined.
4. Add remaining ingredients and beat until combined.
5. Pour batter into air fryer cake pan and place into the air fryer and cook for 35 minutes.
6. Slice and serve.

440.Macaroon Bites

Servings: 2
Cooking Time: 30 Minutes
Ingredients:
- 4 egg whites
- ½ tsp vanilla
- ½ tsp EZ-Sweet (or equivalent of 1 cup artificial sweetener)
- 4½ tsp water
- 1 cup unsweetened coconut

Directions:
1. Preheat your fryer to 375°F/190°C.
2. Combine the egg whites, liquids and coconut.
3. Put into the fryer and reduce the heat to 325°F/160°C.
4. Bake for 15 minutes.
5. Serve!

441.Cranberry Jam

Servings: 8
Cooking Time: 20 Minutes
Ingredients:
- 2 pounds cranberries
- 4 ounces black currant
- 2 pounds sugar
- Zest of 1 lime
- 3 tablespoons water

Directions:
1. In a pan that fits your air fryer, add all the ingredients and stir.
2. Place the pan in the fryer and cook at 360 degrees F for 20 minutes.
3. Stir the jam well, divide into cups, refrigerate, and serve cold.

442.Seeds And Almond Cookies

Servings: 6
Cooking Time: 9 Minutes
Ingredients:
- 1 teaspoon chia seeds
- 1 teaspoon sesame seeds
- 1 tablespoon pumpkin seeds, crushed
- 1 egg, beaten
- 2 tablespoons Splenda
- 1 teaspoon vanilla extract
- 1 tablespoon butter
- 4 tablespoons almond flour
- ¼ teaspoon ground cloves
- 1 teaspoon avocado oil

Directions:
1. Put the chia seeds, sesame seeds, and pumpkin seeds in the bowl. Add egg, Splenda, vanilla extract, butter, avocado oil, and ground cloves. Then add almond flour and mix up the mixture until homogenous. Preheat the air fryer to 375F. Line the air fryer basket with baking paper. With the help of the scooper make the cookies and flatten them gently. Place the cookies in the air fryer. Arrange them in one layer. Cook the seeds cookies for 9 minutes.

443.Pineapple Cake

Servings:4
Cooking Time: 50 Minutes
Ingredients:
- 8 oz self-rising flour
- 4 oz butter
- 7 oz pineapple chunks
- ½ cup pineapple juice
- 1 egg
- 2 tbsp milk
- ½ cup sugar

Directions:
1. Preheat the air fryer to 390 F, place the butter and flour into a bowl, and rub the mixture with your fingers until crumbed. Stir in pineapple, sugar, chocolate, and juice. Beat eggs and milk separately, and then add to the batter. Transfer the batter to a previously prepared (greased or lined) cake pan, and cook for 40 minutes. Let cool for at least 10 minutes before serving.

444.Classic Vanilla Mini Cheesecakes

Servings: 6
Cooking Time: 40 Minutes + Chilling Time
Ingredients:
- 1/2 cup almond flour
- 1 ½ tablespoons unsalted butter, melted
- 1 tablespoon white sugar
- 1 (8-ounce) package cream cheese, softened
- 1/4 cup powdered sugar
- 1/2 teaspoon vanilla paste
- 1 egg, at room temperature
- Topping:
- 1 ½ cups sour cream
- 3 tablespoons white sugar
- 1 teaspoon vanilla extract
- 1/4 cup maraschino cherries

Directions:
1. Thoroughly combine the almond flour, butter, and sugar in a mixing bowl. Press the mixture into the bottom of lightly greased custard cups.
2. Then, mix the cream cheese, 1/4 cup of powdered sugar, vanilla, and egg using an electric mixer on low speed. Pour the batter into the pan, covering the crust.
3. Bake in the preheated Air Fryer at 330 degrees F for 35 minutes until edges are puffed and the surface is firm.
4. Mix the sour cream, 3 tablespoons of white sugar, and vanilla for the topping; spread over the crust and allow it to cool to room temperature.
5. Transfer to your refrigerator for 6 to 8 hours. Decorate with maraschino cherries and serve well chilled.

445.Berry Crumble

Servings:6
Cooking Time: 30 Minutes
Ingredients:
- 7 oz fresh raspberries
- 5 oz fresh blueberries
- 5 tbsp cold butter

- 2 tbsp lemon juice
- 1 cup flour
- ½ cup sugar
- 1 tbsp water
- A pinch of salt

Directions:
1. Mass the berries, but make sure there are chunks left. Mix with lemon juice and 2 tbsp of sugar. Place the berry mixture at the bottom of a prepared round cake. Combine the flour with the salt and sugar, in a bowl. Add the water and rub the butter with your fingers until the mixture becomes crumbled. Arrange the crisp batter over the berries. Cook in the air fryer at 390 F for 20 minutes. Serve chilled.

446.Fruity Tacos

Servings:2
Cooking Time: 5 Minutes
Ingredients:
- 2 soft shell tortillas
- 4 tablespoons strawberry jelly
- ¼ cup blueberries
- ¼ cup raspberries
- 2 tablespoons powdered sugar

Directions:
1. Set the temperature of air fryer to 300 degrees F. Lightly, grease an air fryer basket.
2. Arrange the tortillas onto a smooth surface.
3. Spread two tablespoons of strawberry jelly over each tortilla and top each with berries.
4. Sprinkle each with the powdered sugar.
5. Arrange tortillas into the prepared air fryer basket.
6. Air fry for about 5 minutes or until crispy.
7. Remove from the air fryer and transfer the tortillas onto a platter.
8. Serve warm.

447.Ultimate Lemon Coconut Tart

Servings: 8
Cooking Time: 15 Minutes + Chilling Time
Ingredients:
- 2 eggs plus 6 egg yolks
- 1/4 cup lemon juice
- 4 tablespoons unsalted butter
- 1/2 cup powdered swerve
- 4 tablespoons heavy cream
- Crust:
- 1 cup blanched almond meal
- 3/4 cup shredded coconut
- 1 ¼ cups cream cheese, room temperature
- 1 teaspoon apple pie spice blend
- 1 teaspoon pure vanilla extract
- 1/8 teaspoon salt
- 1/2 teaspoon ground anise star

Directions:

1. In a mixing bowl, whisk the eggs. Add in lemon juice, zest, butter, powdered swerve. Place in a double boiler or place a stainless-steel bowl over simmering water.
2. Continue to mix until the temperature reaches 170 degrees. Remove from heat and fold in heavy cream.
3. Place plastic wrap over top and let it cool in your refrigerator.

448.Sugar Butter Fritters

Servings: 16
Cooking Time: 30 Minutes
Ingredients:
- For the dough:
- 4 cups flour
- 1 tsp. kosher salt
- 1 tsp. sugar
- 3 tbsp. butter, at room temperature
- 1 packet instant yeast
- 1 ¼ cups lukewarm water
- For the Cakes
- 1 cup sugar
- Pinch of cardamom
- 1 tsp. cinnamon powder
- 1 stick butter, melted

Directions:
1. Place all of the ingredients in a large bowl and combine well.
2. Add in the lukewarm water and mix until a soft, elastic dough forms.
3. Place the dough on a lightly floured surface and lay a greased sheet of aluminum foil on top of the dough. Refrigerate for 5 to 10 minutes.
4. Remove it from the refrigerator and divide it in two. Mold each half into a log and slice it into 20 pieces.
5. In a shallow bowl, combine the sugar, cardamom and cinnamon.
6. Coat the slices with a light brushing of melted butter and the sugar.
7. Spritz Air Fryer basket with cooking spray.
8. Transfer the slices to the fryer and air fry at 360°F for roughly 10 minutes. Turn each slice once during the baking time.
9. Dust each slice with the sugar before serving.

449.Air Fried Snickerdoodle Poppers

Servings:6
Cooking Time: 30 Minutes
Ingredients:
- 1 can of Pillsbury Grands Flaky Layers Biscuits
- 1 ½ cups cinnamon sugar
- melted butter, for brushing

Directions:

1. Preheat air fryer to 350 F. Unroll the flaky biscuits; cut them into fourths. Roll each ¼ into a ball. Arrange the balls on a lined baking sheet, and cook in the air fryer for 7 minutes, or until golden.
2. Prepare the Jell-O following the package's instructions. Using an injector, inject some of the vanilla pudding into each ball. Brush the balls with melted butter and then coat them with cinnamon sugar.

450.Vanilla Yogurt Cake

Servings: 12
Cooking Time: 30 Minutes
Ingredients:
- 6 eggs, whisked
- 1 teaspoon vanilla extract
- 1 teaspoon baking powder
- 9 ounces coconut flour
- 4 tablespoons stevia
- 8 ounces Greek yogurt

Directions:
1. In a bowl, mix all the ingredients and whisk well. Pour this into a cake pan that fits the air fryer lined with parchment paper, put the pan in the air fryer and cook at 330 degrees F for 30 minutes.

451.White Chocolate Cheesecake

Servings:6
Cooking Time: 34 Minutes
Ingredients:
- 3 eggs, whites and yolks separated
- 1 cup white chocolate, chopped
- ½ cup cream cheese, softened
- 2 tablespoons cocoa powder
- 2 tablespoons powdered sugar
- ¼ cup apricot jam

Directions:
1. In a bowl, add the egg whites and refrigerate to chill before using.
2. In a microwave-safe bowl, add the chocolate and microwave on high heat for about 2 minutes, stirring after every 30 seconds.
3. In the bowl of chocolate, add the cream cheese and microwave for about 1-2 minutes or until cream cheese melts completely.
4. Remove from microwave and stir in cocoa powder and egg yolks.
5. Remove the egg whites from refrigerator and whisk until firm peaks form.
6. Add 1/3 of the mixed egg whites into cheese mixture and gently, stir to combine.
7. Fold in the remaining egg whites.
8. Set the temperature of air fryer to 285 degrees F.
9. Place the mixture into a 6-inch cake pan.

10. Arrange the cake pan into an air fryer basket.
11. Air fry for about 30 minutes.
12. Remove from the air fryer and set aside to cool completely.
13. Refrigerate to chill before serving.
14. Just before serving, dust with the powdered sugar.
15. Finally, spread the jam evenly on top and serve.

452.Pumpkin Custard

Servings: 6
Cooking Time: 32 Minutes
Ingredients:
- 4 egg yolks
- 1/2 tsp cinnamon
- 15 drops liquid stevia
- 15 oz pumpkin puree
- 3/4 cup coconut cream
- 1/8 tsp cloves
- 1/8 tsp ginger

Directions:
1. Preheat the air fryer to 325 F.
2. In a large bowl, combine together pumpkin puree, cinnamon, swerve, cloves, and ginger.
3. Add egg yolks and beat until combined.
4. Add coconut cream and stir well.
5. Pour mixture into the six ramekins and place into the air fryer.
6. Cook for 32 minutes.
7. Let it cool completely then place in the refrigerator.
8. Serve chilled and enjoy.

453.Peppermint Chocolate Cheesecake

Servings: 6
Cooking Time: 40 Minutes
Ingredients:
- 1 cup powdered sugar
- 1/2 cup all-purpose flour
- 1/2 cup butter
- 1 cup mascarpone cheese, at room temperature
- 4 ounces semisweet chocolate, melted
- 1 teaspoon vanilla extract
- 2 drops peppermint extract

Directions:
1. Beat the sugar, flour, and butter in a mixing bowl. Press the mixture into the bottom of a lightly greased baking pan.
2. Bake at 350 degrees F for 18 minutes. Place it in your freezer for 20 minutes.
3. Then, make the cheesecake topping by mixing the remaining ingredients. Place this topping over the crust and allow it to cool in your freezer for a further 15 minutes. Serve well chilled.

454.Aromatic Baked Plum Dessert

Servings:4
Cooking Time:45 Minutes
Ingredients:
- 1/3 cup honey
- 1 teaspoon orange extract
- 3/4 teaspoon candied ginger, minced
- 1 teaspoon vanilla essence
- 3/4 pound purple plums, pitted and halved
- 2 tablespoons cornstarch
- 1/3 teaspoon ground cinnamon
- 1 cup whipped cream, for garnish

Directions:
1. Spritz a baking dish with a nonstick cooking spray or melted coconut butter; arrange plums on the bottom of the baking dish.
2. Then, combine the remaining ingredients, minus whipped cream. Spread this mixture over the plum layer.
3. Bake at 380 degrees F for 35 minutes. Serve topped with cream. Enjoy!

455.Classic White Chocolate Cookies

Servings: 10
Cooking Time: 40 Minutes
Ingredients:
- 3/4 cup butter
- 1 2/3 cups almond flour
- 1/2 cup coconut flour
- 2 tablespoons coconut oil
- 3/4 cup granulated swerve
- 1/3 teaspoon ground anise star
- 1/3 teaspoon ground allspice
- 1/3 teaspoon grated nutmeg
- 1/4 teaspoon fine sea salt
- 8 ounces white chocolate, unsweetened
- 2 eggs, well beaten

Directions:
1. Put all of the above ingredients, minus 1 egg, into a mixing dish. Then, knead with hand until a soft dough is formed. Place in the refrigerator for 20 minutes.
2. Roll the chilled dough into small balls; flatten your balls and preheat the Air Fryer r to 350 degrees F.
3. Make an egg wash by using the remaining egg. Then, glaze the cookies with the egg wash; bake about 11 minutes. Bon appétit!

456.Blueberry Cake

Servings:6
Cooking Time:25 Minutes
Ingredients:
- 3 eggs
- 1 cup almond flour
- 1 stick butter, room temperature
- 1/3 cup blueberries
- 1½ teaspoons baking powder
- ½ cup sour cream
- 2/3 cup swerve
- 2 teaspoons vanilla

Directions:
1. Preheat the Air fryer to 370 °F and grease a baking pan lightly.
2. Mix all the ingredients in a bowl except blueberries.
3. Pour the batter in the baking pan and fold in the blueberries.
4. Mix well and transfer the pan in the Air fryer basket.
5. Cook for about 25 minutes and cut into slices to serve.

457.Classic Pound Cake

Servings: 8
Cooking Time: 35 Minutes
Ingredients:
- 1 stick butter, at room temperature
- 1 cup swerve
- 4 eggs
- 1 ½ cups coconut flour
- 1/2 teaspoon baking powder
- 1/2 teaspoon baking soda
- 1/4 teaspoon salt
- A pinch of freshly grated nutmeg
- A pinch of ground star anise
- 1/2 cup buttermilk
- 1 teaspoon vanilla essence

Directions:
1. Begin by preheating your Air Fryer to 320 degrees F. Spritz the bottom and sides of a baking pan with cooking spray.
2. Beat the butter and swerve with a hand mixer until creamy. Then, fold in the eggs, one at a time, and mix well until fluffy.
3. Stir in the flour along with the remaining ingredients. Mix to combine well. Scrape the batter into the prepared baking pan.
4. Bake for 15 minutes; rotate the pan and bake an additional 15 minutes, until the top of the cake springs back when gently pressed with your fingers. Bon appétit!

458.Espresso Cinnamon Cookies

Servings: 12
Cooking Time: 15 Minutes
Ingredients:
- 8 tablespoons ghee, melted
- 1 cup almond flour
- ¼ cup brewed espresso
- ¼ cup swerve
- ½ tablespoon cinnamon powder
- 2 teaspoons baking powder
- 2 eggs, whisked

Directions:
1. In a bowl, mix all the ingredients and whisk well. Spread medium balls on a cookie sheet

lined parchment paper, flatten them, put the cookie sheet in your air fryer and cook at 350 degrees F for 15 minutes. Serve the cookies cold.

459.Apple Crumble

Servings:4
Cooking Time: 25 Minutes
Ingredients:
- 1 (14-ounces) can apple pie filling
- ¼ cup butter, softened
- 9 tablespoons self-rising flour
- 7 tablespoons caster sugar
- Pinch of salt

Directions:

1. Set the temperature of air fryer to 320 degrees F. Lightly, grease a baking dish.
2. Place apple pie filling evenly into the prepared baking dish.
3. In a medium bowl, add the remaining ingredients and mix until a crumbly mixture forms.
4. Spread the mixture evenly over apple pie filling.
5. Arrange the baking dish in an air fryer basket.
6. Air fry for about 25 minutes.
7. Remove the baking dish from air fryer and place onto a wire rack to cool for about 10 minutes.
8. Serve warm.

OTHER AIR FRYER RECIPES

460.Italian Eggs With Smoked Salmon

Servings: 4
Cooking Time: 25 Minutes
Ingredients:
- 1/3 cup Asiago cheese, grated
- 1/3 teaspoon dried dill weed
- 1/2 tomato, chopped
- 6 eggs
- 1/3 cup milk
- Pan spray
- 1 cup smoked salmon, chopped
- Fine sea salt and freshly cracked black pepper, to taste
- 1/3 teaspoon smoked cayenne pepper

Directions:
1. Set your air fryer to cook at 365 degrees F. In a mixing bowl, whisk the eggs, milk, smoked cayenne pepper, salt, black pepper, and dill weed.
2. Lightly grease 4 ramekins with pan spray of choice; divide the egg/milk mixture among the prepared ramekins.
3. Add the salmon and tomato; top with the grated Asiago cheese. Finally, air-fry for 16 minutes. Bon appétit!

461.Colby Potato Patties

Servings: 8
Cooking Time: 15 Minutes
Ingredients:
- 2 pounds white potatoes, peeled and grated
- 1/2 cup scallions, finely chopped
- 1/2 teaspoon freshly ground black pepper, or more to taste
- 1 tablespoon fine sea salt
- 1/2 teaspoon hot paprika
- 2 cups Colby cheese, shredded
- 1/4 cup canola oil
- 1 cup crushed crackers

Directions:
1. Firstly, boil the potatoes until fork tender. Drain, peel and mash your potatoes.
2. Thoroughly mix the mashed potatoes with scallions, pepper, salt, paprika, and cheese. Then, shape the balls using your hands. Now, flatten the balls to make the patties.
3. In a shallow bowl, mix canola oil with crushed crackers. Roll the patties over the crumb mixture.
4. Next, cook your patties at 360 degrees F approximately 10 minutes, working in batches. Serve with tabasco mayo if desired. Bon appétit!

462.Southwest Bean Potpie

Servings: 5
Cooking Time: 30 Minutes
Ingredients:
- 1 tablespoon olive oil
- 2 sweet peppers, seeded and sliced
- 1 carrot, chopped
- 1 onion, chopped
- 2 garlic cloves, minced
- 1 cup cooked bacon, diced
- 1 ½ cups beef bone broth
- 20 ounces canned red kidney beans, drained
- Sea salt and freshly ground black pepper, to taste
- 1 package (8 1/2-ounce) cornbread mix
- 1/2 cup milk
- 2 tablespoons butter, melted

Directions:
1. Heat the olive oil in a saucepan over medium-high heat. Now, cook the peppers, carrot, onion, and garlic until they have softened, about 7 minutes
2. Add the bacon and broth. Bring to a boil and cook for 2 minutes more. Stir in the kidney beans, salt and black pepper; continue to cook until everything is heated through.
3. Transfer the mixture to the lightly greased baking pan.
4. In a small bowl, combine the muffin mix, milk, and melted butter. Stir until well mixed and spoon evenly over the bean mixture. Smooth it with a spatula and transfer to the Air Fryer cooking basket.
5. Bake in the preheated Air Fryer at 400 degrees F for 12 minutes. Place on a wire rack to cool slightly before slicing and serving. Bon appétit!

463.Double Cheese Mushroom Balls

Servings: 4
Cooking Time: 30 Minutes
Ingredients:
- 1 ½ tablespoons olive oil
- 4 ounces cauliflower florets
- 3 garlic cloves, peeled and minced
- 1/2 yellow onion, finely chopped
- 1 small-sized red chili pepper, seeded and minced
- 1/2 cup roasted vegetable stock
- 2 cups white mushrooms, finely chopped
- Sea salt and ground black pepper, or more to taste
- 1/2 cup Swiss cheese, grated
- 1/4 cup pork rinds
- 1 egg, beaten
- 1/4 cup Romano cheese, grated

Directions:

1. Blitz the cauliflower florets in your food processor until they're crumbled (it is the size of rice).
2. Heat a saucepan over a moderate heat; now, heat the oil and sweat the cauliflower, garlic, onions, and chili pepper until tender.
3. Throw in the mushrooms and fry until they are fragrant and the liquid has almost evaporated.
4. Add the vegetable stock and boil for 18 minutes. Now, add the salt, black pepper, Swiss cheese pork rinds, and beaten egg; mix to combine.
5. Allow the mixture to cool completely. Shape the mixture into balls. Dip the balls in the grated Romano cheese. Air-fry the balls for 7 minutes at 400 degrees F. Bon appétit!

464.Breakfast Pizza Cups

Servings: 4
Cooking Time: 30 Minutes
Ingredients:
- 12 slices pepperoni, 2-inch
- 2 tablespoons butter, melted
- 4 eggs, beaten
- 1/4 teaspoon ground black pepper
- Salt, to taste
- 4 slices smoked ham, chopped
- 1 cup mozzarella cheese, shredded
- 4 tablespoons ketchup

Directions:
1. Start by preheating your Air Fryer to 350 degrees F. Now, lightly grease a muffin tin with nonstick spray.
2. Place pepperoni into a mini muffin pan. In a mixing bowl, thoroughly combine the remaining ingredients.
3. Bake in the preheated Air Fryer for 20 minutes until a toothpick inserted comes out clean. Let it cool for 5 minutes before removing to a serving platter.
4. Bon appétit!

465.Omelet With Mushrooms And Peppers

Servings: 2
Cooking Time: 20 Minutes
Ingredients:
- 1 tablespoon olive oil
- 1/2 cup scallions, chopped
- 1 bell pepper, seeded and thinly sliced
- 6 ounces button mushrooms, thinly sliced
- 4 eggs
- 2 tablespoons milk
- Sea salt and freshly ground black pepper, to taste
- 1 tablespoon fresh chives, for serving

Directions:

1. Heat the olive oil in a skillet over medium-high heat. Now, sauté the scallions and peppers until aromatic.
2. Add the mushrooms and continue to cook an additional 3 minutes or until tender. Reserve.
3. Generously grease a baking pan with nonstick cooking spray.
4. Then, whisk the eggs, milk, salt, and black pepper. Spoon into the prepared baking pan.
5. Cook in the preheated Air Fryer at 360 F for 4 minutes. Flip and cook for a further 3 minutes.
6. Place the reserved mushroom filling on one side of the omelet. Fold your omelet in half and slide onto a serving plate. Serve immediately garnished with fresh chives. Bon appétit!

466.Beer-braised Short Loin

Servings: 4
Cooking Time: 15 Minutes
Ingredients:
- 1 ½ pounds short loin
- 2 tablespoons olive oil
- 1 bottle beer
- 2-3 cloves garlic, finely minced
- 2 Turkish bay leaves

Directions:
1. Pat the beef dry; then, tenderize the beef with a meat mallet to soften the fibers. Place it in a large-sized mixing dish.
2. Add the remaining ingredients; toss to coat well and let it marinate for at least 1 hour.
3. Cook about 7 minutes at 395 degrees F; after that, pause the Air Fryer. Flip the meat over and cook for another 8 minutes, or until it's done.

467.Breakfast Eggs With Swiss Chard And Ham

Servings: 2
Cooking Time: 20 Minutes
Ingredients:
- 2 eggs
- 1/4 teaspoon dried or fresh marjoram
- 2 teaspoons chili powder
- 1/3 teaspoon kosher salt
- 1/2 cup steamed Swiss Chard
- 1/4 teaspoon dried or fresh rosemary
- 4 pork ham slices
- 1/3 teaspoon ground black pepper, or more to taste

Directions:
1. Divide the Swiss Chard and ham among 2 ramekins; crack an egg into each ramekin. Sprinkle with seasonings.
2. Cook for 15 minutes at 335 degrees F or until your eggs reach desired texture.

3. Serve warm with spicy tomato ketchup and pickles. Bon appétit!

468.Mini Bread Puddings With Cinnamon Glaze

Servings: 5
Cooking Time: 50 Minutes
Ingredients:
- 5 tablespoons butter
- 1/2 pound cinnamon-raisin bread, cubed
- 1 cup milk
- 1/2 cup double cream
- 2/3 cup sugar
- 1 tablespoon honey
- 1 teaspoon pure vanilla extract
- 2 eggs, lightly beaten
- Cinnamon Glaze:
- 1/4 cup powdered sugar
- 1 teaspoon ground cinnamon
- 1 tablespoon milk
- 1/2 teaspoon vanilla

Directions:
1. Begin by preheating your Air Fryer to 370 degrees F. Lightly butter five ramekins.
2. Place the bread cubes in the greased ramekins. In a mixing bowl, thoroughly combine the milk, double cream, sugar, honey, vanilla, and eggs.
3. Pour the custard over the bread cubes. Let it stand for 30 minutes, occasionally pressing with a wide spatula to submerge.
4. Cook in the preheated Air Fryer at 370 degrees F degrees for 7 minutes; check to ensure even cooking and cook an additional 5 to 6 minutes.
5. Meanwhile, prepare the glaze by whisking the powdered sugar, cinnamon, milk, and vanilla until smooth. Top the bread puddings with the glaze and serve at room temperature. Bon appétit!

469.Italian Creamy Frittata With Kale

Servings: 3
Cooking Time: 20 Minutes
Ingredients:
- 1 yellow onion, finely chopped
- 6 ounces wild mushrooms, sliced
- 6 eggs
- 1/4 cup double cream
- 1/2 teaspoon cayenne pepper
- Sea salt and ground black pepper, to taste
- 1 tablespoon butter, melted
- 2 tablespoons fresh Italian parsley, chopped
- 2 cups kale, chopped
- 1/2 cup mozzarella, shredded

Directions:
1. Begin by preheating the Air Fryer to 360 degrees F. Spritz the sides and bottom of a baking pan with cooking oil.

2. Add the onions and wild mushrooms, and cook in the preheated Air Fryer at 360 degrees F for 4 to 5 minutes.
3. In a mixing dish, whisk the eggs and double cream until pale. Add the spices, butter, parsley, and kale; stir until everything is well incorporated.
4. Pour the mixture into the baking pan with the mushrooms.
5. Top with the cheese. Cook in the preheated Air Fryer for 10 minutes. Serve immediately and enjoy!

470.Cheese And Chive Stuffed Chicken Rolls

Servings: 6
Cooking Time: 20 Minutes
Ingredients:
- 2 eggs, well-whisked
- Tortilla chips, crushed
- 1 1/2 tablespoons extra-virgin olive oil
- 1 ½ tablespoons fresh chives, chopped
- 3 chicken breasts, halved lengthwise
- 1 ½ cup soft cheese
- 2 teaspoons sweet paprika
- 1/2 teaspoon whole grain mustard
- 1/2 teaspoon cumin powder
- 1/3 teaspoon fine sea salt
- 1/3 cup fresh cilantro, chopped
- 1/3 teaspoon freshly ground black pepper, or more to taste

Directions:
1. Flatten out each piece of the chicken breast using a rolling pin. Then, grab three mixing dishes.
2. In the first one, combine the soft cheese with the cilantro, fresh chives, cumin, and mustard.
3. In another mixing dish, whisk the eggs together with the sweet paprika. In the third dish, combine the salt, black pepper, and crushed tortilla chips.
4. Spread the cheese mixture over each piece of chicken. Repeat with the remaining pieces of the chicken breasts; now, roll them up.
5. Coat each chicken roll with the whisked egg; dredge each chicken roll into the tortilla chips mixture. Lower the rolls onto the air fryer cooking basket. Drizzle extra-virgin olive oil over all rolls.
6. Air fry at 345 degrees F for 28 minutes, working in batches. Serve warm, garnished with sour cream if desired.

471.Easy Cheesy Broccoli

Servings: 4
Cooking Time: 25 Minutes
Ingredients:

- 1/3 cup grated yellow cheese
- 1 large-sized head broccoli, stemmed and cut small florets
- 2 1/2 tablespoons canola oil
- 2 teaspoons dried rosemary
- 2 teaspoons dried basil
- Salt and ground black pepper, to taste

Directions:
1. Bring a medium pan filled with a lightly salted water to a boil. Then, boil the broccoli florets for about 3 minutes.
2. Then, drain the broccoli florets well; toss them with the canola oil, rosemary, basil, salt and black pepper.
3. Set your air fryer to 390 degrees F; arrange the seasoned broccoli in the cooking basket; set the timer for 17 minutes. Toss the broccoli halfway through the cooking process.
4. Serve warm topped with grated cheese and enjoy!

472.English Muffins With A Twist

Servings: 4
Cooking Time: 15 Minutes
Ingredients:
- 4 English muffins, split in half
- 2 eggs
- 1/3 cup milk
- 1/4 cup heavy cream
- 2 tablespoons honey
- 1 teaspoon pure vanilla extract
- 1/4 cup confectioners' sugar

Directions:
1. Cut the muffins crosswise into strips.
2. In a mixing bowl, whisk the eggs, milk, heavy cream, honey, and vanilla extract.
3. Dip each piece of muffins into the egg mixture and place in the parchment-lined Air Fryer basket.
4. Cook in the preheated Air Fryer at 360 degrees F for 6 to 7 minutes, turning them over halfway through the cooking time to ensure even cooking.
5. Dust with confectioners' sugar and serve warm.

473.Scrambled Egg Muffins With Cheese

Servings: 6
Cooking Time: 20 Minutes
Ingredients:
- 6 ounces smoked turkey sausage, chopped
- 6 eggs, lightly beaten
- 2 tablespoons shallots, finely chopped
- 2 garlic cloves, minced
- Sea salt and ground black pepper, to taste
- 1 teaspoon cayenne pepper
- 6 ounces Monterey Jack cheese, shredded

Directions:

1. Simply combine the sausage, eggs, shallots, garlic, salt, black pepper, and cayenne pepper in a mixing dish. Mix to combine well.
2. Spoon the mixture into 6 standard-size muffin cups with paper liners.
3. Bake in the preheated Air Fryer at 340 degrees F for 8 minutes. Top with the cheese and bake an additional 8 minutes. Enjoy!

474.Salted Pretzel Crescents

Servings: 4
Cooking Time: 20 Minutes
Ingredients:
- 1 can crescent rolls
- 10 cups water
- 1/2 cup baking soda
- 1 egg, whisked with 1 tablespoon water
- 1 tablespoon poppy seeds
- 2 tablespoons sesame seed
- 1 teaspoon coarse sea salt

Directions:
1. Unroll the dough onto your work surface; separate into 8 triangles.
2. In a large saucepan, bring the water and baking soda to a boil over high heat.
3. Cook each roll for 30 seconds. Remove from the water using a slotted spoon; place on a kitchen towel to drain.
4. Repeat with the remaining rolls. Now, brush the tops with the egg wash; sprinkle each roll with the poppy seeds, sesame seed and coarse sea salt. Cover and let rest for 10 minutes.
5. Arrange the pretzels in the lightly greased Air Fryer basket.
6. Bake in the preheated Air Fryer at 340 degrees for 7 minutes or until golden brown. Bon appétit!

475.Snapper With Gruyere Cheese

Servings: 4
Cooking Time: 25 Minutes
Ingredients:
- 2 tablespoons olive oil
- 1 shallot, thinly sliced
- 2 garlic cloves, minced
- 1 ½ pounds snapper fillets
- Sea salt and ground black pepper, to taste
- 1 teaspoon cayenne pepper
- 1/2 teaspoon dried basil
- 1/2 cup tomato puree
- 1/2 cup white wine
- 1 cup Gruyere cheese, shredded

Directions:
1. Heat 1 tablespoon of olive oil in a saucepan over medium-high heat. Now, cook the shallot and garlic until tender and aromatic.

2. Preheat your Air Fryer to 370 degrees F.
3. Grease a casserole dish with 1 tablespoon of olive oil. Place the snapper fillet in the casserole dish. Season with salt, black pepper, and cayenne pepper. Add the sautéed shallot mixture.
4. Add the basil, tomato puree and wine to the casserole dish. Cook for 10 minutes in the preheated Air Fryer.
5. Top with the shredded cheese and cook an additional 7 minutes. Serve immediately.

476.Chive, Feta And Chicken Frittata

Servings: 4
Cooking Time: 10 Minutes
Ingredients:
- 1/3 cup Feta cheese, crumbled
- 1 teaspoon dried rosemary
- ½ teaspoon brown sugar
- 2 tablespoons fish sauce
- 1 ½ cup cooked chicken breasts, boneless and shredded
- 1/2 teaspoon coriander sprig, finely chopped
- 3 medium-sized whisked eggs
- 1/3 teaspoon ground white pepper
- 1 cup fresh chives, chopped
- 1/2 teaspoon garlic paste
- Fine sea salt, to taste
- Nonstick cooking spray

Directions:
1. Grab a baking dish that fit in your air fryer.
2. Lightly coat the inside of the baking dish with a nonstick cooking spray of choice. Stir in all ingredients, minus Feta cheese. Stir to combine well.
3. Set your machine to cook at 335 degrees for 8 minutes; check for doneness. Scatter crumbled Feta over the top and eat immediately!

477.Savory Italian Crespelle

Servings: 3
Cooking Time: 35 Minutes
Ingredients:
- 3/4 cup all-purpose flour
- 2 eggs, beaten
- 1/4 teaspoon allspice
- 1/2 teaspoon salt
- 3/4 cup milk
- 1 cup ricotta cheese
- 1/2 cup Parmigiano-Reggiano cheese, preferably freshly grated
- 1 cup marinara sauce

Directions:
1. Mix the flour, eggs, allspice, and salt in a large bowl. Gradually add the milk, whisking continuously, until well combined.
2. Let it stand for 20 minutes.

3. Spritz the Air Fryer baking pan with cooking spray. Pour the batter into the prepared pan.
4. Cook at 230 degrees F for 3 minutes. Flip and cook until browned in spots, 2 to 3 minutes longer.
5. Repeat with the remaining batter. Serve with the cheese and marinara sauce. Bon appétit!

478.Potato Appetizer With Garlic-mayo Sauce

Servings: 4
Cooking Time: 19 Minutes
Ingredients:
- 2 tablespoons vegetable oil of choice
- Kosher salt and freshly ground black pepper, to taste
- 3 Russet potatoes, cut into wedges
- For the Dipping Sauce:
- 2 teaspoons dried rosemary, crushed
- 3 garlic cloves, minced
- 1/3 teaspoon dried marjoram, crushed
- 1/4 cup sour cream
- 1/3 cup mayonnaise

Directions:
1. Lightly grease your potatoes with a thin layer of vegetable oil. Season with salt and ground black pepper.
2. Arrange the seasoned potato wedges in an air fryer cooking basket. Bake at 395 degrees F for 15 minutes, shaking once or twice.
3. In the meantime, prepare the dipping sauce by mixing all the sauce ingredients. Serve the potatoes with the dipping sauce and enjoy!

479.Old-fashioned Beef Stroganoff

Servings: 4
Cooking Time: 20 Minutes
Ingredients:
- 3/4 pound beef sirloin steak, cut into small-sized strips
- 1/4 cup balsamic vinegar
- 1 tablespoon brown mustard
- 2 tablespoons all-purpose flour
- 1 tablespoon butter
- 1 cup beef broth
- 1 cup leek, chopped
- 2 cloves garlic, crushed
- 1 teaspoon cayenne pepper
- Sea salt flakes and crushed red pepper, to taste
- 1 cup sour cream
- 2 ½ tablespoons tomato paste

Directions:
1. Place the beef along with the balsamic vinegar and the mustard in a mixing dish;

cover and marinate in your refrigerator for about 1 hour.

2. Then, coat the beef strips with the flour; butter the inside of a baking dish and put the beef into the dish.
3. Add the broth, leeks and garlic. Cook at 380 degrees for 8 minutes. Pause the machine and add the cayenne pepper, salt, red pepper, sour cream and tomato paste; cook for additional 7 minutes.
4. Check for doneness and serve with warm egg noodles, if desired. Bon appétit!

480.Rosemary Roasted Mixed Nuts

Servings: 6
Cooking Time: 20 Minutes
Ingredients:
- 2 tablespoons butter, at room temperature
- 1 tablespoon dried rosemary
- 1 teaspoon coarse sea salt
- 1/2 teaspoon paprika
- 1/2 cup pine nuts
- 1 cup pecans
- 1/2 cup hazelnuts

Directions:
1. Toss all the ingredients in the mixing bowl.
2. Line the Air Fryer basket with baking parchment. Spread out the coated nuts in a single layer in the basket.
3. Roast at 350 degrees F for 6 to 8 minutes, shaking the basket once or twice. Work in batches. Enjoy!

481.Frittata With Porcini Mushrooms

Servings: 4
Cooking Time: 40 Minutes
Ingredients:
- 3 cups Porcini mushrooms, thinly sliced
- 1 tablespoon melted butter
- 1 shallot, peeled and slice into thin rounds
- 1 garlic cloves, peeled and finely minced
- 1 lemon grass, cut into 1-inch pieces
- 1/3 teaspoon table salt
- 8 eggs
- 1/2 teaspoon ground black pepper, preferably freshly ground
- 1 teaspoon cumin powder
- 1/3 teaspoon dried or fresh dill weed
- 1/2 cup goat cheese, crumbled

Directions:
1. Melt the butter in a nonstick skillet that is placed over medium heat. Sauté the shallot, garlic, thinly sliced Porcini mushrooms, and lemon grass over a moderate heat until they have softened. Now, reserve the sautéed mixture.
2. Preheat your Air Fryer to 335 degrees F. Then, in a mixing bowl, beat the eggs until frothy. Now, add the seasonings and mix to combine well.
3. Coat the sides and bottom of a baking dish with a thin layer of vegetable spray. Pour the egg/seasoning mixture into the baking dish; throw in the onion/mushroom sauté. Top with the crumbled goat cheese.
4. Place the baking dish in the Air Fryer cooking basket. Cook for about 32 minutes or until your frittata is set. Enjoy!

482.Delicious Hot Fruit Bake

Servings: 4
Cooking Time: 40 Minutes
Ingredients:
- 2 cups blueberries
- 2 cups raspberries
- 1 tablespoon cornstarch
- 3 tablespoons maple syrup
- 2 tablespoons coconut oil, melted
- A pinch of freshly grated nutmeg
- A pinch of salt
- 1 cinnamon stick
- 1 vanilla bean

Directions:
1. Place your berries in a lightly greased baking dish. Sprinkle the cornstarch onto the fruit.
2. Whisk the maple syrup, coconut oil, nutmeg, and salt in a mixing dish; add this mixture to the berries and gently stir to combine.
3. Add the cinnamon and vanilla. Bake in the preheated Air Fryer at 370 degrees F for 35 minutes. Serve warm or at room temperature. Enjoy!

483.Japanese Fried Rice With Eggs

Servings: 2
Cooking Time: 30 Minutes
Ingredients:
- 2 cups cauliflower rice
- 2 teaspoons sesame oil
- Sea salt and freshly ground black pepper, to your liking
- 2 eggs, beaten
- 2 scallions, white and green parts separated, chopped
- 1 tablespoon Shoyu sauce
- 1 tablespoon sake
- 2 tablespoons Kewpie Japanese mayonnaise

Directions:
1. Thoroughly combine the cauliflower rice, sesame oil, salt, and pepper in a baking dish.
2. Cook at 340 degrees F about 13 minutes, stirring halfway through the cooking time.
3. Pour the eggs over the cauliflower rice and continue to cook about 5 minutes. Next, add the scallions and stir to combine. Continue

to cook 2 to 3 minutes longer or until everything is heated through.
4. Meanwhile, make the sauce by whisking the Shoyu sauce, sake, and Japanese mayonnaise in a mixing bowl.
5. Divide the fried cauliflower rice between individual bowls and serve with the prepared sauce. Enjoy!

484.Two Cheese And Shrimp Dip

Servings: 8
Cooking Time: 25 Minutes
Ingredients:
- 2 teaspoons butter, melted
- 8 ounces shrimp, peeled and deveined
- 2 garlic cloves, minced
- 1/4 cup chicken stock
- 2 tablespoons fresh lemon juice
- Salt and ground black pepper, to taste
- 1/2 teaspoon red pepper flakes
- 4 ounces cream cheese, at room temperature
- 1/2 cup sour cream
- 4 tablespoons mayonnaise
- 1/4 cup mozzarella cheese, shredded

Directions:
1. Start by preheating the Air Fryer to 395 degrees F. Grease the sides and bottom of a baking dish with the melted butter.
2. Place the shrimp, garlic, chicken stock, lemon juice, salt, black pepper, and red pepper flakes in the baking dish.
3. Transfer the baking dish to the cooking basket and bake for 10 minutes. Add the mixture to your food processor; pulse until the coarsely is chopped.
4. Add the cream cheese, sour cream, and mayonnaise. Top with the mozzarella cheese and bake in the preheated Air Fryer at 360 degrees F for 6 to 7 minutes or until the cheese is bubbling.
5. Serve immediately with breadsticks if desired. Bon appétit!

485.Scrambled Eggs With Sausage

Servings: 6
Cooking Time: 25 Minutes
Ingredients:
- 1 teaspoon lard
- 1/2 pound turkey sausage
- 6 eggs
- 1 scallion, chopped
- 1 garlic clove, minced
- 1 sweet pepper, seeded and chopped
- 1 chili pepper, seeded and chopped
- Sea salt and ground black pepper, to taste
- 1/2 cup Swiss cheese, shredded

Directions:

1. Start by preheating your Air Fryer to 330 degrees F. Now, spritz 6 silicone molds with cooking spray.
2. Melt the lard in a saucepan over medium-high heat. Now, cook the sausage for 5 minutes or until no longer pink.
3. Coarsely chop the sausage; add the eggs, scallions, garlic, peppers, salt, and black pepper. Divide the egg mixture between the silicone molds. Top with the shredded cheese.
4. Bake in the preheated Air Fryer at 340 degrees F for 15 minutes, checking halfway through the cooking time to ensure even cooking. Enjoy!

486.Decadent Frittata With Roasted Garlic And Sausage

Servings: 6
Cooking Time: 20 Minutes
Ingredients:
- 6 large-sized eggs
- 2 tablespoons butter, melted
- 3 tablespoons cream
- 1 cup chicken sausage, chopped
- 2 tablespoons roasted garlic, pressed
- 1/3 cup goat cheese such as Caprino, crumbled
- 1 teaspoon smoked cayenne pepper
- 1 teaspoon freshly ground black pepper
- 1/2 red onion, peeled and chopped
- 1 teaspoon fine sea salt

Directions:
1. First of all, grease six oven safe ramekins with melted butter. Then, divide roasted garlic and red onion among your ramekins. Add chicken sausage and toss to combine.
2. Beat the eggs with cream until well combined and pale; sprinkle with cayenne pepper, salt, and black pepper; beat again.
3. Scrape the mixture into your ramekins and air-fry for about 13 minutes at 355 degrees F.
4. Top with crumbled cheese and serve immediately.

487.Country-style Apple Fries

Servings: 4
Cooking Time: 20 Minutes
Ingredients:
- 1/2 cup milk
- 1 egg
- 1/2 all-purpose flour
- 1 teaspoon baking powder
- 4 tablespoons brown sugar
- 1 teaspoon vanilla extract
- 1/2 teaspoon ground cloves
- A pinch of kosher salt
- A pinch of grated nutmeg

- 1 tablespoon coconut oil, melted
- 2 Pink Lady apples, cored, peeled, slice into pieces (shape and size of French fries
- 1/3 cup granulated sugar
- 1 teaspoon ground cinnamon

Directions:
1. In a mixing bowl, whisk the milk and eggs; gradually stir in the flour; add the baking powder, brown sugar, vanilla, cloves, salt, nutmeg, and melted coconut oil. Mix to combine well.
2. Dip each apple slice into the batter, coating on all sides. Spritz the bottom of the cooking basket with cooking oil.
3. Cook the apple fries in the preheated Air Fryer at 395 degrees F approximately 8 minutes, turning them over halfway through the cooking time.
4. Cook in small batches to ensure even cooking.
5. In the meantime, mix the granulated sugar with the ground cinnamon; sprinkle the cinnamon sugar over the apple fries. Serve warm.

488.Stuffed Mushrooms With Cheese

Servings: 5
Cooking Time: 15 Minutes
Ingredients:
- 1/2 cup parmesan cheese, grated
- 2 cloves garlic, pressed
- 2 tablespoons fresh coriander, chopped
- 1/3 teaspoon kosher salt
- 1/2 teaspoon crushed red pepper flakes
- 1 ½ tablespoons olive oil
- 20 medium-sized mushrooms, cut off the stems
- 1/2 cup Gorgonzola cheese, grated
- 1/4 cup low-fat mayonnaise
- 1 teaspoon prepared horseradish, well-drained
- 1 tablespoon fresh parsley, finely chopped

Directions:
1. Mix the parmesan cheese together with the garlic, coriander, salt, red pepper, and the olive oil; mix to combine well.
2. Stuff the mushroom caps with the parmesan filling. Top with grated Gorgonzola.
3. Place the mushrooms in the Air Fryer grill pan and slide them into the machine. Grill them at 380 degrees F for 8 to 12 minutes or until the stuffing is warmed through.
4. Meanwhile, prepare the horseradish mayo by mixing the mayonnaise, horseradish and parsley. Serve with the warm fried mushrooms. Enjoy!

489.Easy Pork Burgers With Blue Cheese

Servings: 6

Cooking Time: 44 Minutes
Ingredients:
- 1/3 cup blue cheese, crumbled
- 6 hamburger buns, toasted
- 2 teaspoons dried basil
- 1/3 teaspoon smoked paprika
- 1 pound ground pork
- 2 tablespoons tomato puree
- 2 small-sized onions, peeled and chopped
- 1/2 teaspoon ground black pepper
- 3 garlic cloves, minced
- 1 teaspoon fine sea salt

Directions:
1. Start by preheating your air fryer to 385 degrees F.
2. In a mixing dish, combine the pork, onion, garlic, tomato puree, and seasonings; mix to combine well.
3. Form the pork mixture into six patties; cook the burgers for 23 minutes. Pause the machine, turn the temperature to 365 degrees F and cook for 18 more minutes.
4. Place the prepared burger on the bottom bun; top with blue cheese; assemble the burgers and serve warm.

490.Cheesy Pasilla Turkey

Servings: 2
Cooking Time: 30 Minutes
Ingredients:
- 1/3 cup Parmesan cheese, shredded
- 2 turkey breasts, cut into four pieces
- 1/3 cup mayonnaise
- 1 ½ tablespoons sour cream
- 1/2 cup crushed crackers
- 1 dried Pasilla peppers
- 1 teaspoon onion salt
- 1/3 teaspoon mixed peppercorns, freshly cracked

Directions:
1. In a shallow bowl, mix the crushed crackers, Parmesan cheese, onion salt, and the cracked mixed peppercorns together.
2. In a food processor, blitz the mayonnaise, along with the cream and dried Pasilla peppers until there are no lumps.
3. Coat the turkey breasts with this mixture, ensuring that all sides are covered.
4. Then, coat each piece of turkey in the Parmesan/cracker mix.
5. Now, preheat the air fryer to 365 degrees F; cook for 28 minutes until thoroughly cooked.

491.Frittata With Turkey Breasts And Cottage Cheese

Servings: 4
Cooking Time: 50 Minutes
Ingredients:

- 1 tablespoon olive oil
- 1 pound turkey breasts, slices
- 6 large-sized eggs
- 3 tablespoons Greek yogurt
- 3 tablespoons Cottage cheese, crumbled
- 1/4 teaspoon ground black pepper
- 1/4 teaspoon red pepper flakes, crushed
- Himalayan salt, to taste
- 1 red bell pepper, seeded and sliced
- 1 green bell pepper, seeded and sliced

Directions:
1. Grease the cooking basket with olive oil. Add the turkey and cook in the preheated Air Fryer at 350 degrees F for 30 minutes, flipping them over halfway through. Cut into bite-sized strips and reserve.
2. Now, beat the eggs with Greek yogurt, cheese, black pepper, red pepper, and salt. Add the bell peppers to a baking pan that is previously lightly greased with a cooking spray.
3. Add the turkey strips; pour the egg mixture over all ingredients.
4. Bake in the preheated Air Fryer at 360 degrees F for 15 minutes. Serve right away!

492.Easy Frittata With Mozzarella And Kale

Servings: 3
Cooking Time: 20 Minutes
Ingredients:
- 1 yellow onion, finely chopped
- 6 ounces wild mushrooms, sliced
- 6 eggs
- 1/4 cup double cream
- 1/2 teaspoon cayenne pepper
- Sea salt and ground black pepper, to taste
- 1 tablespoon butter, melted
- 2 tablespoons fresh Italian parsley, chopped
- 2 cups kale, chopped
- 1/2 cup mozzarella, shredded

Directions:
1. Begin by preheating the Air Fryer to 360 degrees F. Spritz the sides and bottom of a baking pan with cooking oil.
2. Add the onions and wild mushrooms, and cook in the preheated Air Fryer at 360 degrees F for 4 to 5 minutes.
3. In a mixing dish, whisk the eggs and double cream until pale. Add the spices, butter, parsley, and kale; stir until everything is well incorporated.
4. Pour the mixture into the baking pan with the mushrooms.
5. Top with the cheese. Cook in the preheated Air Fryer for 10 minutes. Serve immediately and enjoy!

493.Broccoli Bites With Cheese Sauce

Servings: 6
Cooking Time: 20 Minutes
Ingredients:
- For the Broccoli Bites:
- 1 medium-sized head broccoli, broken into florets
- 1/2 teaspoon lemon zest, freshly grated
- 1/3 teaspoon fine sea salt
- 1/2 teaspoon hot paprika
- 1 teaspoon shallot powder
- 1 teaspoon porcini powder
- 1/2 teaspoon granulated garlic
- 1/3 teaspoon celery seeds
- 1 ½ tablespoons olive oil
- For the Cheese Sauce:
- 2 tablespoons butter
- 1 tablespoon golden flaxseed meal
- 1 cup milk
- 1/2 cup blue cheese

Directions:
1. Toss all the ingredients for the broccoli bites in a mixing bowl, covering the broccoli florets on all sides.
2. Cook them in the preheated Air Fryer at 360 degrees for 13 to 15 minutes.
3. In the meantime, melt the butter over a medium heat; stir in the golden flaxseed meal and let cook for 1 min or so.
4. Gradually pour in the milk, stirring constantly, until the mixture is smooth. Bring it to a simmer and stir in the cheese. Cook until the sauce has thickened slightly.
5. Pause your Air Fryer, mix the broccoli with the prepared sauce and cook for further 3 minutes. Bon appétit!

494.Easy Greek Revithokeftedes

Servings: 3
Cooking Time: 30 Minutes
Ingredients:
- 12 ounces canned chickpeas, drained
- 1 red onion, sliced
- 2 cloves garlic
- 1 chili pepper
- 1 tablespoon fresh coriander
- 2 tablespoons all-purpose flour
- 1/2 teaspoon cayenne pepper
- Sea salt and freshly ground pepper, to taste
- 3 large (6 ½ -inch pita bread

Directions:
1. Pulse the chickpeas, onion, garlic, chili pepper and coriander in your food processor until the chickpeas are ground.
2. Add the all-purpose flour, cayenne pepper, salt, and black pepper; stir to combine well.

3. Form the chickpea mixture into balls and place them in the lightly greased Air Fryer basket.
4. Cook at 380 degrees F for about 15 minutes, shaking the basket occasionally to ensure even cooking.
5. Warm the pita bread in your Air Fryer at 390 degrees F for around 6 minutes.
6. Serve the revithokeftedes in pita bread with tzatziki or your favorite Greek topping. Enjoy!

495.Italian Sausage And Veggie Bake

Servings: 4
Cooking Time: 20 Minutes
Ingredients:
- 1 pound Italian sausage
- 2 red peppers, seeded and sliced
- 2 green peppers, seeded and sliced
- 1 cup mushrooms, sliced
- 1 shallot, sliced
- 4 cloves garlic
- 1 teaspoon dried basil
- 1 teaspoon dried oregano
- 1/4 teaspoon black pepper
- 1/4 teaspoon cayenne pepper
- Sea salt, to taste
- 2 tablespoons Dijon mustard
- 1 cup chicken broth

Directions:
1. Toss all ingredients in a lightly greased baking pan. Make sure the sausages and vegetables are coated with the oil and seasonings.
2. Bake in the preheated Air Fryer at 380 degrees F for 15 minutes.
3. Divide between individual bowls and serve warm. Bon appétit!

496.Grilled Cheese Sandwich

Servings: 1
Cooking Time: 15 Minutes
Ingredients:
- 2 slices artisan bread
- 1 tablespoon butter, softened
- 1 tablespoon tomato ketchup
- 1/2 teaspoon dried oregano
- 2 slices Cheddar cheese

Directions:
1. Brush one side of each slice of the bread with melted butter.
2. Add the tomato ketchup, oregano, and cheese. Make the sandwich and grill at 360 degrees F for 9 minutes or until cheese is melted. Bon appétit!

497.Grilled Chicken Tikka Masala

Servings: 4
Cooking Time: 35 Minutes + Marinating Time

Ingredients:
- 1 teaspoon Tikka Masala
- 1 teaspoon fine sea salt
- 2 heaping teaspoons whole grain mustard
- 2 teaspoons coriander, ground
- 2 tablespoon olive oil
- 2 large-sized chicken breasts, skinless and halved lengthwise
- 2 teaspoons onion powder
- 1 ½ tablespoons cider vinegar
- Basmati rice, steamed
- 1/3 teaspoon red pepper flakes, crushed

Directions:
1. Preheat the air fryer to 335 degrees for 4 minutes.
2. Toss your chicken together with the other ingredients, minus basmati rice. Let it stand at least 3 hours.
3. Cook for 25 minutes in your air fryer; check for doneness because the time depending on the size of the piece of chicken.
4. Serve immediately over warm basmati rice. Enjoy!

498.Farmer's Breakfast Deviled Eggs

Servings: 3
Cooking Time: 25 Minutes
Ingredients:
- 6 eggs
- 6 slices bacon
- 2 tablespoons mayonnaise
- 1 teaspoon hot sauce
- 1/2 teaspoon Worcestershire sauce
- 2 tablespoons green onions, chopped
- 1 tablespoon pickle relish
- Salt and ground black pepper, to taste
- 1 teaspoon smoked paprika

Directions:
1. Place the wire rack in the Air Fryer basket; lower the eggs onto the wire rack.
2. Cook at 270 degrees F for 15 minutes.
3. Transfer them to an ice-cold water bath to stop the cooking. Peel the eggs under cold running water; slice them into halves.
4. Cook the bacon at 400 degrees F for 3 minutes; flip the bacon over and cook an additional 3 minutes; chop the bacon and reserve.
5. Mash the egg yolks with the mayo, hot sauce, Worcestershire sauce, green onions, pickle relish, salt, and black pepper; add the reserved bacon and spoon the yolk mixture into the egg whites.
6. Garnish with smoked paprika. Bon appétit!

499.Easy Roasted Hot Dogs

Servings: 6
Cooking Time: 25 Minutes
Ingredients:

- 6 hot dogs
- 6 hot dog buns
- 1 tablespoon mustard
- 6 tablespoons ketchup
- 6 lettuce leaves

Directions:
1. Place the hot dogs in the lightly greased Air Fryer basket.
2. Bake at 380 degrees F for 15 minutes, turning them over halfway through the cooking time to promote even cooking.
3. Place on the bun and add the mustard, ketchup, and lettuce leaves. Enjoy!

500.Sausage, Pepper And Fontina Frittata

Servings: 5
Cooking Time: 14 Minutes
Ingredients:
- 3 pork sausages, chopped
- 5 well-beaten eggs
- 1 ½ bell peppers, seeded and chopped
- 1 teaspoon smoked cayenne pepper
- 2 tablespoons Fontina cheese
- 1/2 teaspoon tarragon
- 1/2 teaspoon ground black pepper
- 1 teaspoon salt

Directions:
1. In a cast-iron skillet, sweat the bell peppers together with the chopped pork sausages until the peppers are fragrant and the sausage begins to release liquid.
2. Lightly grease the inside of a baking dish with pan spray.
3. Throw all of the above ingredients into the prepared baking dish, including the sautéed mixture; stir to combine.
4. Bake at 345 degrees F approximately 9 minutes. Serve right away with the salad of choice.

9 781922 547637